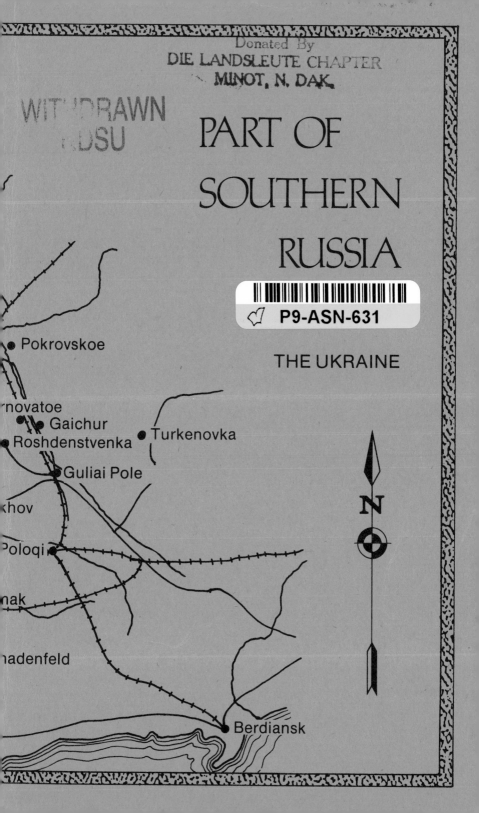

PART OF

SOUTHERN

RUSSIA

THE UKRAINE

Pokrovskoe

rnovatoe
Gaichur
Roshdenstvenka
Turkenovka

Guliai Pole

khov

Poloqi

nak

hadenfeld

Berdiansk

N

Gerhard P. Schroeder
Author

MIRACLES

OF GRACE

AND JUDGMENT

MIRACLES

OF GRACE

AND JUDGMENT

A brief account of the personal contacts and experiences
with some of the leaders and followers of the notorious
Makhnovshchina during the civil war in the Ukraine
1914-1923.

by

Gerhard P. Schroeder

Edited by David G. Rempel, Gordon Ginn, and Joan P. Rowe

I dedicate this book to my dear wife Gertrude (Peters) Truda Schroeder, who so faithfully has gone with me through all the good and evil days, now 60 years. Also I dedicate this book to my children, who have helped in various ways and especially now in my declining years are bearing with me.

Library of Congress Catalog Card Number: 74-82258

Typesetting by Reeder Typesetting, Fremont, California
Book Design by Ramspott and Burnett, Livermore, California
Printed by Kingsport Press, Kingsport, Tennessee

Table of Contents

Introduction

These recollections and reflections of Mr. Gerhard P. Schroeder deal with an aspect of one of the bloodiest chapters of the Russian Civil War in the areas of Southern Russia which since 1921 have become commonly known as the Ukraine, but which until the collapse of the Tsarist regime were known since the second half of the eighteenth century as New Russia or *Novorossiia*. More specifically this story of Mr. Schroeder deals with events which transpired between 1914 and 1923 in those portions of the Ekaterinoslav and the continental portions of the Tavrida guberniias which embraced parts of the Berdiansk and Melitopol *uiezds* (districts) of the latter guberniia, and the Ekaterinoslavskii, Alexandrovskii, Mariupol'skii and Bakhmutskii *uiezdy* of the former. The events described here were part and parcel of a series of peasant partisan movements during the years in question. Among these numerous movements—brought forth, initially, by the November Revolution of 1917, and later intensified by succeeding upheavals in this area during 1918 and 1919—none reached the extent and the degree of significance than the one commonly called the Makhnovshchina. Nor did any of these jaqueries anywhere in Russia play such an important and complex role in the fate of the revolution and counter-revolution as did this one which took its name from that of its chief leader, Nestor Makhno.

The Makhnovshchina, more than any similar movement throughout the length and breadth of Russia, carried on a great struggle against oppression and crushing exactions of a number of foreign invaders and tyrannical regimes of domestic origin which followed each other in rapid succession during the course of three years of civil strife. As far as most Ukrainian peasants were concerned, there was not much choice between any of them—be they the German-Austrian-Hungarian occupying troops, the Varta police force of the Central Powers' stooge, Hetman Skoropadskii, the short-lived and equally ineffective government of Simon Petliura, and such other counter-revolutionary leaders as Generals Denikin and Wrangel, and finally, the most authoritarian, dictatorial and crushing regimes of them all, the Bolshevik dictatorship. All of them were determined to force their forms of government upon them, to bend them to their will, and to live off the fruits of their labor. Therefore, the peasants throughout Southern Russia, under innumerable leaders—Dovgalenko, Sekira, Gladchenko, Shuba, Burlak, Grigoriev, Seropashka, Makhno, and a host of others—sought to hold on to the land and other forms of goods and properties they had commenced to appropriate at the height of the late fall of 1917, and continued to seize at feverish pitch under the Bolshevik slogan "plunder the plunderers" after October of that year. As long as the Bolshevik government was faced with greater counter-revolutionary dangers from within and without, it was of necessity compelled to tolerate, if not to incite, such partisan movements against its enemies. The final collapse of the counter-revolution and of intervention in the late fall of 1920 freed the Bolshevik government from any necessity to permit this state of affairs in the countryside to continue, and the latter, in fact, found it imperative to liquidate such forms of opposition as speedily as possible.

General Causes of the Partisan Movements

A brief discussion of the general causes which gave rise to the peasant uprisings, often going under the name of *povstantsy* (up-risers) in the Ukraine might help the reader to understand more fully what was taking place in the Schoenfeld and the Chortitza Mennonite settlements as highlighted by Mr. Schroeder's experiences and observations.

These causes were complex and varied with the leadership of a particular partisan movement and the locality's past history, its current economic condition, and to a considerable degree upon its national composition. The character of the different movements, therefore, showed considerable variations in detail. Most of them began as regular jaqueries—for example, Dovgalenko in the Chernigov guberniia, Selenchik in the Kiev, and Burlak and Seropashka in the Kharkov guberniia—and remained such until overwhelmed by Bolshevik power. The Makhnovshchina, on the other hand, which was led by an alleged Anarchist, Nestor Makhno, and apparently guided by several philosophical and syndicalist anarchists, and having initially enjoyed widespread support among the rural population in the Ekaterinoslav and Tavrida guberniias, especially among the kulak element in the countryside, and having fought various occupying forces—Red, White, and Green, including armed forces from abroad—to a standstill for a considerable period of time, ended up as a rabble mass of men plundering the crucified country, raping women and wreaking a frightful revenge upon all whom it hated or disliked.

At the bottom of the Makhnovshchina—as with the other partisan groups—which raised its head in the summer of 1918 in the Guliai Polie district of the Ekaterinoslav guberniia, lay the agrarian question. The peasants, in what was to become the heartland of this movement—Guliai Polie, Zalivnoe, Liubimovka, Zherebets, and other places nearby—had seized most of the areas' estates from the gentry and goodly portions of the land which belonged to the very numerous onetime so-called foreign settlers, Mennonites, Lutherans, Catholics, Evangelicals, and so forth. They had barely accomplished this, when in the spring of 1918 Hetman Skoropadskii's regime, solely supported by German and Austrian bayonets, endeavored to deprive them of their ill-gotten fruits. Soon after the occupation of the Ukraine by the Central Powers had gotten underway many of the former landlords reappeared from their places of hiding with punitive expeditions of their own formation or with detachments of soldiers from the occupying powers, and they usually succeeded in reclaiming their former possessions. In the process of doing so, they managed to inflict cruel punishment upon the neighboring peasant villages of a devastated estate. Many Mennonite estate owners, as well as quite a number of well-to-do farmers in the colonies, were not averse to appeal to the German military authorities for assistance in their efforts to regain their seized lands, livestock, farm machinery, and other goods. All of them were to pay dearly for this after the German-Austrian forces were forced to leave the Ukraine in the late fall of 1918.

These repressive measures, combined with the requisitions of large amounts of grain for the Central Powers, at prices fixed by the latter, soon produced great dissatisfaction among the peasantry. The first open revolt took place in the middle of May in the Kiev guberniia. It was brutally suppressed, but from then on partisan bands, usually comprising 50 to 100 men, began to make their appearance throughout the Ukraine. They attacked small German army detachments sent out to collect grain, but in the main they sought to interrupt rail communications, to loot restored estates and to kill the landowners and their families. The Hetman's police, the Varta, was utterly incapable to cope with the *povstantsy* (partisans), for the latter disappeared as swiftly after a raid as they had surprised a landowner or a military unit. It was as if the steppe had simply swallowed them. It was an endless game of hide and seek, of fleeing and pursuing, and an undertaking which a number of German soldiers disliked and resented to pursue.

Disrespect for government, irrespective of its form and content, was another cause of the Makhnovshchina. The Tsarist regime had broken down ingloriously. The Provisional government, with its high-sounding phrases, but of masterly inactivity, was not one to restore among the anarchistically-minded peasants obedience to law and order. And the Bolsheviks had for some time been preaching the slogans of "plunder the plunderers", and of seizing the land of the gentry and of the one-time foreign settlers, who were mostly of German descent, in addition to being incomparably more prosperous than their peasant neighbors. Such slogans were a language which the peasants understood well and upon which they acted immediately.

However, once in power, the Bolsheviks commenced to plunder the plunderers of yesterday by ruthless grain expropriations. As long as the grain and livestock requisitions affected the economically well-off rural inhabitants, that is, the so-called *kulaks*, the generality of the peasantry was not particularly concerned nor alienated by the Bolsheviks policies. In part, this was also due to the fact that the broad mass of the peasants was still intoxicated with the seizure of the land which it had effected earlier. But when the Communist government's expropriation policies of grain, horses and cattle commenced to be applied to the *seredniak* (middle) level among the peasants, the latter came to the conclusion that all governments only wished to bleed him white for the benefit of bureaucrats, party officials and the urban laboring people, and so he reasoned that all forms of government were bad, and therefore all forms of government which tried to establish themselves in the Ukraine should be opposed.

A very important stimulant of the Makhnovshchina was the instinctive dislike of the ignorant peasantry for the city, while at the same time being irresistibly allured by the prospect of a big plunder. Nestor Makhno's actual fighting force prior to the summer and fall of 1919 was perhaps never larger than 5-6,000 men. But his strength rested not so much in his excellently equipped and well-mounted cavalry and infantry units being transported with ease and great speed from place to place on the 'light spring-wagons, called *tachanki*, and which were usually drawn by a span of three fleet horses, but rather in the mass following of peasant looters which usually followed his swift raids upon a city, town or German colonists' village. As soon as the fighting arm of the Makhnovtsy captured such a place, or places, hundreds of peasant wagons from the heartland of the Makhnovshchina-Guliai Polie, Liubimovka, and other neighboring villages in the district, would stream into the seized place and loot for days on end, starting, as a rule, with the business section, and later, or simultaneously fanning out throughout the residential area, taking everything that could be carried away. Anything that was of no immediate use to such a looting mob was usually taken to the nearest market place for disposal. Men, women and children, all would be kept busy throughout the day in gathering up loot, and their rapacity was such that often it would lead to bloody encounters between peasants of different villages.

While the looting process was going on, Makhno's fighting men would either engage in the same sport of seizing anything they could lay their hands on, or else engage in drunken revalries. Makhno, the leader of this movement, had little use for urban areas except to loot them. It is important to note that Makhno never found much support among the urban laboring classes.

Hatred of Communists, Commissars and the Cheka (the secret police of the Bolshevik government), on one side, and of the officers of the White Army or those of the Petliura government on the other side, as well as anti-Semitism, were another cause of the Makhnovshchina. "Death to the Cadets (officers), Communists, Commissars and Jews" were the slogans of most of the partisan movements, including that of the Makhnovshchina, this despite the fact that there were some Jews in prominent place at Makhno's headquarters.

The unbridled excesses of the Makhnovshchina, perhaps, rested in part also in the tradition of lawlessness which had characterized this one-time frontier region for centuries prior to the abolition of the independence of the Zaporozhian Cossacks in 1775. At least some of Makhno's followers would occasionally engage in talking about their leader's dream of resurrecting the famous *Zaporozhian Siech* (headquarters of Zaporozhian or Dnieper Cossacks. Makhno's biographer, P. Arshinov, observes in his book *Istoriia makhnovskogo dvizheniia, 1918-1921 gg.* Berlin, 1923, that in 1918 Makhno had briefly entertained the idea of organizing the revolting peasants of the Southern Ukraine into an independent peasant republic. Such an idea had little, if any, connection with Ukrainian nationalism, for Makhno was not a Ukrainian himself nor did he know anything of the history of the Ukraine.

Finally, the Makhnovshchina, unlike most, if not all, other partisan movements in the Ukraine, had an incalculably valuable asset in its favor from which it could draw a variety of forms of sustenance for itself for a period of almost three years. This favorable factor derived from the fact that the heartland of his following was located in an area which was completely surrounded for scores of miles with numerous large settlements, separate colonies, hamlets and innumerable *khutors* (individual farms or estates) of Mennonites, Lutherans, Catholics, and members of other faiths and alien nationality, all of whom, by Russian standards or, for that matter, by any European standards, were exceedingly prosperous farmers, and therefore had long been the envy of the Russian peasant. It was from them that Makhno requisitioned, or rather plundered, most of the wherewithal to clothe, feed, transport and mount his armed men and his large camp-following. The collapse of his entire movement in the last months of 1919 and the early months of 1920 was not caused merely by the fact that his usefulness to the Bolsheviks had ceased with the utter defeat of the counter-revolution, the exhaustion of much of his army due to the ravages of epidemic diseases, but to a very considerable degree to the fact that the sources for his sustenance in food and materielle the Mennonite, Lutheran and Catholic villages, had been utterly exhausted. And the neighboring Russian peasants lost all stomach for a continuation of a partisan movement when faced with the situation where they would have to sustain it out of their own means.

DAVID G. REMPEL

Professor David G. Rempel, who rewrote the entire first half of this book, taught Russian History for many years at the College of San Mateo, San Mateo, California. He was born in the colony Nizhniaia Khortitza (Nieder Chortitza). Educated in the Chortitza high school and teacher's seminary, he later attended several American colleges and universities, receiving his doctorate in history from Stanford University, Stanford, California.

During the fateful years of 1918-1920 he was a student at the teacher training institute in Chortitza. He observed and experienced at first hand a number of the tragic events related by Gerhard Schroeder.

Preface

Fifty years have passed into the ocean of Eternity since August 1923 when we came across the ocean on the S.S. Bruton into Canada and thirteen years later in 1936 as missionary in the U.S.A. My diary had made many trips with us, but we did not have any desire to read our own writings, because most of it was and is very unpleasant. Time and again people have tried to encourage me to write my memoirs, but I had no real desire to do so, neither was there time for this. I was too busy preaching and teaching in various places in four languages. I hope in the next book: "In THE NEW WORLD" I'll be able to give you more details about our very pleasant life in Canada and in the U.S.A., the Lord willing.

My life and that of our family has been a long chain of miracles which God performed, and the simple fact that now at the age of 84 I am still able to work, to preach and teach, to eat and drink, sleep and sing and produce music on a number of instruments—after being almost dead in 1922 from hunger—that is a great miracle of the grace of God and we praise Him for it. We thank God for the Mennonite organization through whose help and guidance we were able to come to Canada. We say this with our deepest sincerity and thanks, that without this Mennonite organization we would have perished in Russia. I want all of our children and grandchildren to be mindful and grateful for this. Also we want to praise God for our Baptist brethren who, through the many years found it possible to use us in missionary work and to support us when we needed special help.

One day Virginia (Mrs. Charles Rowland) phoned me declaring herself willing to type for me, if I wanted her help in writing my memoirs. She had heard me speak on Russia. This started the stone rolling. Virginia deserves our praise and credit. Without her help at this given time I would never have started the work of typing close to 400 pages.

Next we must mention professor David G. Rempel of Menlo Park, Calif. who had read my writings in a Canadian German paper. He encouraged me in my writing and later edited the first 144 pages. He has put a great deal of work into the first 144 pages rewriting everything sentence by sentence.

After awhile letters began to come from professor John B. Toews of Calgary, Alberta, Canada. He, too, has helped me with proper advice and otherwise.

And now the Goehring brothers, Elmer and Clifford, are trying their best to see to it that the manuscript will be properly printed and published in a book.

Above all others we praise our Heavenly Father who day by day has been supplying us with health and strength and loving care and all that makes this world so fair. We praise Him for our salvation through Jesus Christ and the impetus He gives us to testify to others about this.

Some of my writing—over 100 pages is in German and at the proper time I may publish some in German, the Lord willing.

I have a list of former Makhnovtsy who turned to Christ. You will read some letters from them. Since they became Christians the communist government had no use for them. They already had a nice Baptist Church with over 60 members. But nothing is left of it. I shed my tears because of their premature death because of their faith in Jesus Christ. It is hard to understand the fallacy and folly of communism, why they persecute the best citizens of their own country, who are honest and would be the best supporters any government could wish to have.

A Russian and an American were debating about their countries and the form of government. The American remarked that he and others had so much freedom of speech that he could even speak against his president, who at that time happened to be Harry S. Truman. "Oh", said the Russian, "I, too, can talk as much as I desire against president Truman and nothing will be done against me by the soviet government."

Having brought out quite a few negative points of others, I strongly feel that I and others should be willing to recognize the negative features of our lives and correct them.

May God richly bless everyone who is reading these lines.

Humbly and sincerely yours,

Gerhard P. Schroeder
Lodi, California, 1974

My Ancestors

My ancestry leads to Holland, where my forefathers lived till about the middle of the sixteenth century, when they moved to Germany in the Danzig-Elbing area. My great-grandfather, Johann Schroeder, at the age of about 33 years, from *Krebswalde*, south of Elbing, Germany moved to *Rosental*, Russia and lived in the latter on Franz Janzen's (Johann Penner) farmstead. Here my grandfather, also Johann Schroeder, was born in the year 1807 on November 11th. As a young man of about 29 years or so, he, along with many others, moved to *Bergtal*, in the Mariupol district north of the Azov Sea. Here in the year 1852 on January 18, my father, Peter John Schroeder, was born. He attended the public school in Bergtal and after that went to Chortitza, where he studied at the Central High School and later became a teacher in Rosental. About this time all his relatives, parents, brothers, sisters, and friends moved to Manitoba, Canada in the Gretna area in the years 1874-1875. The Bible says: Therefore shall a man leave his father and his mother and shall cleave unto his wife: and the two shall be one flesh" (Gen. 2:24).

As a young teacher in Rosental, Russia, my father had his board and room just across from the school at the Corner-Ungers (later the Corner-Penners). Mr. Unger time and again would tell him, "Peter, it is about time for you to get yourself a 'Handmenschen', i.e., a handyman or a handymaid. He had found one whom he wanted to marry, Maria Klassen, but her father said he could have Maria for his wife only under the condition that he would promise to stay in Russia; and he did stay, though he often had a deep longing to see his parents and relatives in Canada. He died in Russia during the greatest unrest in the revolution, February 12, 1920.

Ironically, we all came to Canada in the years 1923, 1926, and 1927; only my father never reached the shores of America, but was buried in our Rosental, Russia, cemetery. Later, when the collective farms were organized this cemetery was made level to the ground and a pig and cattle ranch was built at this place where my father is buried. The communists showed no respect for things that were dear and sacred to us. My mother Maria (Klassen) Schroeder lived in Morris, Manitoba, along with my sisters from 1926 till 1951, when she, at the age of almost 96, died and was buried at the Morris cemetery.

We often shudder when we think back of what we have gone through in Russia during the years from 1914-1923. There is very little doubt in my mind that I personally, and very probably most of the members of my family, would have died in Russia long ago. The communist slaughter machine did not stop at any instance or place but demanded millions and millions of innocent victims, lives that had to be eliminated until they would have a population of citizens with *absolute obedience*.

The question has come: What if the tsarist government had remained in power? From what I have been able to gather, through various connections, mainly through men who, before the revolution, were in high standing in Petrograd, State Duma, etc., we would not have fared one bit better under the tsarist government.

Whichever way we may turn our thoughts and attention, we all have reasons to be very deeply thankful to God, and to the men who have made it possible for us to leave Russia and come to Canada and to the U.S.A.

When we, on August 19, 1923 arrived on the C.P.R. train in Winnipeg, I had ten cents (and how much sense?) in my pocket, my wife Gertrude (Truda) and four children; Margaret, eight, Peter, six, Katherine, four, and Gerhard, one; owing the C.P.R. company about $600.00 for the trip across the ocean.

When in the fall of 1923 I was offered a position to teach the German language in the Mennonite Educational Institute in Altona, teaching three hours a day with a salary of $50.00, renting a little house for about $5.00 per month, we thought heaven had come down to earth.

This lasted only a short period of time. Some of the readers may know that this school burned down and has never been rebuilt. I at that time was already in missionary work among Russian and German speaking people. The Baptists needed a man with languages and I was willing to go into that service, which I have never regretted. So we became Baptists but always retained a close fellowship with the Mennonites. We love all children of God.

Besides other periodicals, newspapers, and books in various languages we also have Mennonite papers and books and love to read about those Mennonite men who risked so much and unselfishly laboured and sacrificed their time, efforts, and money to bring us out of slavery into the freedom of Canada and the U.S.A. When we were almost dead from hunger in Russia in 1922 the AMRA (American Mennonite Relief Administration) brought us food, opened soup kitchens, and sent us food drafts from Canada and from the U.S.A. We do not keep silent about this; our children are interested to hear about this and we gladly tell them and our grandchildren what God has done to us and for us through men like Bishop David Toews of Rosthern, Saskatchewan, and pastor Benjamin B. Janz in Russia, and through many others who opened their hearts, homes and pocketbooks for us. My dear, dear people, I am writing these lines with tears in my eyes. God bless their memory, God bless their children and children's children. From the bottom of our hearts we as the Schroeder family say a hearty "Thank You!" The Lord willing, we would like to participate at the Anniversary celebrations and GREAT THANKSGIVING for God's marvelous grace. We as the Schroeder family, along with thousands, yea millions love to sing: "O Canada, glorious and free, O Canada, we stand on guard for Thee". . . and here especially we love to sing:

> God bless America, land that I love,
> Stand beside her and guide her
> Through the night with the light from above.
> From the mountains to the prairies,
> To the oceans white with foam,
> God bless America! My home sweet home! Amen!

Two great countries! We will never forget to thank God for all the good people in these countries and for their governments.

In Canada the good Lord gave us three more daughters: Gertrude (Trudie), Joanne and Doris.

MIRACLES
OF GRACE
AND JUDGMENT

CHAPTER I

Life Before The Revolution

It is now 1923. Nine years of unsettled life are behind us. During the major portion of this time the area in which we lived in Southern Russia was the scene of alternating brief spells of relative normality, followed by prolonged periods of chaos and utter lawlessness. Reflecting upon the past, one wonders how we managed to survive those years of hardships. But the present situation is full of instability and uncertainty, and the future looks even more ominous.

How beautiful and flourishing were our Mennonite villages, or colonies, as they were generally called, on the eve of the Revolution of 1917. Each farmer possessed a so-called "full farm", and owned sixty-five desiatins of land, which represented in Canadian terms circa 175 acres. Owners of "half-farms" and "quarter-farms" possessed about eighty-seven and forty-four acres respectively. All of our farmers cut their grains with reapers manufactured in local Mennonite industrial establishments or with imported binders of American make, such as McCormack, Deering, International Harvester, and others. Each owner of a full or half-farm also possessed his own threshing machine, also locally produced, and not an inconsiderable number of the larger farmers propelled these machines with motor power of local or imported manufacture.

The major source of power of the farmers living in villages remained, as before, the horse, and their number per full farm varied from ten to fourteen work horses and a number of colts and yearlings. Those of the smaller farmers were proportionately less numerous; thus, a half-farm owner might have about six or seven work horses and several yearlings.

The majority of the Mennonites and other foreign settlers used what in Russia was called the "colonist" horse. This was not a clearly defined type. At the beginning of the present century definite attempts were made in many Mennonite colonies to improve their horses with stallions from government stud farms, or with imported stallions from abroad, mostly of the Percheron and Ardennes breeds. One may add that in contrast to large estate owners, or the small Ukrainian peasant farmers, who used principally oxen, the horse was the principal draft animal in Mennonite farming.

Dairy cattle on these farms almost invariably consisted of the so-called German Red Cow.

The Mennonite farmers had a good system of working the land properly, a rational distribution of arable land among gain-growing, summer fallow, and truck-crops, and so generally assured themselves a plentiful supply of food for their own use and large amounts for the domestic and the export markets.

We had a good educational system; compulsory through the elementary school level; and a number of secondary schools for boys, called *Zentralschulen* (central or high schools); and in the two major Mennonite settlements, Chortitza and the Molochnaia, several institutions of higher learning. The teaching staffs generally consisted of an excellently prepared corps of teachers. School buildings were invariably of brick construction, usually with a modern system of heating such as steam or water.

That, in briefest form, was the situation which existed in almost all of the approximately 400 Mennonite colonies throughout the length and breadth of the huge Russian empire before World War I. The cataclysmic effects of war, revolution, civil war, anarchy, famine and pestilent diseases destroyed what to most Mennonites and outsiders had seemed an idyllic situation.

And what is the picture today? Hundreds of our people have been massacred by a succession of bandit regimes, notably that of Nestor Makhno which held sway over so many of our colonies during the years of 1918 and 1919. Thousands of our people, especially among the male population, have died of typhus or have starved to death. Many of our villages have literally been wiped off the face of the earth, and there is not one of our colonies in Southern Russia which does not show glaring evidence of the ravages of civil war, in the countless buildings damaged or almost totally destroyed, leaving innumerable people homeless. The numbers of orphaned children in every village would be difficult to comprehend by an outsider. Few farmers are left with any draft animals or dairy cattle.

Were it not for the American Relief Administration in general, and the Mennonite Relief Agency in particular, and the adoption by the Soviet government of its New Economic Policy, the situation would be hopeless indeed.

At the beginning of the First World War, I was a teacher in the Schoenfeld high school in the Mennonite settlement called Brasol. It was located in the Alexandrovsk uiezd (district), on the left bank of the Dnieper River, in the large Ekaterinoslav guberniia. To some of the readers Alexandrovsk may be better known as the city and district of Zaporozhie, a name-change which took place after the re-establishment of the Ukraine as a separate republic in the Union of Soviet Socialist Republics, usually called the U.S.S.R.

Just prior to the outbreak of the war, namely on May 27, 1914, I married Miss Gertrude Peters, daughter of Mr. and Mrs. Bernhard J. Peters. On September 3, like thousands of other Mennonite youths all over Russia, I received a summons to report to the city of Ekaterinoslav, now known as Dniepropetrovsk, for substitute military service. I was extremely fortunate to be assigned as a nurses' aid, or orderly (sanitar) to a hospital in the Mennonite colony of Kronsgarten located at not too great a distance from the city of Ekaterinoslav. Two other teachers, Jacob Wiens and David P. Loewen, were also assigned to this hospital, which in the early days of hostilities had been turned over to the Russian Red Cross, who operated it for several years for wounded and sick military personnel. The work we were required to perform was not especially hard, and we had every reason to be grateful for we were situated at a relatively short distance from home, and the people with whom we worked, except for the higher personnel of the staff and those folk with whom we associated most, were all Mennonites.

Service in the Red Cross During World War I

In May of 1915 Count Nicholai Petrovich Urusov, Chief of the Red Cross hospitals in Southern Russia, inclusive of the fronts along the main portions of the Russo-Austro-Hungarian and Rumanian boundaries, the Black Sea and the Caucasion front, happened to inspect our hospital. The Urusovs, an extremely wealthy family, possessed a number of estates in the South of Russia and a palatial home in the city of Ekaterinoslav. He traveled in his private automobile, chauffeured as it happened, by Peter Nicholaevich Golubovskii. Though we were graduates of different colleges, Peter of the Mining Institute, and I of the Teachers Institute, had known each other well from our college days.

And so, when Count Urusov needed another secretary in his office in Ekaterinoslav, my friend had suggested my name. Suddenly during the Count's inspection of our hospital at Kronsgarten (or *Polovitse* as it was known in Russian), he stopped in front of the line of nurses' aides and asked:

"Who is the Orderly Schroeder?"

"I, Your Excellency."

"Where did you study?"

"In the Ekaterinoslav Teachers Institute, Your Excellency."

"Did you graduate?"

"Yes, Your Excellency."

"I will transfer you to the Medical Department in my office."

"At your command, Your Excellency."

Thus I became a secretary in that big office building on Sadovaia Street. My immediate chief was Dr. Anatoly E. Vartminsky, of Polish extraction. He appointed me as First Secretary of the Department of Nurses (*sestry miloserdiia* or "sisters of mercy"). The department kept a roster of all the nurses throughout Southern Russia, and upon its orders they had to report for duty in the cities of the interior or on the front. My staff consisted of a secretary, a typist, and other clerks.

My thoughts were constantly with my loved ones in Schoenfeld and in its high school. At various times my wife, Truda, as I called her, and later with our first child, Margaret, born on April 26, 1915, was permitted to visit me in Ekaterinoslav for brief periods. Fortunately, in June 1915 I managed to find an apartment, and my wife and baby were able to live with me in the city until almost the close of 1916. The apartment was located half a block from the main street, the Ekateriniskii Prospect, and not too far from our headquarters, and it was capacious enough that we were able to room and board several staff members from our office. It was as nice a setup as could have been expected under wartime conditions. Still, in my dreams I always kept on thinking of myself as back in school, teaching, singing and practicing music.

Toward the end of 1916 our entire headquarters was transferred to Odessa, and this meant separation from my wife and child, who now had to move back to her parents in Schoenfeld. Our work consisted of rendering medical services to the Russian armies on the Rumanian Front, specifically the Fourth, Fifth and Ninth Armies, and to military hospitals throughout Southern Russia.

Two hotels in Odessa, the Krymskaia and Slavianskaia Hotels, were placed at the disposal of our staffs. My billet was in the latter hotel where

I shared a room with a fellow secretary from our office, Jacob Wiens. My former assistant secretary in Ekaterinoslav, Abram Unruh, had meanwhile been assigned to head the Section of Nurses, while I was appointed as Executive Secretary of the Finance Office for medical personnel.

My specific duties consisted chiefly in checking the requisitions of the medical personnel and the signing of their vouchers for payment by the cashier. The responsibilities of my position were extensive and often trying, but on the other hand they were also productive in engendering respect and creating genuine friendship toward me on the part of many doctors, nurses and orderlies. One of them I remember in particular, a lady doctor of extraordinary ability and integrity. Her name was Maria Baltazarovna Stanishevskaia. Among her multifarious duties was that of chief Physician of the Fifty-First Evacuation Hospital. This meant that she and her staff were responsible for the examination and distribution of all wounded and sick military personnel from the entire Southern Front into hospitals of the interior of the South Russian guberniias. It was always a pleasure to deal with her whenever her duties brought her to our office, endeavoring to assist her with the solution of her problems or to discourse with her on a variety of subjects. In June of 1917 it was she who managed to obtain for me a furlough to visit my family in Schoenfeld.

Our billets at the Slavianskaia Hotel were almost luxurious in the accommodations as well as services available to us. After office hours I had merely to press a button in my room, and Ivan, the servant would come to get his orders. The steam baths were excellent, and since I had been able to obtain for the niece of the hotel manager her heart's desire, namely assignment to the so-called flying division of the Red Cross on the Front, the manager had become my friend and would often place at my disposal tickets for nice private rooms in the steam bath department. These rooms could accommodate two persons, and so either Unruh, Wiens, or other staff members would be able to go with me.

Meanwhile I had been promoted from the ranks of a private to that of a commissioned officer, with a commensurate increase in pay. This was most welcome since, due to inflation, costs had steadily risen. There was then a saying abroad to the effect that when the government bond, currently worth ninety-five rubles, would be worth five rubles and a good goose selling for about five rubles would fetch ninety-five rubles, the war would be over. Little did we dream at the time that we would not have to wait very long before such a prediction came true.

During the early months of my work in the Red Cross offices my monthly salary was twenty rubles. This was not enough to meet even the minimum living costs of my family and myself, and so I was quite early confronted with the necessity of selling some of the things Truda and I had treasured greatly. First, we sold the German piano which had cost us 500 rubles originally. Though it brought a fair price, we soon had to sell my prized possession, my trotter called *Zabavnik*, ("amuser or entertainer"), whom I had trained and loved dearly. Next to be sold was my English saddle and another cherished possession, namely the cabriolet carriage, a choice bridle, beautiful reins, etc. Last, but not least, came the time to dispose of a second, but smaller horse I had bought in early 1914. It was a pacer, called *Krasavets* ("Beauty") whom I had trained to kneel, to lie down and to perform other acts. Fortunately, the promotions I received brought higher salaries so that by early 1917 my monthly pay had been raised to 200 rubles.

Whether in Ekaterinoslav or in Odessa, there was never a dearth in the numerous special demands that were made upon our staff from higher headquarters, or in the amount of work that fell upon our shoulders in carrying out our specifically assigned tasks. The nature of the organization's functions and duties, the type of people who composed its staff, and the absence of the usual "spit and polish" manifestations so characteristic of the typical military installation made life in our office, then, whether on or off duty not devoid of its lighter moments or humorous side.

To begin with, Count Urusov amused us with certain of his foibles. Thus, for example, he flatly refused to sign any piece of paper with an ordinary pen, but only with a goose feather. And so, Kazakov, the office flunky, every morning had to see to it that the Count's desk was supplied with a holder full of freshly sharpened goose feathers.

Kazakov's duties were not many, consisting in the main of occasionally dusting a desk, and regularly bringing the staff its mid-morning and afternoon teas. For the rest of the day he generally stood at the door, mostly preoccupied with his nose, mostly furiously digging in it while awaiting further orders. Our chief doctor would occasionally call to him: "Kazakov, watch out, you might break your finger." Mother Nature had not endowed Kazakov with special intelligence or any special gifts, but he was a good-natured, obedient soul.

Tea-time in the fall or in winter was prone to take on some of the aspects of the Mennonite *faspa* (afternoon coffee break), for during hog-butchering time at home, some of our men would receive packages of home-made sausages which were shared with the rest of the office workers. Needless to add that some of our Mennonite medical corps men were well-to-do or even rich landowners.

Among my co-religionists in the office I recall particularly Cornelius Martens, Friesen, Neufeld and especially Dr. Abram Unruh. All of us were young, and Unruh, a teacher of religion and a minister, had a strong influence upon us. With him we often discussed significant questions affecting our brotherhood, or issues of national import. I feld particularly drawn to him and have ever been grateful for the influence he had upon me. For a considerable period of time in Ekaterinoslav, when he was my assistant secretary, our desks were adjoining each other, and it was not an unusual occurrence when at tea-break I would find in my desk drawer not the lunch of homebaked goodies, such as *Schnettje* which my wife had packed for me, but a bag of cookies and other sundries from a commercial bakery. There was no mystery to this exchange, for all I had to do was to look toward Unruh's desk where I would usually observe him eating my homemade goodies which he greatly preferred to his bakery purchase. Many years later when we would meet in different places in Canada, he would always remind me of the good pastries which my Truda had baked during our service days in Ekaterinoslav.

It was fun to look at him when we would get a new issue of uniforms. He was most difficult to fit because of his enormous weight, and his waist was so huge that it invariably required the stitching together of two belts to cover the circumference of his "baywindow."

Our office, in Ekaterinoslav as in Odessa, was divided into three sections or bureaus, the Main Administrative Office, the Medical Department, and the Business Office. The last one was under the supervision of the well-known Mennonite engineer and business man, John J. Esau, former mayor of Ekaterinoslav, holder of numerous other offices in that city, and close acquaintance of Count Urusov. As mentioned previously, Dr. Anatoly E. Vartminsky headed the medical branch during our stay in Ekaterinoslav. There were other well-known doctors on the staff of this department, among whom might be mentioned Dr. Shmarovin and the famous surgeon Dr. Peter B. Kolesnikov. The ladies of the secretarial staff were also well-educated people. There was; therefore, no lack of intellectually stimulating conversation, discussion or debate.

In keeping with military regulations, an officer was kept on duty day and night. One night I happened to be on duty, a young man, a lawyer by profession, named Goldberg, who had recently been appointed to our staff, came to visit me. Frankly, I had been puzzled over the appointment since we were in no need of additional secretarial help. However, it was an open secret that a letter had recently been received by Count Urusov from Baron Meyendorf, head of the National Red Cross, a member of the upper house of the Russian Parliament, the Council of State, inquiring about the possibility of Count Urusov finding an assignment for this fine young man "with high moral qualifications", to quote from the Baron's letter.

The inquiry from Petrograd was of sufficient weight to necessitate a favorable response, and the young gentleman was given a post in our office, with a good salary, little work to do, and with plenty of time to use his legal qualifications for services to private clients on the side.

On this particular night, when the two of us were all alone in the office, the lawyer asked me whether I was interested to hear how he happened to be recommended to the Count by the Baron. Naturally, I was interested in this case of obvious political pull from someone on high. With that he pulled out his wallet and showed me a piece of paper on which there was a brief note with the signature of "Gregory" (Rasputin). To the best of my recollection, it was scribbled on a torn piece of ordinary paper, and read, as best as I can recall, "Dear Baron Meyendorf. Please accept the young man named Goldberg, with high moral qualifications, into one of the offices of the Red Cross, preferably in the South." It was signed simply: "Gregory."

I never asked Mr. Goldberg how much he paid for that piece of paper, but as was generally known at the time, such intercession by the famous, or shall one say notorious, priest, also known as the "Holy Man", did cost many hundreds of dollars.

Odessa

Red Cross Headquarters. The incidents related herewith illustrate some of the problems and frustrations which Count Nicholai Petrovich Urusov, Chief of the Russian Red Cross Society of the Southern Front and the Southern Region of Russia, encountered during the closing months of Tsarist Russia from Rumanian officials in his endeavors to fulfill requisitions of various kinds coming from the Red Cross officials of the three Russian armies which manned the Russian front against the enemy on Rumanian soil. These were the Fourth, Fifth and Ninth Russian armies. The requests would usually embrace medical supplies, means of transport such as horses and wagons, and many other kinds of supplies. The housekeeping and material branch of our headquarters, under the capable leadership of John J. Esau, always managed to assemble and to load the requested items and goods with unaccustomed speed as far as the usual Russian bureaucratic practices were concerned.

If and whenever practicable, Count Urusov would personally accompany the train to the front, taking with him his adjutant and a sufficient number of soldiers to guard the contents of each separate railroad car. Difficulties invariably ensued upon reaching the Rumanian boundary, for here the authorities insisted upon a Rumanian locomotive with a native engineer to replace the Russian machine and its engineer. Just imagine this train now moving towards the front on Rumanian territory. It is night, the train has stopped . . . one minute, two minutes, five minutes, ten minutes. Finally the adjutant realizes that something must be wrong with the whole train. He gives the orders to investigate the matter. It all takes time, especially when you are stopped with a whole trainload for the front and you discover that the train has stopped far from any buildings and far from a railroad station. One of the soldiers reports that the train is without the locomotive. No matter how angry or how impatient the adjutant might be, there is but one solution, and that is to wait till finally dawn will break. Two soldiers on horseback ride to the nearest railroad station and report the matter. It again takes a lot of time, till another locomotive can be found. I recall that when Count Urusov returned from this journey he would vow that this experience would not happen to him again—this was sabotage, and he was not going to tolerate its recurrence.

A few weeks later, another trainload was dispatched to the same front from the Odessa headquarters. Count Urusov decided to accompany it once more. As a precautionary measure, he had placed his adjutant alongside the engineer of the Rumanian locomotive as soon as the latter had replaced the Russian locomotive after crossing the boundary into Rumania. The train had traveled a relatively short distance when the new engineer at a railroad station insisted that the engine would have to take on an additional supply of water before the train could proceed further toward the front. Would the adjutant permit him to unhitch the locomotive to go only a short distance to the watertower at the station? The adjutant agreed to this move, only to find that once more the Rumanian engineer had tricked him. The locomotive never returned from its "watering" expedition. Count Urusov now sought out the stationmaster and lodged the strongest protest; however, neither threats nor pleas succeeded in getting another locomotive from this official. And so Count Urusov decided upon a rather drastic action. He instructed a group of his soldiers to fetch the stationmaster, place a rope around his neck, and string the recalcitrant Rumanian up a pole right in the railroad yard.

This act had the desired effect, the official now really bestirred himself, and a locomotive was soon hitched to the train, sending it on its destination to the front.

It can readily be seen that the Rumanians were held in very low esteem at our Odessa Red Cross headquarters.

CHAPTER 2

Beginning of the Revolution

Other interesting memories of Odessa I recall from March 1917. One day I was standing at the harbor watching a number of naval vessels coming in, and I observed how they were signaling to each other with their flags. Our office was on the *Ekaterininskaia Ploshchad* ("Catherine's Square"), near the monument of Catherine the Great. Close by was the famous Richelieu Esplanade with its beautiful stairway of some 198 stairs leading down to the water's edge. As I stood and watched I could see the sailors disembarking from the ships and assembling in formations to march into the city. When the march began they were singing the *Marseillaise*, the thrilling song of Revolutionaries then being sung in countless cities and towns throughout Russia. It is still ringing in my ears, and I believe I could sing it today without any difficulty. The tune is French, but the words were in Russian, "Away with all that we have had up until now!"

Shortly after mid-March word reached Odessa that Tsar Nicholas II had abdicated. The tempo of revolutionary fervor increased by the moment. Everywhere there were speeches, demonstrations, slogans without end, music and general jubilation. Endlessly one heard, "Long live this and long live that," and countless masses of people would answer in shouts of "Hurrah! Da zdravstvuyet Konstitutsia!" (Long live the Constitution). Since the word *konstitutsia* in Russian is of the feminine gender, someone would shout: "Why only the *konstitutsia*? I say: Da zdravstvuyet Konstantin!" (Long live Constantin). Many of the demonstrators had no real idea what they were marching and yelling for. The one clear idea everyone had grasped was the Tsar had abdicated and that now there was freedom. They were weary of the war, they wished an end to it and hoped that peace would now come soon.

But I was much more concerned at this moment over other matters and deeply worried, for my wife was about due to give birth to another child, and neither one of us was able to get in touch with the other by telegraph. Messages of this kind could simply not get through floods of the exciting political news of the day. And so I decided that I must get home, come what may. I did manage to obtain a two-weeks leave of absence; the question was how to get there. I went to the railroad station and found huge crowds milling around the depot. Trains were arriving and departing, many with windows already broken by frantic people endeavoring to get onto a train. Tickets were unavailable and so I decided to board any train going in an easterly direction hoping that I eventually might be able to make it to a station at not too great a distance from my home. I did succeed in getting a seat on a rough plank. It was far from comfortable, but it was a seat. I observed an army officer on an upper berth in our car, stretching out and trying to sleep. A soldier soon crawled up onto the berth and demanded that the officer move. When the latter refused, the soldier simply stretched himself on the berth with his feet right under the nose of the officer. Revolution had abolished privileges and established equality and freedom.

A Trip to Schoenfeld

The same attributes now riding high, equality and freedom, soon also touched my belongings. Ere long I found myself relieved of them. When finally I reached the station nearest my home, Gaichur, it was night. It was snowing and raining intermittently, and I was about fourteen miles from home. My wife's parents had a telephone in their home, but there was no use trying to get through to them, for no telephones were working. There was no other way of getting home except to walk the distance to Schoenfeld which, since I had been relieved of my belongings, was not an insurmountable task except for the nasty weather. On the lapel of my uniform I had a red ribbon as a sign of being in tune with the times. Still, for protection's sake, I got myself a big club to be prepared for any eventualities. And so, tired, sleepy and hungry I set out on my journey. About two miles from my home village Schoenfeld, I met one of its farmers, unfortunately driving a team of horses in the opposite direction.

Though I was thoroughly soaked by now and hungry, the news which this farmer, John Fast, was able to impart to me filled me with joy. He reported that my family was well and that the new baby, a boy named

Peter, had been born March 27.

The two weeks leave passed all too soon, and I had to go back to Odessa. My immediate superior, Dr. Fomiliant, Dr. Vartminskii had remained in Ekaterinoslav, was glad to see me back and informed me of some staff changes that had taken place as well as of the new "democratic" spirit and procedures which were to characterize our work from now on. Instructions just received from a Revolutionary Committee directed that from now on certain limits were to be placed on the authority of our superior officers. The new chief of the office was a man named Mardanov, who seemed to get a satisfaction out of disciplining the secretaries and to scream, threaten or yell at the officers. We were, of course, directed to elect our own representatives to a staff's soviet, which election picked one Kolosov and myself to these tasks. It was quite a blow to Mardanov that from now on the two of us would have to be consulted by him on any matter pertaining to the office staff. "Democracy" was hard to swallow by this little despot.

I have mentioned previously the name of Dr. Maria Baltazarovna Stanishevskaia. Some time in May another secretary, Ivan Kolesnichenko, and I decided to make an attempt to obtain through her a hearing and examination before a doctor's committee for an extended leave, or perhaps even a discharge from the service. At a propitious moment I called her office and broached the subject of such an examination by an appropriate medical committee. Her response was that at this particular time, due to a large number of sick patients with typhoid fever, it would be impossible for her to assign to the two of us a room in the hospital for "observation and examination" of our physical condition. However, not very long after this she called our office and told us that beds and a room were now available for a customary two-weeks stay for such an examination. We went there and found the time a veritable oasis in the desert. She had arranged all sorts of privileges for us in the matter of visiting hours by friends and walks to the seashore in the immediate vicinity of the hospital.

Three Months Leave of Absence

After fourteen days of this kind of luxury we were told that we would have to be examined by a special medical board to determine the state of our health for further service or discharge. The board consisted of three doctors and a sailor. The former agreed that both of us were unfit for further service and so should receive our discharge papers. However, the sailor said "no". The voice of the Revolutionary Committee, which the sailor represented, insisted that we deserved only a three-month sick leave. My friend Kolesnichenko was extremely disappointed and discouraged, but I told him, "Why worry? We will get three months pay and clothing and other rations, and never return anyway."

By now Alexander Kerensky was at the head of The Provisional Government in Petrograd, a government which without any difficulty had obtained control of the situation throughout the country. At least so it seemed on the surface. But neither Kerensky nor the other members of the government or, for that matter the higher ups in the military command really fully grasped how desperately tired the broad masses of the Russian people were of the war and how deeply they hoped for peace and fundamental transformation of the Russian political and economic systems. In accordance with agreements made with Russia's allies, Kerensky rushed from city to city, from one sector of the front to another in attempts to bolster public morale at home and to inspire the flagging spirits of the troops to "fight to a victorious end of the war."

In the meantime the Socialist Parties, especially the Bolsheviks, were telling the masses at home and the soldiers at the front to support them, for they alone claimed to be able to give them "peace, bread and land," and that virtually at once by either bringing all the warring countries to the peace table, or by making a separate peace with Russia's enemies on the Western and Southern Fronts. But all the while, while the Kerensky government was still exhorting the troops to fight, the workers to continue to work, and the peasants to refrain from seizing the lands of large and medium-sized landholdings, soldiers by the thousands were deserting from the front and did so fully armed.

On the homeward journey from Odessa about June 20 I was fortunate to find a ride on a freight train, for passenger trains were already running far behind schedule and with prolonged layovers. I did manage to get to Ekaterinoslav, where I had spent three years during my college education, spent a day there, and then as luck would have it I managed to catch a passenger train in the direction of my home. To my surprise I happened to meet the president of our high school board, Mr. W.H. Janzen on this train. It was a happy reunion, and we had time to discuss many problems regarding our school and our nation.

How wonderfully quiet it was in Schoenfeld. The fruit trees were loaded with ripening fruit, the nightingales were singing as beautifully as ever; there were no marching demonstrators or soldiers, and there was no shouting anywhere. What a blessing to behold and to enjoy.

As a teacher before the outbreak of hostilities, it was natural that I thought above all about the fate of our high school which the Tsarist government, in its insane hatred against everything German, had closed in 1915. Its doors were still sealed since that day in the spring of 1915 when the government school inspector, Maidachenko, had locked and sealed them. Imbued, I suppose, with the revolutionary spirit of the time, I decided that there were no further reasons why this school should not be reopened and be used by our Mennonites as before the war. The Tsar's government was dead and gone. I am not sure of the exact date, but I think it was June 28, just a few days after my home coming that I went to the school building, tore off the seal, and entered the classrooms which had been shut tight for over two years.

When the neighbors of the school heard what I had done, they were quite apprehensive over possible consequences which might flow from my act. However, I assured them that nothing would happen since the old regime was dead and buried. What a satisfaction it gave the school board and us teachers to write Maidachenko to inform him of our action. We did not ask him for permission, but just wrote him that the school was open and that announcements of resuming instruction had been issued to the people of Schoenfeld and of the neighboring Mennonite colonies.

Such, then, in briefest terms is the story of my military service from early September of 1914 to about mid-June 1917 when, to judge from the turn of events on the Russian front as well as in the zones of the interior of the country, the war to all intents and purposes was winding down for the once greatly feared giant of the east.

What startling changes had taken place in Russia during the months of March to June 1917. The Tsarist regime, so awesomely powerful and seemingly invincible until just yesterday, had toppled in March like a house of cards. With its collapse, the Autocrat of all the Russians had by June been relegated forever to the dustbins of history. To untold millions of Russians, ruthlessly exploited and brutally oppressed for centuries, the changes which had taken place in every branch of the government and had touched every facet of their lives during those heady spring and early summer days of 1917, seemed at the moment to augur well for the initiation of a brighter and happier future. And all this appeared during those days to have been brought about with so little bloodshed that Russians everywhere were congratulating themselves as the only European peoples who had ever brought off a feat of such magnitude in so short a time and with so little loss of life. The wave of patriotism, the elation of national spirit and the sense of common purpose which had characterized such broad masses of the Russian people during the opening months of the war, only to vanish completely during the terrible autumn reverses of 1914 and the incredible corruption at home during 1915 and 1916, seemed to have momentarily come alive once more during the early months of the First Revolution of 1917.

But what effects had the events of August 1914 to June 1917 wrought upon the feelings and attitudes of the Mennonites at home and upon the nearly 13,000 of us who had either volunteered or had been drafted for service in the cause of our motherland? Although we had always insisted upon calling ourselves "die Stillen im Lande" (i.e., the quiet and unobtrusive ones in the land), there had not been the slightest question where our loyalties and our patriotism were. As an unemotional, undemonstrative, and socially and religiously conservative folk, the overwhelming majority of the Mennonites were a political, and most of them, perhaps, had never given much thought to the subject of patriotism as an abstract idea, but simply taking it for granted that in practice it meant obedience "to the government which God had instituted over men." More specifically, to most of them this meant unquestioned loyalty to the Tsar and to a monarchical form of government, to pray in church and school for his safety and its security, in giving obedience to the laws of the land, and in the rendering of various forms of assistance to their country and its people whenever they were called upon to do so, or whenever they felt they should act upon their own initiative as, for example, in the case of widespread famines or in times of war, as long as the latter did not infringe upon or did no violence to their principle of conscientious objection to war. Such had been the ideals which had always been brought home to us in the past in church and in school.

Drastic Changes in Our Private Life

The outbreak of World War I temporarily bolstered the security of the Tsarist government since the broad masses of the Russian people approved of the actions which their government had taken prior to Germany's declaration of war and had caused them to stage tremendous demonstrations of patriotic fervor during the first months of the conflict.

The Mennonites quite generally were swept up in this wave of patriotism, though not to the frenzied degree as their Slavic neighbors. ' When the news of the outbreak of hostilities reached our villages there was a great outpouring among our people of a genuine feeling of loyalty to Russia. Large sums of money were immediately collected for the assistance to the Red Cross and various other voluntary organizations.

Hundreds of young men volunteered their services in non-military capacity for work in the medical agencies organized by different organizations to take care of the wounded and sick in the armed forces. Their own hospitals were offered to be available for use by the medical branches of the armed services or of other voluntary agencies. In various localities Mennonite farmers immediately volunteered to assist their peasant neighbors with the harvests, whose male members had already been called to the colors, with the bringing in of the harvests.

Since the agreements of the 1870's had abolished the historic Mennonite privilege of complete exemption from any form of military duties, in favor of substitute service in times of peace and war, prominent lay and church leaders immediately entered into negotiations with the government as to the form such service was to take. The agreements reached provided that approximately half of the Mennonites subject to call now and during the duration of the war would be placed at the disposal of the different agencies, generally referred to as the Voluntary Organizations (the Red Cross, the All-Russian Union of Zemstvos, etc.) These agencies assumed exclusive responsibility for taking care of wounded and sick military personnel. The remaining Mennonites would be assigned to road work, taking care of the government's forest reserves, and a few other non-combat duties. Relatively few Mennonites abandoned the principle of conscientious objection to war to join the armed forces. In the course of World War I about 13,000 Mennonite volunteers and draftees loyally rendered their duties to the motherland in the mentioned branches of the service. In proportion to the total number of Mennonites in Russia on the eve of the war (approximately 104,000), the number of these servicemen was larger than the rest of the population.

Despite all these efforts by the Mennonites to bear their share of the burdens and responsibilities, there was from the very outset of hostilities, a great feeling of uneasiness and apprehension among them, especially among a number of leading men of the laity and the church.

The war was primarily with Germany. In the early 1890's and again during the years of 1910 to 1912, various segments of the extreme nationalist press and the public, lay as well as that of the State Church, had carried on a most vicious campaign against the one-time foreign colonists, particularly those which it chose to label as of "German descent" (which tended to include the Mennonites, contrary to what had been the prior practice). Would the Russian government, if placed in an exceeding predicament on the front and at home, resort to its old and tried strategem of finding, or conveniently inventing, a scapegoat upon whom to place

the blame for its reverses? Miserable failures occured at home in providing arms for the military and food for the civilians. Would it now
throw us as one would throw a bone to the land-hungry peasant masses?
The old canard whom State and Church had so often used in the past
when in dire straits, namely the Jew, with the slogan *Beei zhidev, spassi
Rossiiu* ("Beat the Jew, save Russia"), would no longer suffice to save
either Tsar, the autocracy, the aristocracy or other large landholders. The
answer was not long in forthcoming.

There were thousands of us in the service of our country, and what was
the frequent refrain in the messages which we received from home? It was
often highly disturbing. How could it have helped but to have an adverse
effect upon our morale and our feelings of patriotism.

Born in Russia, as were my ancestors for a number of generations back,
educated in Russian schools, always in contact with a number of fine and
genuine Russian, i.e., Slavic, friends, I considered myself as much a
Russian patriot as they. The names of many of my friends in college
ended with the characteristic South Russian, or Ukrainian,
"enko"—Alexeienko, Babenko, Bondarenko, Stetsenko, and then came
my name Schroeder, or Shreder, as it was pronounced and written in
Russian. Some of these friends had suggested that they would call me
"Shredenko", which was alright with me. At our Mennonite youth parties in Ekaterinoslav we used the Russian language, more often perhaps
than Low or High German, and we considered ourselves Russians, even
though ethnically we were not Slavic.

And now, all at once, because of this war with Germany, our people at
home were given to understand and made to feel that they were no longer
considered full-fledged Russian citizens. The high school at Schoenfeld
(Krasnopolie), in which I had taught before being called into the service
of my country, though entirely maintained by the Mennonites and
teaching all prescribed subjects in the Russian language except Bible and
German, had been closed in the spring term of 1915 by the Tsarist government. And yet I recalled an event from the spring term of 1914 when the
government school inspector, Maidachenko, visited our school; he was so
impressed with its buildings, library, laboratory facilities, etc., that I
heard him make the statement, "This is not a mere high school; we could
call it an institution of higher learning." During the same spring term of
1914 he delegated the principal of our school, Peter Sawatzky, and myself
to represent him at a neighboring high school and to supervise the giving
of its final examinations. This surely spoke of his confidence in us. And
yet, one year later this same Maidachenko came to Schoenfeld and in the

name of the government closed our school, placed the official seal on the door with strictest instructions not to open that door. It will readily be seen that receipt of such news from home had a disturbing affect upon me.

Even earlier there had come the news that the use of the German language on the street and in any other public place was prohibited. There were frequent reports from home that in the evenings police informers would hide behind bushes or fences on private properties to report anyone who had been overheard using the German, really the Low German tongue, the almost universally used language in Mennonite homes. The guilty person could consider himself or herself fortunate to get off the agent's hook by the payment of a substantial bribe, otherwise there was the threat of being banished to Siberia.

I could cite many illustrations (of the tendency of the ruling class to incriminate the German speaking people at any and every occasion) from my diary kept in those days, but a few will suffice. In Schoenbrunn, a neighboring village to Schoenfeld, the owner of a small mill, John Berg, happened to be overheard one day in calling his miller to come in for dinner in German. The agent's report to the local police accused Berg of having said "Kaiser Wilhelm will soon be here", a totally unsubstantiated charge, and Berg found himself enroute to Siberia simply by police fiat and without any trial whatsoever.

Similar cases of police arbitrariness, and in large numbers, could be listed. For example, when our high school was closed and its doors sealed, my father-in-law, B.J. Peters, asked the official why this was done and received the curt reply from the inspector Maidachenko, "Mr. Peters, would you like to breathe the air of Vologodsk?" Anyone familiar with Russian history knows, of course, that Vologodsk was a place for political exiles in extreme northern Russia.

A most glaring example of outrageous official arbitrainess, because it reached into the highest offices of the Ekaterinoslav guberniia, was the case of three important Mennonite leaders, namely the head of the Old Colony church, Elder Isaak Dyck, the president of the volost (district) council, Franz Paetkau, and the secretary to this council, Jacob Klassen. The accusation against them was that at a large congregation meeting in the Chortitza church they allegedly had voiced pro-German sentiments, when in actuality the meeting had been called for the purpose of raising money for the Russian Red Cross. Only by the intervention of other prominent Mennonite leaders, who had influence in various high places, were the three men released from prison, and then only after the Chortitza volost had paid a fine of 3,000 rubles.

Two prominent Mennonite landowners, brothers by the name of Heinrichs, were exiled to Siberia because many years ago they had contributed money to a Russian Evangelical Baptist Church for the construction of a new sanctuary. In this case the accusing agents were representatives of the State Church, for the Heinrichs brothers were accused of having subverted the Russian faith. Another great danger loomed on the horizon for the Mennonites from certain legislation passed by the government on February 2, 1915, commonly referred to as the *Zakon o likvidatsii nemetskogo zemlevladeniia* (The Law about the Liquidation of German Land Ownership). Involved actually were two laws, the first one entitled "On Land Ownership and Land Tenure of Certain Categories of Russian Subjects of Austrian, Hungarian or German Descent", and the second one "On the Liquidation of Land Ownership and Land Tenure of Russian Subjects of Austrian, Hungarian or German Descent in the Boundary Zones."

Stripped of all legal niceties and bureaucratic verbiage, these laws were simply and solely designed to apply to those Russian subjects of German descent who generations ago had received an allotment of land from the government and had comprised that category of citizens who, until the reforms of the 1860's and 1870's had been legally classified as colonists. It did not affect a single Russian subject of German descent, be he a Baltic Baron, general, merchant prince, ordinary office holder, or land owner irrespective of how many thousands of desiatins of land he might own. The lands of the former colonists were to be expropriated at forced sales, the times of such sales depending upon certain specified boundary zones in which such "liquidations of the German Yoke" were to take place. By an additional law, passed on December 3, 1915, the Peasant Land Bank was declared to be the privileged purchaser of lands, for which it was not to pay in cash but by registered bonds, bearing four-and-a-half per cent interest, redeemable in twenty-five years, non-transferable, and inheritable only in direct line. The former owners themselves were to be sent to certain locations in Siberia.

This was class expropriation, to all intents and purposes confiscation of private property without compensation, and forced exile to Siberia.

The way these policies were carried out in the Western guberniias, the first ones in which the laws were applied during 1915, 1916 and early 1917, there was little difference between the Tsarist policies and those of the Bolshevik government during the "dekulakization of agriculture" during the years 1929 on.

As far as the Mennonites were concerned, there was from the very inception of this legislation until about the collapse of the Tsarist regime, a tremendous amount of uncertainty at the national and local government levels as to whether the laws applied to the Mennonites or not, since the latter maintained that they were of Dutch origin, their forebears having come to Danzig and environs originally from the Low Countries, that none of them had ever been German subjects, since there existed no Germany until 1871, and that with but few exceptions their ancestors had been Prussian subjects only since the several partitions of Poland.

This uncertainty as to whether the laws were applicable to the Mennonites protected most of them in the Ekaterinoslav and Tavrida guberniias against early implementation. But on the other hand, the lack of certainty exposed many of them to endless chicanery by the monstrously corrupt Russian officialdom. Meanwhile, Russian peasants from neighboring villages were often openly driving through Mennonite colonies and telling a particular owner of a farm that soon he would be its possessor, and that without having to pay any compensation for either the land or the homestead.

Actual expropriation of Mennonite lands had taken place in relatively few areas of the Tavrida, Kherson and Ekaterinoslav guberniias by late January 1917 when the Tsarist government decided that the Mennonites, not being of "German descent", were not subject to the application of the laws in question. The Provisional Government in March of 1917 set the laws aside entirely as far as any former colonist was concerned.

It can readily be seen how we servicemen felt when we received letters from home telling us about the prospects they faced and the chicaneries to which they were subjected by high and low officials of various governmental agencies. And here we were, loyal Russian subjects, having been invited by the government in the first place to come to its extensive uncultivated lands of the South, having called Russia our motherland for some 120 years, and now serving it in its hours of need. Now our folks, having made the land fertile over the period of several generations of the hardest work and intelligent use of the land, were to be expropriated of their belongings and like common criminals to be exiled to Siberia.

And all this was merely done as a sop to a land-hungry peasantry, relatively few of whom, even if parcelled out in very small amounts, could have appreciably improved their hard lot from such a program of wholesale robbery of private property. And all this in the incredibly naive belief "that this would save the Russian nobility for another century from all agrarian troubles and from expropriation on the part of the Constitutional Democrats"—as one large landowner in the Ekaterinoslav guberniia near the Chortitza settlement, by the name of Strukov, a member of the Council of State, was quoted as putting it.

I suppose it would be difficult for an American and Canadian citizen, except a member of those scores of thousands of American and Canadian Japanese people who experienced a somewhat similar fate as was facing us in those days, to understand and to appreciate our feelings and attitudes during those years.

Schoenfeld High School 1917

During the latter part of the summer plans were readied for the resumption of instruction in our high school on the usually designated date for the opening of the secondary schools, namely September 1. In all our planning we completely ignored the once powerful government inspector Maidachenko. This, at the moment, seemed as real progress for who could have thought at the beginning of this year that a Mennonite school district would dare to ignore such an "upholder of law and order" of the mighty autocratic Tsarist government. The school board had designated me as the schools' principal, and now some of my first duties were to recruit a small teaching staff. Because of the prolonged interruption which our school had experienced, our decision had been to open with only the first two classes. In addition to myself there was a young teacher, Jacob Thiessen, whose assigned subjects of instruction were religion and German. Another young teacher, Miss Suzanna Loewen, had been engaged to teach several subjects, including singing and music. The addition of a lady teacher to a high school teaching staff was, perhaps, also quite an innovation, for such practices too had been great rarities in pre-Revolutionary Russia. Though young and somewhat inexperienced she was eager and enthusiastic, and we enjoyed her greatly on our staff. My own duties, in addition to administration, included instruction in the following fields: Russian language, mathematics, physics and chemistry.

Teaching or Military Service

We opened school on schedule with a fair-sized enrollment. Everything ran smoothly, and my health began to improve noticeably under the prevailing normal conditions. The only immediate issue which faced me was the possibility that I might have to return to military service, since I had only been granted a three-months sick leave. The issue seemed to be of greater concern to the trustees of the school and to my dear wife, Truda, for all of them often called this to my attention. However, I did not wish to hear them broach this subject, though there were times when it bothered me too. I was supposed to report to a military commander in Alexandrovsk, a city of some forty miles distance from Schoenfeld. I had some connections in that city, which gave me confidence to anticipate there a complete realization of the absurdity of sending a teacher back into the army when there was such a crying need for the resumption of schooling to the fullest degree possible after an interruption of three years. Evidence also abounded that the public was most anxious for the work of peace and schooling to be resumed as fully as possible under the prevailing conditions. In our own school matters were running smoothly and pupils and teachers were working harmoniously.

At last the time came for me to report to Alexandrovsk, and to the relief of all concerned I was given an unconditional discharge from the service. I was now free to devote all my energies and enthusiasm to the school.

The names from the various military fronts continued to sound more ominous with each passing day. Despite Kerensky's barrage of entreaties and exhortations to the soldiers to fight to a victorious end, the morale in the armed services continued on its path of precipitous decline. The rate of desertions grew to alarming proportions. In the cities, at railroad stations and railroad junctions one could see thousands of deserters, all bent upon getting home, or at least as far away from the scene of military action as possible. It was obvious to anyone but the completely foolhardy that the days of the Provisional Government were numbered. Bolshevik slogans and promises to the Russian masses of immediate peace "without indemnities and annexations" of land to the peasant-soldier which he had craved for so many centuries, bread to the city worker, higher wages, shorter hours and control of the factories, mills, shops, or wherever else they happened to be employed.

And to the surprise of few of us who had watched the trend of events since the summer months, the Bolsheviks did successfully stage their seizure of power in late October of 1917. The news of the bloody events at Petrograd and in Moscow spread like wildfire throughout the country, and soon they witnessed their counterparts in most of the larger cities of European Russia.

CHAPTER 3

Bolshevik Revolution

To us in the country the Bolshevik Revolution in the capital and other large and small cities seemed at first not to affect our lives too directly and personally. But this was illusory, for in a very short time larger numbers of soldiers, at times of greater number than batallion strength, came streaming home from the front fully armed, and at times with machine guns and comprising entire cavalry detachments, poured into our villages demanding and taking food, fodder, clothing, or whatever suited them. These forays were soon followed by demands of peasants from nearby and distant villages for land, livestock, farm machinery, and other equipment. In this they were strongly encouraged by local city and rural soviets. Where compliance with such demands was refused or even delayed, bloody scenes ensued. Decrees from the newly established Bolshevik Government compelled the owners of factories, shops, flour mills, business and commercial enterprises, and other undertakings to surrender their property to agents of the government. In the rural areas any owner of a farm of around 200 acres or more was directed to turn the property over to representatives or emisaries of the new government, with the requirement that quarters be furnished to these representatives in the owner's home. In many instances the owners were summarily evicted from their homes and left to shift for themselves, and a larger or smaller number of peasant families moved in. Protests were, of course, to no avail except in rare cases where former laborers of the expropriated farmer agreed to let them take some personal belongings with them. Overt resistance usually resulted in imposition of monetary fines, and if not collectible, ended up in brutal beatings or summary execution on the spot.

Soon we teachers also faced the grim question of our own future exist-ence. How and where were we to obtain our sustenance when the people who bore the expense of maintaining our private high school were them-selves deprived of their own property and thus severely restricted in their own means of subsistence? However, the most immediate problem which we teachers faced a few weeks after the change of government, though it was not a question of bread and butter but of professional interest to us, was, "How are we going to be able to attend a teacher's conference which had been slated to take place in a village of about twenty miles distance from ours?" Ordinarily the attendance of such a conference might not have been of too vital significance. However, after years of having been away from professional meetings, and with schools hopefully reopening throughout our district after a three-year interval due to war, and now our facing all kinds of shortages of supplies of every kind, we were indeed anxious to attend and to meet old and new colleagues and to discuss with them how we were going to meet our responsibilities.

Teachers Conference

But twenty miles was a good distance, really too far to make it per *pedus apostolorum*. And the horses of our farmers had generally been divided among a number of newcomers to the village, with none of the former owners having the right to offer us any assistance without the per-mission of the newly appointed emissar named Trifon. He lived across the street from the school, sharing the house of its former owner Henry B. Wiens. Since Trifon's younger brother was a student in our school, I decided to approach the emissar with whom I already, of necessity, had been compelled to deal. And so I went to him and greeted him with the salutation, "Good morning, Comrade."

"Good morning, Comrade, "he replied. "What can I do for you?"

"I am a teacher of the high school. We have to go to a teacher's con-ference. But since that is to be held in a community some twenty miles from here, I wish to ask you a favor, namely to place at our disposal a team of horses to take us there."

"Oh, I see. It is nice that you have come to see me about this matter. I surely wish to do everything for the promotion of education. You shall be provided with a team to take you to the conference."

"Thank you for your kindness, and I hope we will understand each other."

"Yes, I wish the same thing. I noticed, by the way, that you called me

'Comrade', and you did right in doing so. Now we are all comrades, and henceforth there are not to be any class differences in our country any longer."

"But I nearly forgot to ask you about another matter. My wife would like to have two pounds of butter. We always used to buy butter from this farm, and since you are the emissar, I would like to ask you about it."

"Certainly, you have a right to have the butter. I will tell Mrs. Wiens to give you two pounds of butter and make it a present to you."

"That is very kind of you. I thank you."

When Mrs. Wiens had to give me the amount of butter in question, she was smiling. It seemed funny to weigh out the specified product to the teacher at the command of a person of much lower status than we thought ourselves to be at the time.

It was a nice November day when the three of us from the high school and Gerhard Doerksen from the local public elementary school drove to the conference. I chose to be the driver. At the conference there was a good deal of discussion taking place about our new government, and all wondered what the outcome of the revolutionary changes of October would be. Everyone had something to report of the changes which the events of the past few weeks had wrought in their households and in their communities, of the endless demands that had been made by peasants upon the Mennonite landowners—in livestock, food provisions, furniture and furnishings, clothing, machinery, etc. To the former owners the new situation was, of course, hell on earth, but to the peasants the new order, at least as long as their demands were met or allowed to be met by the new government, was most satisfactory, not only in improving their lot but also because it seemed to offer them the opportunity to even scores with some of their former landlords.

This state of affairs was most unsatisfactory to the former landowners, to say the least, since often they were compelled to either vacate their homes or to share them with a group of peasants whose level of education, standards of behavior and codes of ethics left very much to be desired. But at any rate, thus far no murders had taken place in the villages.

Personally, I was often reminded of the message of Isaiah 48:18, which reads, "Oh, that thou hadst harkened to my commandments, then had thy peace been as a river and thy righteousness as the waters of the sea." Notice that the message reads "thy peace [would have] been as a river." And I also often recalled the message from the New Testament, namely the words of Jesus spoken over the city of Jerusalem shortly before his crucifixion. I have referred to Luke 19:42, "If thou hadst known even thou, at least in this thy day, the things which belong unto thy peace! But now they are hid from thine eyes for the days shall come upon them that thine enemies shall cast a trench about thee and compass thee round and keep thee on every side." The entire passage was appropriate to the conditions in which we found ourselves at this time. If only we would know what belongs to our peace, and to us that now meant giving up many of our possessions.

The German Occupation

"Did you hear the cannons thunder this morning?" asked one neighbor of another.

"Yes, they say it is the German army which is coming closer to our vicinity. Our storekeeper came from the city last night, and he brought us the news that the Germans are only about twenty miles from here."

"That is great. We will get all our property back from these thieves and let them feel how wrong it is to steal and plunder."

"If only the German army would come a little bit faster," said the next neighbor. "Don't you think we should send a delegation secretly and tell them that we will help them if only they will help us to get back our property?"

"I think it is very risky to do, since you cannot tell how things will turn out. I prefer to wait."

That is how some of our landowners were talking. But it was quite different among the poor peasants. They wished they would have the chance to keep everything they had gotten from their wealthier neighbors. It was so nice to sleep on these cozy pillows, the like of which they had never had before. It was so bright by the light of these good kerosene lamps, the like of which they had never possessed previously. And these good horses . . . It was such a pleasure to work the fields with them.

The time came when the German and Austro-Hungarian armies marched into our villages. And there now was one German word which the Russian peasants had to learn, "Zurueck" (Back). Wherever he wanted to go, and whatever he wanted to do, the peasant would hear the word "Zurueck." That was a command, and he had to obey it. And how they hated this word!

But the most bitter anger he felt was when the former rich landowner came accompanied with foreign soldiers and demanded his property back. "Zurueck" was the command used with whatever the peasant had taken—horses, cows, and numerous other things. Some of these poor children were now left without the milk they had enjoyed so much. Not only the livestock, but all other articles had to be returned. It seemed funny at times to see and hear how these rich women went to the houses of the poor and demanded back their pillows, lamps, chickens, pets and jars. Here is where the real hatred was engendered.

We had two bricklayers in our district; both were from the north and were very good of character and competent in their work. They were brothers, Alexander and Prokofy. How often these two men, observing what was going on in our area and themselves not knowing what was taking place in their home districts, would comment about of how the Russian peasant had been struggling in poverty to improve his lot, while the country was in the midst of revolution, and in various places people had been killed; yet, in our immediate vicinity there had not been any bloodshed. I well remember Alexander's frequent remark that "these rich landowners do everything to make the muzhik angrier." And how bitter the peasants did become. We, including myself, did not realize that by being tolerable and willing to part with some of our earthly possessions, we could perhaps have saved many lives later on.

The German occupation also gave a tremendous impetus to translate into reality plans which a number of young Mennonites, with support from prosperous farmers, had recommended in various Mennonite colonies even prior to the arrival of foreign troops. Their contemplated plans, strongly resisted by the Mennonite clergy and many of the elder servicemen of World War I, urged the organization of a *Selbstschutz* (self-defense) unit from amongst their midst for the protection of colonies and separate estates from the ever-increasing raids of plunder upon them by highly-organized and armed-to-the-teeth gangs of bandits, and the inordinate demands of peasant brigands. Such agitation, it should be pointed out, was not confined to the Mennonite colonies but was as strong, if not stronger, in colonies of other faiths, and was particularly advocated with vehemence in colonies situated to the south-east of Alexandrovsk, in the vicinity of Guliai Polie and neighboring villages, which was the very heartland of South Russian agrarian brigands and well-organized gangs of unbridled bandits.

German officers, and, to a lesser extent, Austrian officers strongly encouraged the institution of such self-defense units, in part because of the serious dangers which their own small garrisons in many mining towns and villages suffered especially their lines of communications, from the constant threat of groups of bandits and peasant guerillas.

In our area a landowner, a man with a good education, was appointed secretary of the county. He was a minor version of what during World War II became known as a *Gauleiter*. He felt strongly that the time had come for the landowners to take revenge for the depredations they had suffered. Under the instruction of a German soldier, the secretary's son, a high school student, and another young man from the vicinity armed themselves with revolvers and went into some of the neighboring peasant villages, allegedly seeking out Communists and Anarchists on whom to vent their hatred. The father seemed to be quite proud when his son, upon return from such visitations, would tell him "Oh father, how I smashed such and such fellow's face with the revolver. We will teach them the price of stealing."

Bible and Prayer Meetings

I was highly disturbed by such practices. One dark night I went to see my neighbor, Doerksen, the teacher. He was also the minister in our church and I felt that perhaps he could help me spiritually. I needed peace. And so, after he had put his school work aside we talked at length and he helped me to understand some PASSAGES in the Bible. Afterwards, I suggested that perhaps we could have private Bible studies. He seemed to be quite happy with the suggestion, and from then on we had Bible studies in various private homes. We had free discussions with questions and answers, together with prayers. Ere long there was peace in my heart, and also in my dear wife's and in many others'. My favorite passage was the twenty-third psalm.

Our good neighbor Henry Wiens and his wife took part in these studies, which pleased me a great deal. I may add that this good friend and brother in Christ died in Leamington, Ontario, at the age of ninety-one. We always loved to visit with them.

During the late months of 1917 and during most of 1918 we were still able to have our regular church services in the Mennonite church of Schoenfeld. We were fortunate to have the services of Pastors Jacob Leonard Dyck, John Driedger, and Gerhard Doerksen. The latter, it will be recalled, was also the local elementary school teacher.

As time went on it was becoming more and more difficult to buy almost any kind of household good, including drygoods and food products. My father-in-law had lost the ownership of his store, but for the time being was allowed to stay on as its manager, a thankless position, made all the more difficult since it was impossible to replenish the depleted stocks in almost any line of goods.

Our Bible studies continued. One verse from the Sermon on the Mount

(Luke 6:30) often occupied our minds, and we discussed the verse quite often. It reads, "Give to every man that asketh of thee and of him that taketh away thy goods ask them not again." What did Jesus really mean by this instruction? We came to the conclusion that if we could learn to apply this verse in our time and the circumstances under which we were living, we could perhaps live and not be killed. The question of peace is included here too, but many did not learn this lesson and, as we shall see later, they did lose their lives. How hard it is for man to part with earthly possessions, to leave the worldly goods and hope only for the heavenly reward. Jesus spoke against the rich with many words, and told us that only by separation from worldly things, forsaking all that we have, can we be his disciples. Our regular Thursday evening meetings were a real study of the Bible and a practical lesson.

Most of the participants agreed that we should follow only the Bible and not to try to recover from the poorer people all the property we had lost to them. It is quite a different thing when a thief breaks into the house, and we are compelled to ask the arm of the law and of the government to protect us against a thief. The latter knows that he is stealing, and also knows that he is doing the wrong thing. But these poor peasants were told by the government that they had a right to take others' property. Whatever anyone may think about the matter, we have to learn and to study the scriptures and particularly the Sermon on the Mount.

Another Bible passage often came up for discussion among our group. It is contained in Hebrews 10:34 and reads, "For ye had compassion of me in my bonds, and took joyfully the spoiling of your goods, knowing in yourselves that ye have in heaven a better and an enduring substance."

I shall cite a little illustration. I happened to be at the home of my father-in-law, B.J. Peters, when a group of bandits came to rob his home clean, as well as taking most of the goods in the store. Next to me stood the gang's leader, pistol held in readiness to shoot anyone for offering the slightest resistance. He asked me a question which ever since I have felt to have been worth more than a $64,000 question. It was, "Do you feel sorry that we are taking all this?" My reply was, "Oh, no. I don't feel sorry at all. Do you wish me to help carry the things outside to your wagon?" His reply, "No, we will do that."

We had now to learn the lesson between higher and lesser values, a lesson aptly illustrated in Psalm 73:25, the psalm of Asaph. It reads, "Whom have I in heaven but thee? and there is none upon earth that I desire beside thee." Luther's version, freely translated reads, "When I have only Thee I do not ask for neither heaven or earth." With that lesson learned in a very hard way, my family and I came to Canada and later to the United States, and God grant we would never forget this lesson.

Someone has said that "Life is a university of hard knocks." We have received plenty of them. It is for us Christians to learn to take hard knocks without complaining and to learn the lesson for which the Lord has sent them to us. The sooner we learn the lesson, the sooner God will change the situation.

Many a poor peasant possessed next to nothing. In the spring of 1918, before the German-Austrian occupation of Southern Russia, the poor farmers were told by the Bolshevik government to settle on big farms in groups of about five or ten families, depending upon the size of the farm. In some places the owners, as I have pointed out before, were allowed to live on the same farm and work and share with his new "partners." After the German occupation, the rich landowners got their lands back again, and the poor peasants in many places were left without a piece of land from which they could derive their sustenance. It so happened that a group of them came to a big landowner with a petition which read, "We were appointed by the Communist government to work on your farm and we have done so until May. Now we have been driven away and we have no land, no potatoes, no wheat or barley. We will help you to bring in the crop and would ask you to give us a part of the crop." The owner replied, "You have helped, you have been working on my farm, you lazy people. Away from my farm and don't you ever dare come back here again. Off with you!" And he called his dogs and told them, "Sig them down there!" He chased them away with his dogs. The poor muzhiks had no alternative but to leave the farm without anything. It would not have been too difficult to come to an agreement with them, and most of them would have remained in good fellowship with him, and that on relatively easy terms. But the wealthier people thought they had the power to turn everything to their own benefit or in their favor.

Family and Social Life

After I returned from the service with The Red Cross in Odessa toward the end of June 1917, my family and I lived with our parents, that is, my wife's parents, B.J. Peters. They had two main buildings—one along the street which comprised the store, and attached to it were the living quar-ters for the family. The other building was a machine shop. Both structures were of brick construction with metal roofs. The heating system was water heating with radiators. Some people in America will not understand this since they have the idea that all houses in Russia were very primitive buildings. But these buildings could compare favorably with such structures in the United States.

The community also had its own telephone system, and the two aunts of my wife, Susanna and Tina Toews, were the telephone operators. As young people we would often go to the telephone office to keep company with the aunts.

Our family of four, that is myself, my wife and our two children, Margaret and Peter, did not live in the main building but in the machine shop, at the end of which building was an apartment where we lived during the months of July and August of 1917.

When school got underway, we moved to the high school campus on which were located four brick buildings. The first one, along the street, was a long two-story building with four classrooms and an assembly hall. This building was also equipped with a water-heating system. On the ground floor was the heating plant, and at each end an apartment. For the time being we lived at the end of the building. The other apartment was occupied by the school custodian, Mr. H. Riesen.

There were many nice trees on the campus, including walnut, apple, and pear trees. I shall always remember the beautiful trees along the street, which were silver spruce. The next spring (1918) we moved into another house on the campus, one of three separate buildings for the teaching staff of the high school. They too were well equipped, with each also having an outdoors, or summer kitchen, so that Truda, my wife, could cook outside and not have all the heat in the living quarters.

It seems strange to me to mention that now; although, we had almost no income, at least money-wise, we managed to have two girls to serve us. One of them helped my wife with cooking and cleaning. Her name was Katharina Knelsen, though we usually called her Tina. The other girl, Marie Knelsen, fulfilled the role of what we in Russia called a "nianka", that is a nurse who helped with the children. Both of these girls came from Rosental, the place where I was born. I am not sure whether they were related to each other, but they were not sisters. I don't recall how much of a salary we paid them. To the best of my recollection Marie stayed only during the winter of 1918 with us, and in the spring I took her back to Rosental. I must mention at this time that there was no desire in any of us to acquire nice things during those days, for we realized that we were living in a period of time when all such things could very easily be taken away from us. I consider this a very profitable lesson for us as we behold the materialism so rampant in America and all over the world. We learned this lesson, so we were satisfied with the bare necessities of life.

We also had to keep our own cows, one or two as the circumstances permitted. And I had a horse which I named Cossack. It was a chestnut colored horse, some twenty-one years old, and the subject of a considerable amount of teasing by friends and acquaintances who used to say that my Cossack was old enough to be drafted into the army. This of course made reference to the system under the Tsarist government when young men at that age had to report for military service. But age and lack of beauty were precisely Cossack's assets, for a younger and better looking horse would have been taken away from us in no time during those civil war days.

We had a little wagon. It was nothing fancy and we had acquired it for a very small sum of money. It was without springs, and so on bumpy roads we bumped along with every slight heave in the road. The upholstered seat was to no great avail in lessening the bumping noticeably. But horse and wagon were a valuable asset at the time, for it allowed us to visit my relatives in Rosental, a distance of better than fifty miles from Schoenfeld. We had a number of fine friends on that route and I shall never forget how wonderfully hospitable these Russian people were to us each time we came through their villages, feeding not only us but our trusted Cossack.

The conditions of the time necessitated that in addition to a cow or two we also raised our own chickens and pigs. One time we had a litter of seventeen piglets. These animal possessions were more valuable than money since the latter had lost all its value due to inflation. And speaking of piggies, one time we permitted ourselves the luxury of butchering one of them and roasting it whole. For so sumptuous a repast we invited the president of our school board for dinner.

And so, though we had little money, we did not as yet fare too badly as far as food was concerned. More difficult was the situation in regard to footwear and wearing apparel. These things simply were not available, and even thread for sewing on a patch or buttons became a rare item as time went on.

Our children, Margaret and Peter, were quite happy children. How memorable are the nice times we all used to have with their grandparents, the Bernhard Peters family. I happen to recall in particular the happy times of Easter we had with them. In early morning the children would be hunting Easter eggs, and the exciting shouts that would ensue when they happened to find them. Later in the morning we all would go to church and then enjoy the family dinner. If the weather was nice we would all gather outside after dinner, and the children and young people would play ball. Even Grandpa Peters could at times not resist the temptation to play with the youngsters. Our son Peter was usually called by the Russian diminutive "Petia", while Margaret went by the nickname of "Gritza." Naturally my wife and I, as parents in general, felt so sorry that our children had to hear and witness so many unpleasant things in their young lives, and we tried as best we could to make life more pleasant for them.

Schoenfeld was known for its friendliness. It was a small enough place so that you did not have to worry as to whether or not friends and acquaintances would remember the date of your birthday. It could be taken for granted that on the day in question there would be plenty of baked goodies for the traditionally famous Mennonite custom of "faspa" (vesper time), or coffee time at around three or four o'clock in the afternoon. Of course it did not require a birthday for good Mennonites to interrupt even the busiest of days for an afternoon coffee-break. Still, birthdays were special occasions when delicious pastries would be prepared, when such was possible at all.

A special time in Schoenfeld was also the hog-butchering time in late October or early November, an event which undoubtedly was equally significant in just about every Mennonite settlement. The size of the farm and the farmer's household largely determined the number of hogs that were killed on such an occasion, and might very well vary from two to five pigs. It was always an affair where the neighbors, friends and relatives got together for the work, which might start at four o'clock in the morning and last until the early hours of the evening. But among the participants were always several men who were known for their particular skills in this undertaking. A variety of preparations preceded the event. For example, the pigs were not fed the day before the butchering was to take place. Huge kettles for the boiling of water, a trough for the scalding of the pigs; scaffolds, ropes, etc., for the hanging of the pigs to be drawn and cleaned; tables for the cutting of the meat, sausage stuffers and various other pieces of equipment too numerous to mention here, were assembled the preceding day. Nor should one fail to mention that a sizeable bottle of vodka was an essential element for starting the day's work and capping it just before supper time. Needless to say, this was something in which only the menfolk indulged. Some of the tasks, like smoking the sausage and curing the hams, could not be completed on this day and were left for the owner of the farm to finish in due course. However, when the main tasks of the day were accomplished, the participants would end the day with a real feast, and before leaving for home each of them was as a rule given a present of fresh pork meat, be that in spare-ribs, sausages or other kinds.

Nor was the school teacher, or teachers, as the case might be, forgotten during the hog-butchering season, being remembered with an assortment of pork meat.

For school-age boys this annual event was one of a good deal of fun and pranks, not necessarily always confined to members of their own group but also with taking puns at the oldsters, especially in trying to pin the pigs tails to one or another of the *Ohmtjes* (men).

A favorite pastime in Schoenfeld was organized singing. We loved to sing and as Goethe says, "Where people sing, there you dwell in peace, for evil men have no songs." As was the custom in many Mennonite villages we had a community choir and we usually practiced on Monday evenings. My friend, brother in Christ and colleague, teacher Jacob Thiessen, was the choir director. It was wonderful to get together to sing and to have fellowship with one another. Now, after these many years I wonder what the purpose was for this choir to go on practicing week after week, because it never gave a single performance during the regular Sunday services. For some reason or another, our Mennonite churches did not believe in having choir music in church. Nor were there, with possibly very few exceptions, any musical instruments in our churches. So our choir practiced faithfully, but very seldom performed except on some special occasions. This in itself was a blessing for the participants.

School Conditions

During the winter of 1917-1918, despite frequently unsettled conditions, we managed to conduct classes regularly and on the whole with quite satisfactory results. A sufficient amount of coal had been obtained by the board of trustees to keep the school building and the teachers' quarters tolerably warm. The school equipment such as desks, books, and laboratory equipment had not deteriorated during the years of the school's forced closure to an extent which made instruction too difficult.

During the succeeding year, that is, in 1918-1919, conditions became almost intolerable. Fuel could not be gotten and the whole heating system broke down. Classes were often interrupted for days on end because of the proximity to the shifting fronts of the civil war, or because of bandit raids. Families often had to flee and so our enrollment declined. Despite these handicaps we somehow managed to keep the school going until the end of the spring term, conducting the classes in private homes.

CHAPTER 4

Anarchism

Situated four miles to the south of Schoenfeld was Liubimovka, a typically big peasant village. Here we had many friends, but also some enemies. The enmity was not of a personal nature, but stemmed from the fact that much of its population was so anarchistically inclined that it refused to recognize any form of authority above itself and, instead, preferred strongly to practice the then widely advocated policy of "plunder the plunderers", or to state it more accurately, their leaders liked to call themselves anarchists. They represented merely the characteristically Russian peasant proclivity toward brigandage in times of great social and political upheavals, as shown in past centuries in the following of Stenka Razin and Pugachev, and currently by the very numerous adherents of the many bat'kos (leaders, or little fathers) who roamed throughout large portions of Southern Russia during the years 1918-1920.

Here let me mention first of all, the name of one of these bat'kos, Simeon Panteleimon Pravda, an interesting but also frightening man. In the first place, his last name Pravda means "Truth". One may recall that this is also the name of the official organ of the Russian Communist Party, Pravda or the "Truth". In the second place, Simeon Pravda's physical appearance was bound to leave an impression upon anyone who saw him which would be difficult to erase from one's memory. Many years back, while working as a miner in the Don Coal Basin, he had lost both legs up to his knees when he had tried to board a moving train in a heavily inebriated condition. Not having been provided with prosthesis, he walked on the stumps of his legs. In early 1918 he had succeeded in placing himself at the head of a sizeable group of local brigands who, as already pointed out, liked to call themselves anarchists.

I shall use both terms in this story but I would like to emphasize that few, if any, of the local bat'kos or their followers knew anything about anarchism as a philosophy or as a program of action, except that they were opposed to any form of restraint upon themselves. This was also generally true of the supreme "anarchist leader" of these years in Southern Russia, namely Bat'ko Makhno, about whom much will be related below. This is not to say that the individual Bat'ko might not personally kill on the spot one of his close associates or ordinary followers for a slight infraction of an order issued by the leader, or for excessive plunder, but this was solely an expression of momentary anger of the despot over personally sustained embarrassment or inconvenience.

Simeon Pravda had two brothers, generally known in our vicinity as Grishka and Mit'ka, diminutives for the names of Grigorii and Dimitrii. These two also played a prominent role in the general Makhno movement (commonly called the Makhnovshchina) though not at all commensurate with that of Simeon. Unless otherwise indicated, reference to Bat'ko Pravda simply as Pravda here pertains to Simeon.

Pravda, in years prior to the revolution, had made his living primarily as a beggar. He would frequently visit our villages driving a small horse hitched to a tiny wagon, and invariably accompanied his begging with the playing of an accordian.

Several other families from Liubimovka should be mentioned here. First, there was the family of Saveli Evtushenko. His wife's name was Maria. She was a blessing to us all, for she was a God-fearing woman with a Godless and stubborn husband. I recall two daughters of this family. The elder one we called Zin'ka (from Zinovia), and the younger one, Sashka (from Alexandra). The latter had served at my wife's grandparents', a family by the name of Toews, while the former had served in the house of Truda's parents. Both of these girls; therefore, had heard the gospel and later became, together with their husbands, real Christian people. Sashka's husband was called Peter Policarpov, and Zin'ka's was called Michael Peresypkin. The latter was generally known to us simply as Mishka. At the start of the anarchist movement Peter and Mishka went along with its freedom from any restraint and the use of unbridled liberty to plunder. Several years later they changed their ways and became fine Christian men. We shall hear more about them later.

As already mentioned before, I, as well as the other teachers, had milch cows to supplement our reduced support from the constituency of our school. Obtaining cattle feed was a difficult matter. The farmers in our neighborhood had been generally expropriated, or had been left in an economic situation which barely left them fodder for their own depleted livestock. Hence, there was little else for me to do but to take the scythe and to go into the fields in search of grass. I found a patch near a brook and went to work. After the passage of some time I noticed a man at the stream a short distance away trying to catch some fish. In need of a rest, I decided to walk over to him and before long we were engaged in an animated conversation. His name was Grigorii Kurilenko. I had not yet been elected to the post of a preacher and, in fact, had never given any thought to such a calling. However, I deeply believed in Jesus Christ who had said, "Out of the fulness of the heart, the mouth speaketh", and I spoke earnestly about Christ to Kurilenko. Some years later this man did become a true believer in God and follower of Christ.

Nestor Makhno

I wish that I would not have to write about this man, who was just about my age. He was a peasant who lived only about twenty miles from our home in Schoenfeld. Like Pravda, Makhno also came from a very large nearby peasant village, this one called Guliai Polie. Literally translated, it would mean the village of "Pleasure Field." A number of books have been written about Nestor Makhno as the most influential, and for a few years, the most powerful of all brigands or, if one prefers, of all anarchist leaders of the Russian Revolution in Southern Russia during the years 1918-1920.

Let me cite here a conversation which I had in 1918 with the president of our school board, Mr. Neufeld, about this man Makhno. It is based upon lengthy notes I kept at that time about the political developments in our area, but these notes, though extensive, are somewhat jumbled because in those days one had to be extremely careful of what one put down in one's diary. Hence, I am reproducing the conversation with Mr. Neufeld as best as I am able to recall it.

S.: "Mr. Neufeld, do you think this Makhno will find many adherents and supporters in this region and thus possibly cause much damage to our area?"

N.: "Naturally, I do believe so. Just think of it; what is easier in our time than to become the leader of a large group of bandits, and Makhno has all the qualifications for such a position."

S.: "Do you know Makhno personally?"

N.: "No, Mr. Schroeder, and I do not wish any personal acquaintanceship with this inhuman being. However, I have some knowledge of him from one of the landowners in our vicinity. Mr. X, whose estate is not far from Guliai Polie."

S.: "That is interesting. It must not be comfortable or convenient for a Mennonite landowner like Mr. X to live in the neighborhood of a man like Makhno."

N.: "Naturally not. But you know, Makhno has promised Mr. X not to touch his property or him personally. The question is whether anyone can trust the words of a man like this one. When the period of anarchy broke out, Mr. X tried to resist the plundering raids with the help of several German soldiers, and succeeded for awhile in repelling the bandits. However, one day Makhno sent a messenger to this Mennonite landowner. The message read, 'Jake Martynovich [this is not Mr. X's real name], I have not forgotten how in 1906 I found a place of refuge on your estate. There I succeeded in eluding the cruel dogs of the Tsarist police. It was only through your help and cooperation that in 1906 I succeeded in eluding the police and thus was saved from being shot by them. I have not forgotten the old practice of extending *khleb-sol* [the Russian practice of greeting someone, or reciprocating a favor, with the offer of bread and salt]. Do not shoot anymore, and we promise not to touch either you or your property.' "

S.: "That was quite nice of Mr. Makhno."

N.: "Oh, no. You musn't say 'Mr.' Since the Bolshevik seizure of control we have only 'Comrades' in our country, and no more 'Misters.' " After a brief pause of laughter over this change of terminology, I continued, "Yes, Comrade Makhno, that sounds real trustworthy."

N.: "Only you can't trust him. It has not taken him long to reveal what kind of a man he is."

S.: "But how did Makhno get to hide in this Mennonite landowner's property?"

N.: "That is simple. After he participated in some uprising in 1905-1906, the police instituted an extensive hunt for him, but he managed to hide on Mr. X's property. Had the owner reported him to the police, he would have had the whole gang of revolutionaries, or terrorists, against himself and might have been killed. Hence, Mr. X decided to keep quiet."

S.: "But I believe Makhno spent a number of years in prison."

N.: "Yes, he was later arrested by a troop of Cossacks. The fact that he is still alive Makhno attributes to a general manifesto of amnesty issued by the Tsar after the Revolution of 1905, which commuted the death sentences of a number of prisoners to life imprisonment. The last act of grace he received came from Kerensky, now the head of our government, who issued a decree of general amnesty to all political prisoners. So now you can see that we have to thank our friend Kerensky for having this man in our neighborhood."

S.: "Has he caused much disturbance by now?"

N.: "No, until now he has not been too bad, only he has placed himself in the position of leadership in the village soviet. As you know, we now have freedom for all people who previously were suppressed. It was obvious to anyone in Guliai Polie that if he did not vote for Makhno, he would be killed."

S.: "And so we can assume that he has the reigns in his hands and thus can do as he pleases. This is what we call 'svoboda' (freedom), and for this kind of freedom I am not very grateful. It is reported that he has already commenced with the division of land in his district."

N.: "Yes, for the time being he is sailing under the Communist banner, but anarchism is his program. One of his followers explained to me the different types of anarchists, and that Makhno belongs to the individualist anarchists. Russia is supposed to be a free country for all people, and so does not need a government any longer. Everyone should live and do as he or she pleases. This could mean that he, with his gang of adherents, could go and seize any and every kind of property he desires. The bad part of this is that he has started to organize his band of partisans and everyone is supposed to call him 'father', or in the Little Russian language, 'bat'ko.' And so his name is now Bat'ko Makhno. You should see how the people follow him and take his advice. He not only promises them land and other properties, as does Kerensky, but he gives it to them immediately. Not so long ago he toured portions of his district, murdered and robbed as he and his band pleased, and then called the people together and gave each one part of the loot—horses, cows, wagons, machines, clothing, bedding, and food. All this was divided among hundreds of people. From the landowners and the businesses in the area which he had visited, he took anything he enjoyed or wanted. This is 'svoboda.' But Mr. Schroeder, it will soon be evening and I must attend to some business."

S.: "I am sorry that you have to go now, but I greatly appreciate that you took the time to give me this information about Makhno. Good-bye."

Waves and Billows

Master, the tempest is raging! The billows are tossing high!
The sky is o'ershadowed with blackness, no shelter or help is nigh.
Carest Thou not that we perish? How canst Thou lie asleep?

When each moment so madly is threat'ning, a grave in the angry deep.
Refrain: The winds and the waves shall obey my will, Peace, be still!
Whether the wrath of the stormtossed sea,
Or demons, or men or whatever it be,
No water can swallow the ship where lies,
The Master of ocean and earth and skies;
They all shall sweetly obey My will; Peace, be still!

There were, of course, no radio stations in 1918. An occasional news-paper would reach us but it contained little news of the outside world, or even of what was transpiring in our own guberniia or of those bordering it. However, no particular antennae or extrasensory perception were required to tell us of what was coming. Poverty, dissatisfaction and dis-orders were all around us. Even in the more populated places in our vicinity which once enjoyed a relatively high standard of living and pos-sessed such amenities and conveniences of life such as doctors, pharma-cies, bookstores, etc., were now totally without them. Telephone com-munication had all but ceased to exist except between larger cities and between railroad junctions. The signs of the times abounded, and they looked ominous to anyone but the foolhardy.

The beginning of the 16th chapter of St. Matthew reads; "He answered and said unto them, When it is evening, ye say, it will be fair weather: for the sky is red. And in the morning, It will be foul weather today: for the sky is red and lowering. Oh, ye hypocrites, ye can discern the face of the sky; but can ye not discern the signs of the times?" This passage indicates that Jesus wishes us to be intelligent enough to interpret the signs of the times. We did so, though we did not always make the right diagnosis. Still, we saw the clouds coming and what they might bring to us. I won-der whether here in America we are able to interpret the signs of our times?

The occupation of the Ukraine by the armed forces of the Central Powers brought us more suffering. To be sure, there were optimists aplenty amongst us who were confident that the Germans and the Aus-trians would bring to us in South Russia machinery and many other goods which we needed so badly. Instead, the occupying powers took grains and all kinds of food-stuffs and shipped them to their respective countries. Their military forces perpetrated many deeds for which later we were to pay a heavy price, particularly for the arbitrary manner in which they arrested real and alleged enemies, such as terrorists and brigands, and then executed them summarily. Such acts engendered more violence. Few of us at the time realized that only twenty miles distant from us, in the village of Guliai Polie, a political prisoner had returned to his home in 1917 from the notorious prison Lubianka in Moscow. This was Nestor Makhno, a man who in a very short time was to become famous throughout the area as the leader of the broad masses of the peasantry who took it upon themselves to vent their unbridled fury and age-old hatreds against each and every one who allegedly had exploited them in the past. Among such real or imagined enemies were any landowners of a holding larger than theirs, be they Russian or so-called German colonists; former government officials, army officers, policemen, or clergymen of the former State Church.

Nestor Makhno had spent many years in the Lubianka Prison and claimed to have been won over to the philosophy of Anarchism by some of his fellow prisoners. Throughout Russian history the peasant, especially of the southern and southeastern regions of the empire, has been notorious for his proclivities toward brigandage or banditry. While to some readers the connotation between these two terms might be slightly different, in reality there was none at this time in any of the areas in which during 1918-1920 a host of bands had not ravaged and killed at will.

It required; therefore, no great effort on the part of Makhno to arouse the masses in and around Guliai Polie, an area which ere long and for several years to come was to be known as "the Heartland of the Makhnovshchina" (Makhno movement), with such slogans as "go and plunder the plunderers", a slogan which already had been made very popular by the Bolsheviks. Terror, pillage and murder soon became the order of the day by all who embraced the exhortations of Makhno and recognized him as their unchallenged leader. Soon he was dubbed by them as their "Batjko Makhno", i.e., their "Little Father Makhno", not entirely unlike many of the peasants had formerly regarded their emperor as "Batiushka Tsar," i.e., "Little Father Tsar."

It did not take· much time before Makhno arrogated for himself many of the trappings of an "Autocrat of All the Anarchists,"—a fine carriage drawn by a beautiful team of four white horses, driven by a liveried coachman, surrounded at all times by a bodyguard armed with rifle, pistol, sword, handgrenade and the fearsome Nagaika, the whip of frightful memory during Tsarist days when Cossack punitive detachments would terrorize the peasantry. Moreover, he assumed and used the instant power over life and death of the many "little batjkos" among his armed troops, and of course, over any human being who for some reason, or none at all, happened to arouse his displeasure. Except, possibly, for the officially instituted policy of terror by the Bolsheviks in the second half of 1918, few places in Russia experienced such an unbridled era of wanton slaughter, rape and pillage as those areas of Southern Russia which during 1918-1919 came, for shorter or longer periods of time, under control of this "Little Father Makhno." It was a period when everyone from the lower strata of society with a real cause of suffered injury, or imagined grievance had license to avenge himself.

During the summer and fall of 1918, Makhno and his followers, as did brigands in general all over Southern Russia, at first confined their major operations against the occupying German-Austrian forces for their support of the recently returned landowners and their exactions against the peasants of the neighborhood who had plundered their estates. The bandits' operations gradually assumed larger proportions as they felt the whip of the Germans and Austrians for their interference with the shipments of grains, cattle, and other foodstuffs to the Central Powers. And as the instances where these foreign punitive forces not only executed numerous individual bandits, but occasionally also levelled to the ground entire villages suspected of housing guerrillas, or bandits if you will, the latter retaliated more openly against the colonists who were suspected, often not without reason, for being on the side of the occupying troops.

Some of us were greatly troubled by such practices of the Central Powers. On one occasion, when enroute home to Schoenfeld after a visit with my relatives and friends in Rosental, I stopped in Alexandrovsk to visit the headquarters of the German-Austrian command in the eastern area of the Ekaterinoslav guberniia, to plead with one of the high-ranking officers to stop these reprisal tactics, pointing out to him that in the end this would only intensify the terrorist activities. I do not know how much good, if any, my counsel accomplished.

In the late fall of this year, as the Germans and other occupying armies withdrew from the Ukraine, they left plenty of weapons in the hands of the colonists, including many Mennonites. By some, the weapons were intended to be used solely for purposes of self-defense, while others possibly hoped to use them to avenge themselves for the sufferings they had endured at the hands of the Makhnovtsy during preceding months.

As time progressed, Makhno's power and influence mounted, and his armed strength steadily increased. And as the size of his army grew, he appointed a number of his closest friends and henchmen as "batjkos" of different units. One of the most famous of these terrorist-executioners was "Batjko Pravda" (Little Father Truth).

At this time we were expecting our third baby. We were fortunate to have at our disposal the services of a maternity nurse, Miss Elizabeth Harder, who had previously assisted with the delivery of our two older children in 1915 and 1917. She was a well-educated woman and we were tremendously pleased to be able to accommodate her in our own quarters on the high school campus. Since there were no doctors available in our village or in the immediate vicinity, Miss Harder was often called upon for assistance whenever someone was ill in the community, not only by the local citizenry, but also by members of Makhno's troops quartered there.

Another person staying with us was the recently employed teacher in our high school, Miss Helen Froese, the daughter of my cousin Abraham Froese, a teacher in the high school of Nicolaipol. She taught music. And as pointed out earlier we also had the maid, Miss Tina Knelsen. Despite the turmoil all around us we were, on the whole, a happy and congenial group and often would sing songs and praises to God.

One Sunday morning in October of this year, while enroute to church services, I was surprised to see the streets so deserted. There was neither person nor vehicle visible anywhere. My apprehension grew as I entered the church. Our Mennonite churches did not have choirs or organs, and the congregational singing was led by a group of songleaders, usually three or four in number. This morning one sensed an air of apprehension, for the songleaders kept on leading the congregation in one song after another, but neither minister nor deacons made their appearance. Everyone waited with some foreboding. Finally, the pastor, Rev. Jacob L. Dyck entered the sanctuary. He went to the pulpit and quietly announced that word had been received that Makhno with a sizeable force had arrived in a neighboring village about eight miles distant from Schoenfeld. It was clear to everyone what this meant—murder, looting and raping. Thereupon Rev. Dyck asked the assembled for advice as to what the community should do in the imminence of a possible early arrival of the brigands. I recall a man, possibly in his forties, getting up and suggesting that since many of the inhabitants had plenty of rifles and ammunition in their homes the best procedure would be to have everyone go home, pick up his weapons and return to Schoenfeld and be prepared for self-defense. I do not recall whether there was much discussion on this recommendation, but the pastor asked for those in favor of the suggestion to rise. The majority of the men did.

But there were also voices of opposition, particularly from members of our Bible study and prayer group. And then there was the old Mrs. Warkentin, mother of one of the deacons of our church, who advised that we stay in church and pray. Her advice went unheeded. The meeting was closed without any attempt to hold a service. The men went home and soon returned with their arms. The display of resolution and of weapons was devoid of any value and perhaps did us more harm. Of what use would such a small and wholy untrained group have been against a large troop of Makhnovtsy armed to the teeth and ready to slaughter anyone who resisted them? As luck would have it, Makhno did not advance to our village, but sent word the next day that he would leave us unharmed if we surrendered all our weapons at a specified place. This was done.

Self Defense

The Selbst-Schutz, or the self-defense unit in our area crumpled when Makhno later met it with machine gun fire. Our armed men fled, whereupon a hasty evacuation ensued to the large complex of Mennonite colonies on the Molochnaia. I shall not forget how my colleague, Jacob Thiessen, and I happened to encounter on our street some of the members of this self-defense unit returning from the scene of the skirmish with the Makhnovtsy. Some of them accused their comrades of having fled the scene of action at the very start of the encounter. Before long we beheld one wagonload of people after another hastily leaving our beloved Schoenfeld. In many homes people were in such panic that they left their suppers untouched and fled. Thiessen and I were momentarily at a loss of what to do. We had no teams and wagons at our disposal. Moreover, my dear wife was in no condition to undertake such a hasty flight. All we could do was to stay and pray and await the unknown. And how we prayed that God would protect the fleeing ones as well as us.

A third teacher of our school, Mr. Henry P. Neufeld, had his own horse, and throughout the night he repeatedly scouted the streets and the immediate environs of the village to find out whether there were any signs that the Makhnovtsy were advancing in our direction. He was unable to find any evidence of an impending invasion and reported so to us. Still, there was an intense air of apprehension in our quarters on the school campus. Except for the children, who had been put to bed with their clothes on, none of us went to bed, although occasionally one would lie down to rest awhile. We stayed together, alternately praying and discussing the fate that might be in store for us.

The following morning Thiessen and I went out to see what, if anything, was taking place in different parts of our village. The first person we met was the village herdsman who was making his usual round to collect the farmers' cattle to be driven to the pasture. He reported that there was hardly a soul left in the village. As we went from house to house we heard the livestock in the barns bellowing to be fed, and looking through windows we noticed that in many places the previous evening's food still standing on the dining room or kitchen tables. The flight had all been in the direction of one or another of the many colonies in the Molochnaia settlement. However, the fugitives had not gotten very far during the night, and when they got word that all was quiet at home, many decided to risk returning.

Holding school under such conditions was an impossibility. Earlier I made reference to Batjko Pravda. He decided that now was the time for him to make Schoenfeld the base of his depradation operations. Across the street from my in-laws', B.J. Peters', was the homestead of a John Warkentin, a nice brick dwelling. Here is where this batjko, Simeon Pravda, established his headquarters. The horses and tachankas (light spring wagons) used by himself and his staff were housed in the stables and barns of the nearby farms of Henry B. Wiens and Peter Enns.

And so we had a new government with which I, as principal of the high school, from now on had to deal. One day I went to visit our new ruler, Batjko Pravda. The Warkentins had been successful farmers, and everything in house and yard bore testimony to the love and care with which they had treated their possessions. But oh, what a change had taken place in the space of a very short period of time. The house which Mrs. Warkentin had always maintained in immaculate cleanliness bore vivid though mute testimony to the treatment it was receiving from its new occupants. Thick mud covered the floors and there was dirt and filth everywhere. But I also beheld a strange contrast. The samplers with their Biblical mottoes were still hanging on the wall, and the small organ in the living room was still there without any apparent signs of abuse. After awhile I was asked by some of the bandits whether I could play the organ. I told them that I could, and was then immediately asked to play for them. I played and sang some folk and some spiritual songs, all the while praying that it might have a salutary affect upon some of them.

The chief purpose of my going to our new government's leader had been to inquire whether we could reopen our school and resume instruction. The batjko's reply, "By all means you should open the school, and we will protect you." With that he issued orders to his underlings that no one was to molest us and that students from outside of Schoenfeld were to be allowed freely to come and go to school. So a friendly understanding had been reached. The question was, would it be kept?

Meanwhile, the bandits went about their professed business of avenging the alleged injustices which the peasants of the area had suffered at the hands of the Mennonites and other colonists; and of course "To plunder the plunderers". Many an afternoon or towards evening we would see hayracks loaded high with loot from farms and businesses of the surrounding area being driven into the Warkentin yard, now the "benevolent" leader's headquarters. Upon invitation from this modern version of a Robin Hood, the poor peasants from neighboring villages would appear in great numbers to share in the division of the spoils of the day. But we in the school were generally left unmolested except for an occasional prowler or two who might enter a classroom. Thus one day, a group of them entered my room while I was teaching geometry, but they soon learned that they were prowling in the wrong place since they obviously were not interested in the study of geometry.

With the establishment of this leader's headquarters in Schoenfeld we were at the complete mercy of this "Little Father" and his henchmen. Simeon Pravda was of course only one, though admittedly one of the most notorious, underlings of the "Supreme Little Father" on the left bank of the Dnieper, as indeed throughout Southern Russia, during the years 1918-1920, namely Batjko Makhno. Most of these batjkos professed to be Anarchists if not in philosophy, then at least in action. Their slogans were "svoboda" (freedom), which they interpreted as license to do anything they pleased—to steal, rob, plunder, and kill for alleged cause, or simply because at a given moment it happened to strike their fancy to show their contempt for a human life which was not on their level of bestiality, and; therefore, was entered as "expense", to use one of their favorite expressions for such acts of terror.

Let me cite a few examples of the type of experiences most of us were exposed to during the reign of the Makhnovtsy. It was common place for a Makhnovets, like Gregorri F., or for a group of them, to storm into a house at any time of the day or night and demand that a chicken dinner be prepared and be served within so many minutes or the housewife would have to take the consequences. Or some bandit might spot a ring on the finger of a woman and demand there and then that it be surrendered to him. I recall a case of a teacher by the name of Isaak who lived near Schoenfeld. A member of a band happened to notice the wedding ring on the hand of the teacher's wife. He demanded that she give it to him immediately. When she was unable to do so quickly enough because of a swollen finger, he threatened to kill her there and then. A similar incident befell one of the farmers in our school district and with tragic consequence. His name was Warkentin. He was a widower. After the bandits had taken his horses they loaded the wagons with booty of anything they could find in the house. Among the expropriated items was a watch which was particularly dear to this man since it was a gift from his deceased wife. When he begged for its restitution, a member of the gang raised his revolver and killed him with a pointblank shot in the head with the accompanying words: "There, you have your watch."

How hard a lesson it was for us to learn to part with all kinds of things and different pieces of property which we had loved and cherished. But not only were we compelled to learn such lessons, but what was often much more difficult to do was when we were forced to help them load our own goods into wagons just taken from us, or from our neighbors, and to do so in the most expeditious manner and with a smile. May I suggest reading Hebr. 10:32-39, and ponder the advice contained therein.

Knowing that our turn might soon come where we too would face being liberated from some of our cherished possessions, my wife and I decided that we might share some of our belongings with the expropriators. Among other things I decided to give one of my best dark suits to one of the men. His name was Mishka Shinkarenko. He had taken possession of the house of our close friend Peter Enns who had fled to the Molochnaia. Mishka was very proud to strut around among his fellowbandits in such a nice suit.

About this time when so many of the Mennonites from our area had fled south, I was told that in the abandoned farm house of a once prosperous widow was a very nice piano. Some of her friends who had stayed behind, fearing that this valuable instrument might easily be destroyed, suggested that perhaps I could arrange through Batjko Pravda to have the piano moved to our school. Since I had had a pleasant encounter with this man on an earlier occasion, I decided to approach him about this matter. He agreed immediately, and to my surprise he lived up to it, for a few days later the piano was delivered to us, accompanied by a certificate that it was the property of the school and was not to be taken away.

One day Batjko Pravda came to visit us at school. He arrived in a beautiful carriage, a phaeton, drawn by three spirited horses and driven by a coachman in a nice uniform. Pravda was accompanied by one of his trusted men, Fedjka Karpenko. After a brief interval, Pravda told me that he had come expressly to see the piano which he had given to our school, and that he wished to hear some music. I decided to send for our music teacher, Miss Froese (currently a widow named Thiessen and living in Leamington, Ontario), who at the moment happened to be at a neighbor's house. The piano had in fact been placed in her room at the time we received it. Miss Froese was reluctant to comply, but in the end decided to come back to school and play several pieces. Meanwhile my wife, our maid, and Miss Harder, the nurse, busied themselves with preparing as good a meal as it was possible to put together under the prevailing conditions.

We tried to placate this man who possessed such final powers over our lives and those of our friends. The table was covered with a white tablecloth and white napkins were placed at each table setting. Pravda was greatly pleased with the meal and the table setting and soon directed Fedjka to go and fetch a bottle of refreshments from the carriage. Fedjka returned with a bottle of samogon, an evil smelling and vile tasting homebrew. Glasses were ordered, filled and all the men present were expected to consume that filthy stuff. When Fedjka came around to me I told him that I did not drink liquor. Pravda was adamant that I had to drink a toast with him. All my protestations were to no avail and I finally told Pravda that I would drink one glass, but only under his promise that I would not have to touch another drink. The promise was given. Soon Fedjka started filling the glasses again, but I held a hand over my glass and resolutely refused to let him fill it. At last, after repeated insistence by Fedjka that I must drink at least one more glass, I reminded him of Pravda's promise with the words, "I believe Pravda has given me his word. I still trust that he is keeping his promise." At that moment Pravda scolded Fedjka and told him, "Don't you know that when I make a promise, I keep it? You are trying to force the teacher to drink against his wishes and contrary to my promise. I shall let you have it when we get home." Fedjka knew what this meant—a good whipping, and begged not to be punished. The autocrat of the local gang of Makhnovtsy could mete out summary punishment on the spot as an Ivan the Terrible or a Peter the Great. The following case will serve to illustrate how Pravda asserted his unlimited power among his followers where such an assertion was deemed necessary or expedient to his own vanity.

I mentioned earlier that the farms of Wiens and Enns had been appropriated for the stabling and housing of the horses and wagons used by the batjko and his immediate staff. One day, Pravda visited one of the stables to check up on how well his horses were being cared for. In the course of the inspection he noticed that some of the good horse blankets had been carelessly tossed into a corner. Furious about such carelessness, he called several of his men whom he regarded to be guilty of the deed and, with his Nagan (revolver) in one hand and the nagaika in the other, he ordered the men who were by now thoroughly frightened and crying to lie down on the floor where he administered each a thorough whipping.

The frightfulness of our experiences at the hands of the Makhnovtsy was often heightened by the fact that there were rival gangs among them, who at times tried to outdo each other in acts of terror upon the hapless human beings whom they chose at the moment to be the victims of their lust for blood. Thus one day in a neighboring Lutheran village about five miles distant from Schoenfeld, a band of Makhnovtsy seized nine farmers and hanged them in the barn of one of the victims. The local Lutheran pastor and a friend of mine, Mr. Gruenke, who was the teacher in this village, were called to come to the farm house to conduct the mass funeral. The pastor, having been called on another errand of mercy, left immediately after the service but Mr. Gruenke remained. Suddenly, the assembled mourners noticed that the house was being encircled by a group of bandits. Anyone trying to escape was shot on the spot. Soon the frame building was surrounded by piles of straw and set on fire. All inside perished in the flaming structure, including my friend and fellow-teacher with whom only a few weeks earlier I had traveled to attend a district teachers' conference. Truda and I decided to comfort Mrs. Gruenke as far as it was possible for us to do so. She was able to stay with us for a number of days.

In view of the fact that the entire Warkentin family had fled, Batjko Pravda and his immediate entourage who had quartered themselves in the abandoned farm house, needed someone to cook for them. They conscripted for this job a widow, Mrs. Klein, and her two daughters who lived in a small cottage on the Warkentin farmstead. How we trembled over their fate and prayed for their safety. I would see them on occasions when I had to go to Pravda's headquarters, and at times when this leader would order that some food be prepared for us. But the Lord protected these women, for as far as I know they suffered no personal harm from the bandits.

On one of my visits Pravda drew his revolver from his pocket and proudly announced that "with this pistol I have already killed fifty-six people. The last victim was a doctor from Alexandrovsk." Then he added, "You know, I will never be taken alive by my enemies. When my end comes I will simply put this gun to my head." This he did in 1921 at the village of Turkenovka.

At another meeting when he had used a string of simply awful swear words, as was their usual custom, this man who could openly boast of having killed scores of people suddenly halted in his outpouring of foul language with the words, "Excuse me, this must be very unpleasant for you." I often wondered how much of a conscience was left in a man like Pravda.

In our meetings he always insisted that I call him by the familiar ty (thou), not vy (you), on the grounds that both of us were equals, and said, "You are a laborer, a teacher, not a capitalist. We consider you as one of us." He also insisted that I call him Senjka, the Russian endearing version of Simeon. I often complied with this request, and so our relationships were fairly good. Of course, I never for a moment could forget my apprehension as to how far one could trust a man like this.

Victims of Anarchism

In the vicinity of Schoenfeld lived a large number of wealthy Mennonite landowners on their private estates, or khutory, as they were called in Southern Russia. Often a group of closely related families would live on the same khutor or in close proximity to each other, generally having originally purchased a big estate from a Russian noble family or a wealthy member of the gentry or commercial class.

One such large and wealthy Mennonite family near Schoenfeld was named Schroeder (of no blood relationship to my family). All such estate owners as these Schroeders, except for those who in the early fall of 1918 had fled either to the Molochnaia settlement or to the Crimea, suffered indescribable tortures at the hands of the Makhnovtsy and paid a frightful toll in the number of their members murdered by these bandits.

Let me briefly list the fate of a number of members of this particular family. The first to be murdered was Abram Schroeder, and the manager of his estate. They had driven a relatively short distance from the estate to look over some fields when they were surprised by a troop of Makhnovtsy and were forthwith killed by having their throats slit and left to bleed to death. Neighbors accidentally happened to discover their bodies. Next came two nephews of his, Gerhard and Peter, sons of Abram's brother, Gerhard Schroeder, Sr. They were overtaken on the road while driving to Schoenfeld. As they were nearing the Mennonite colony of Brazol, about four miles from our village, they noticed a group of mounted Makhnovtsy coming down the road. They tried to escape but were soon captured and greeted with horrible cursing, "Oh, here you are, you bloody dogs, you blood suckers of the poor. We will settle our account with you today. Back toward Brazol, for we have to present you to our Batjko Makhno. He will be glad to see such boys before eating his supper."

The begging, crying and pleading of the two young men was in vain.

Triumphantly they were brought before Makhno who praised the men for their courageous act of catching the "exploiters of the poor and of the laborers." Makhno reminded them of the fate that was in store for such people and told his men to proceed with their act of revenge. The victims were ordered to undress and then they were hacked to pieces.

The wife of the slain Gerhard Schroeder, Jr. was an expectant mother at this time, and not too long after this terrible tragedy, Mr. Schroeder, Sr. came to Schoenfeld to get the maternity nurse, Miss Harder. I tried as well as I could to extend my sympathies to him and his family and to console him by calling to his attention the words in Revelation 7:14. He expressed his appreciation for my words of sympathy, and then said, "It is so hard to keep faith in these dark times and to believe that there is a just God when we see how such unrighteousness and iniquity are spreading in our country."

What serious thoughts filled many hearts when in evening devotion we would sing that well-known evening prayer, "When from care I seek repose, when in sleep mine eyelids close, Father, let thine eyes now be watching o'er me tenderly." Quite often also we would sing the German version of the song "What a Friend We Have in Jesus. All our sins and griefs to bear, what a privilege to carry everything to God in prayer." Songs such as these had a special meaning in many hearts during those days of terror since every night we were very conscious of the possible harrowing experiences it might bring. In the morning we would often kneel and thank God that we had been able to sleep through the night undisturbed.

Now after many years as I write this, the question arises in my mind, "Have we become so indifferent and complacent that we do not even kneel down in the evening to thank God for the day, and to ask for his protection for the night? May we learn this lesson in good times!

The tragedies for the Schroeder family continued during those terrifying days of late 1918 and during the early part of 1919. Not many weeks after two of his sons had been massacred, Gerhard Schroeder, Sr. and his son, Willy, were slain in the family home after the house had once more been thoroughly ransacked and anything of value loaded and carted away. For reasons known only to this particular band of Makhnovtsy, Mrs. Schroeder was not harmed.

A few days later I accompanied a family from our vicinity to the funeral on the Schroeder estate for the latest victims of the heavily bereaved family. When we reached the outbuildings of the estate we noticed that there were many bandits in the yard and we feared for our lives. But when I asked one of the mounted bandits whether I could go and visit a teacher friend who lived nearby, he said to go ahead. From the teacher's dwelling we could see that the Schroeder place was overrun by Makhnovtsy and we feared that there might be a mass slaughter of people who had come to the funeral. After prolonged waiting; however, we received a message that the bandits were in the process of leaving and that the funeral service was about to take place. The service was very short.

And so two more members of this family were buried. The only survivor of its older members was Henry, brother of the slain Gerhard and Abram Schroeders. I felt strongly that he was risking too much by staying in our area and urged him as insistently as I could to leave for a safer place. But he would not heed my pleas.

At the beginning of September 1919 my family and I decided that it was not safe for us to remain in Schoenfeld and; therefore, we moved to Rosental to stay at the home of my parents. Henry Schroeder stayed, despite increasing signs that the White Armies might not be able to hold on to the territory which, during the late spring and summer of this year, they had wrested from the Red Army and its then ally, the Makhnovtsy bands. Were this to happen, the bandits would be in their home territory in short order around Guliai Polie and Liubimovka, all in the immediate neighborhood of Schoenfeld. The Makhnovtsy did break through the White Army front near Uman during the third week of September, reached the Chortitza-Rosental area on September 21, and a few days later got back to their home base. Although the retreating White forces temporarily forced the Makhnovtsy to retreat back to the right bank of the Dnieper, their acts of terror were immediately resumed. Henry Schroeder happened to be among some of the first to be slain. He was killed in the orchard of his sister who lived in Schoenfeld where he had hoped to be temporarily safe.

Having sketched briefly the tragic fate of this Schroeder family during the course of roughly the period from October 1918 to October 1919, let me go back to my own family and our experiences in Schoenfeld during approximately the same time span. Toward the end of November 1918 our third child, Katherine, was born. Although there was neither a doctor nor a pharmacy in our village we were fortunate, as I have already mentioned earlier, to have a maternity nurse living with us in the teacherage in Schoenfeld. The mother and baby fared well in spite of the unrest and turmoil that were raging all around us.

The terror of the Makhnovtsy continued unabated. One day in early December I saw one of my former students, Jacob Wiens, come running into the schoolyard. Although it was a cold day, I noticed that he was without shoes and in an obvious state of terrible fright. As soon as he saw me he asked whether he could hide in the school from a group of bandits who were searching for him in their home. I told him that the school would be a very unsafe place for him to escape capture, for the bandits had most likely observed him running in its direction. Therefore, I urged him to try to reach an abandoned brickyard at not too great a distance in back of the high school. This he did, and just in time, for not many minutes later a number of Makhnovtsy arrived at the school and told me that, "we are looking for that Wiens boy. We are going to make him pay for what it means to slap someone in the face," and forthwith insisted upon searching the school. In order to give the boy a few minutes extra time to reach a hiding place, I took the searchers into every room, the attic and the basement of the school, asking them to look into every nook and cranny. Having found no trace of the pursued youth in the school building, I then showed them every room of the teacherage in which we lived. And Jacob did manage to elude capture.

However, the father of this youngster, Mr. Henry B. Wiens, was not as fortunate. He was a member of our high school board of trustees and lived only a short distance from the school campus. One day we saw several Makhnovtsy driving into the yard of the Wiens' home, and not much later noticed them coming back in our direction, Mr. Wiens with them. They drove into the yard where Batjko Pravda had his headquarters, straight across the street from our classroom building. This seemed ominous, and we feared greatly for his life. Our apprehensions were confirmed, for scarcely had the bandits with Mr. Wiens disappeared into the headquarters of their leader, when the Wiens' daughter, Agatha, came running to us and informed us that her father had been terribly beaten by these men. Would I come with her and try to help console her mother?

I went with her at once and tried to comfort the family as best I could with word and prayer. In answer to my inquiry as to the charges the bandits had made against Mr. Wiens, I was told that they had made no specific charges but merely accused him of having done something in the past. Actually my inquiry about charges preferred was superfluous, for in those days of the civil war in Russia, and particularly during the period of the Makhnovshchina, warrants for arrest and charges preferred were things which neither bandits nor self-proclaimed governments seldom bothered themselves. Hatred, suspicion or simple dislike of a person by bandits or governments in those days were sufficient causes for that person to be summarily executed or virtually tortured to death. Mr. Wiens, though virtually beaten into unconsciousness, was fortunate in finally being allowed, or rather ordered, to run home under desultory revolver shots being fired in pursuit of him.

CHAPTER 5

Shall We Escape?

The question of whether to stay in Schoenfeld or to try to escape to the Molochnaia as so many Schoenfelders had done already, or whether to attempt to reach Rosental where my parents and so many of my relatives lived, had been seriously considered by us in late 1918 and even more so during the months prior to the fall of 1919. Truda's parents, the B.J. Peters, who lived in the immediate proximity of the high school, had until the advent of the chaotic conditions in 1918 been a very prosperous business family. As such it had naturally been the especial target of numerous visits by a host of bandits long before the establishment of Batjko Pravda's headquarters almost directly across the street from the store owned by Father Peters. All of these day and nocturnal intrusions had the same purposes and end results, and inevitably concluding with such plunder as suited the bandits, be they members of Nestor Makhno's gangs or of some other local batjko. Thus on one of the first major raids upon the store, twelve men loaded four wagons with an assortment of loot, plus a "contribution" of 3,500 rubles. One of the men threatened to kill the owner but was prevented by the leader of the group who happened to know Father quite well. It was not an act of concern for the owner's life which prompted this intercession, but was caused merely for purposes of extortions of money in the future. Such a raid came only a short time later when the same group of men, again with four wagons, arrived and loaded them with all kinds of goods from the store and the machine shop. Fortunately, this time Father Peters was not at home.

Experiences like these compelled us to consider ever more seriously the necessity to resolve the dilemma of whether to stay or to flee, a decision which we weighed repeatedly; but were loath to make it. I should hasten to add that it was not merely a matter of deciding to leave a place which had been a dear and long-time home to the Peters family, or a decision to abandon a heavy investment in a once-flourishing business enterprise. For myself and family it was also the wish to serve the high school as long as it was humanly possible to do so. Finally, it was also a matter of where to seek refuge and the immediate consideration whether flight itself was not just as hazardous as staying and taking a chance on possible survival where we were.

Take, for instance, the tragedy which befell a family by the name of Nicolai Thiessen which lived only a few miles from Schoenfeld. Thiessen, his wife and daughter, and a small child decided to flee to the Molochnaia. They had driven only some ten miles from their abandoned home when they encountered a group of Makhnovtsy. Instead of killing them outright by shooting them, the bandits commenced to hack Thiessen and wife to pieces with their sabers, but leaving daughter and baby unharmed. After assuring themselves that Thiessen was dead, and assuming the same of his wife, the bandits took the slain man's horses and wagon and departed, leaving daughter and baby with the corpses lying on the road. However, Mrs. Thiessen was not dead and lived for a number of hours until another troop of bandits passed by and administered the coup de grace, but again leaving daughter and baby unharmed. Perhaps they had a bit of conscience left, or maybe they were disarmed by the pleas of the young mother that if they killed her they should also kill the baby.

Once Batjko Pravda established his headquarters in Schoenfeld, every home in the village except the teacherage was filled with bandits, and as a rule left the owners, if they were still around, the smallest rooms in the house. The mistress of the house was a matter of course compelled to prepare meals for the unbidden guests at any time of the day or night whenever it struck their fancy to eat.

Father Peters' family, including the parents and several daughters, were left two small rooms. His business was forthwith declared the property of Pravda and his followers. But since they had no competence in running either the store or operating the machine shop, Father Peters and the family were ordered to manage the business for them, without any compensation to any of them. Still, they could regard themselves as fortunate in at least being allowed limited quarters in their own home where in the evenings they could be together, however crowded the conditions might be under which they had to live.

Soon incidents began to take place in the store involving members of the locally quartered bandits which made every member of the family very uneasy about the safety of their father. The incidents were of such a nature that little doubt was left that some of the bandits were determined to kill Mr. Peters. Was Batjko Pravda behind this, or even aware of such a threat? We did not know. And who could place any credence in his disavowal, supposing that one had apprized him of the incidents in the store?

For the time being these incidents were not of too overt a nature, but apparently designed to frighten father. Then one very stormy night in December of 1918, at about 11 o'clock, the family was suddenly aroused by a loud rifle-butt knocking on the door of the room which was occupied by the two daughters. The knocking was accompanied by very excited demands that the door be opened at once. One of the daughters complied and was confronted by five drunk men, each in the usual Makhnovtsy fashion armed with rifle, revolver, saber and hand grenades. In response to her question of what they wanted, the reply was that they wished to see Mr. Peters at once. Four of the men came in and sat down while one positioned himself at the entrance door. Meanwhile, the other daughter had slipped into the parents' bedroom to inform father of the visitors and their demand. He had heard the commotion and, though not completely dressed, went to meet them, and was told by the leader of the group, "Go and get dressed and come with us into the basement. Be sure to bring the keys to the cellar along."

Father B.J. Peters' Flight

The meaning of such a command was all too well known. Almost invariably this, as well as another frequent command of the time, namely to accompany them into the yard, usually meant execution. So when father got back to his room to get dressed, he told mother, "Now it is time. I have to die." Her response was, "Our Heavenly Father for whose protection we have prayed every evening and every morning will not permit this to happen." While father proceeded to dress himself, mother joined the daughters in the front room and talked with the Makhnovtsy. Father used this opportunity to scout for exit possibilities. The door in their room leading to the outside faced the street and he noticed that there were guards near it. So he decided to exit through a window. The ground being muddy and soft allowed him to get out without creating any noise, and silently he made his way through the dark yard and orchard, and thence across a small creek into the open fields. After hours of walking and stumbling over wet and slippery fields in very cold weather he finally succeeded in reaching an empty barn in which he decided to rest for a spell. His clothes were soaking wet, he was chilled to the marrow, and terribly frightened over the possible fate that might have befallen his dear ones at home. After a while he resumed his walk, though without any consciousness of the direction he was going, spurred on by the desperate need to find a warm shelter. At last he stumbled upon the outbuildings of a farm. Afraid to go closer to the dwellings for fear that the dogs whose barking he heard might alert bandits whom he suspected of occupying the main house of the farm, he decided to take shelter in a straw stack. Here he remained the rest of the night and throughout the following day, however cold and uncomfortable this hiding place was. The wisdom of this action was confirmed when during the day he heard voices in the farm yard and dogs barking, as well as some shooting.

When night came he resumed his wandering. Desperately hungry, cold and shivering in his wet clothes, his body racking with pain, he at last chanced to reach the outskirts of a Lutheran village. Noticing light in a small cottage he cautiously approached it and peeked through the uncurtained window. Inside he observed a young couple and a baby in the cradle. The wife was busy with preparing their own bed, while the husband who was sitting at a small table, hymn book in hand, was quietly singing a hymn. The couple's name was Wansiedler whom Father Peters knew slightly, and as he told us later, "Never in my life has a song given me so much joy as the hymn I heard from inside the cottage. Now I knew I would be given shelter." A slight knock on the window caused Mr. Wansiedler to look out. He at once recognized the man at the window, came outside and bid Father Peters to enter. Informed of the fugitive's situation, the young couple did everything possible within their limited means and with borrowed clothing from some neighbors of theirs, to make father comfortable.

Makhnovtsy were prowling day and night in the village, but because of the smallness of this place none came to disturb the Wansiedlers. Father spent nineteen restful days with them and this, no doubt, saved him from having taken seriously ill.

Several days after father's arrival at the Wansiedlers a message about his safety was sent in a very roundabout way to us in the high school, and then cautiously relayed to Mother Peters and the daughters. Our feeling of relief and joy over father's safety can well be imagined. For the moment; however, it was imperative for all of us not to communicate the news to others, though inquiries were continuously made by neighbors and friends as to whether any word of his whereabouts had ever reached us.

But let me briefly report what had been happening in the Peters' residence right after father's escape through the window. The bandits waited quite patiently for him to return and thence to accompany them to the basement. But when he failed to show up they commenced to search for him throughout the house, attic, basement, and the yard. Still, they were not particularly excited about his disappearance, apparently under the assumption that he could not have gotten very far in such stormy weather and during the darkness of the night. The search continued for awhile the next day but was then abandoned. However, word was conveyed to Mother Peters from Pravda's headquarters that in view of her husband's disappearance, his property, as that of an enemy of the people, was forthwith declared to be that of Pravda's followers, and that anyone was free to go and help himself to what he wanted.

Perhaps this had all along been the bandit's objective—not to kill father, but to scare him sufficiently and prompt him to flee for his life and thus to find a "legitimate" excuse to rob the family of all its belongings. Such was often their procedure with entire Mennonite villages situated at some distance from large Mennonite settlements, or with villages lying on the periphery of the Old Colony, as for example Kronsweide, Neuhorst, and others. But whatever the motives of the Makhnovtsy in this particular instance, they had achieved the results that usually followed the arrest of a man of prominence or of property. The man was shot, or perhaps he managed to escape with his life, but for the man's possessions the end result was the same, either "legal" expropriation or simply wholesale looting.

And this is what happened to father's property. The day after his disappearance bandits and ordinary peasants from the surrounding villages showed up with perhaps twenty wagons and proceeded to strip the family dwelling, from attic to cellar, the store and the machine shop of everything that could be lifted, wrenched or broken loose, including furniture, furnishings, dishes, food, clothing, laundry, tools, etc., leaving mother and the daughters with the barest minimum of clothing, food, and furniture.

Sometime after the news of father's safe escape and current whereabouts had reached us in Schoenfeld, mother decided to go to see Batjko Pravda and to ask him what might be his fate were he found to be alive. Pravda's reply was, "Just let him come home. Nothing will happen to him. He can live here in peace. We know he is our friend and I would like to see him first when he comes home." Mother promised that her husband would report to him as soon as he came home.

A message was thereupon sent to father's place of hiding and told of the assurances given by Pravda for his safety at home. However, he was reluctant to place any trust in this leader, and decided for the time being to remain where he felt he was safe. Since the Wansiedlers were very poor people our family and relatives resolved to send them clothing and food. A note was sent to them that if possible they were to dispatch someone to pick up these items in Schoenfeld. Accordingly, two representatives of the poorest people in that village with equally poor houses and a nondescript wagon came to our home and were supplied with a goodly amount of foodstuffs and clothing. On their return journey to their home village, named Kankrin, they were robbed of a large share of the provisions by a number of bandits who prowled over the entire countryside.

Father Peters remained with the Wansiedlers for a week and then decided to take a chance on staying with acquaintances in another Lutheran village. He got there safely but soon found himself in gravest danger of being snared by other bandits. It was by the sheerest luck that he succeeded in eluding them while they were searching the premises of his new hosts. He; therefore, decided to return to Kankrin and to seek refuge once more with the family which so far had harbored him so safely.

It was now eighteen days since father had been forced to leave his family with such suddenness and so unprepared for a lengthy absence from his beloved ones. Christmas was only one day away and he decided that he could no longer bear to be away from the family. A trustworthy man was engaged to take him home. He had shaved off his beard, and the old uniform of a soldier which he had donned made him all but unrecognizable. For fear that his home might be under surveillance, he decided to be taken to a neighbor's home. Word was then sent to mother that father had safely arrived and that he was staying with friends nearby. It can easily be surmised with what joy their reunion took place.

The immediate problem that father and mother now faced was to find out whether Batjko Pravda would keep his word in guaranteeing father's safety. It was decided that a friend would first go to the headquarters and report to Pravda of the return of the fugitive. Pravda's retort was, "Let him come. I want to greet him. He has nothing to fear." He issued orders to the guards to see to it that father be admitted as soon as he reached the headquarters, so father and mother took off to see the batjko. There they met with a friendly reception, father being reassured that he was perfectly safe to remain in his home, for no one would molest him.

And so father was home on Christmas eve. What a joy it was for all of us to have him safely in our midst once more.

Grandpa Peters, Home

Many of the residents of Schoenfeld and of other neighboring Mennonite communities had fled by now, most of them having gone south to the Molochnaia. But those who had stayed behind were glad to see Grandpa Peters safely back, and many came to visit him on Christmas Day.

In Russia we always celebrated Christmas for three whole days. This was also true of Easter and Pentecost. In many communities it was the custom to hold church services the first two days, while the third one was generally devoted to visiting friends and relatives. How different this custom was from that which prevails in Canada and the United States, where only one day is set aside for these festive occasions. In contrast, we really took time to commemorate these great events of Christianity—the birth of Christ, His Resurrection and of the outpouring of the Holy Spirit and the beginning of the Christian era.

On this occasion the first holiday went by quietly. Regular church services were out of the question, but a number of people met for Christian service in a private home. Attendance at such an event in those days was fraught with great danger. Still, many people had come to express to Grandpa Peters and his family their feelings of great relief for his safe return at a time when no one could be sure how long anyone's life might be spared.

On the second day of this holiday season the air seemed full of tension. The partisans, or bandits, if one prefers to call them by their real profession, appeared to be restless from early morning on. Bat'ko Pravda and a group of his men had left Schoenfeld on one of their plundering and killing expeditions to the neighboring colonies. The headquarters was deserted except for the secretary, Antonov, and a few other men.

In keeping with tradition, some of the local residents had gathered for worship at the Peters' home. Grandpa was present. We sang hymns, prayed and read selections from the Holy Scriptures. We tried to comfort ourselves but were able to do so for a short time only. The apprehension would not leave us, for disturbances could occur at any moment. And sure enough, soon we saw two armed men entering our yard and a minute later heard them knock at our door, demanding to know whether Mr. Peters was in our midst. Grandpa responded immediately, "Yes, I am here. Do you want something from me?" The response was that he was to accompany them to headquarters for an interrogation. He went with them. The rest of us, the family members and their friends, had but one thought—this is the last we will see of Grandpa. Summons to the bandits' headquarters for interrogation almost invariably meant death. We prayed hard that the Lord might save his life once more.

The two heavily armed men took Father Peters to the headquarters. Bat'ko Pravda, as mentioned before, was off on one of his periodic plundering and murdering campaigns in the surrounding countryside. Secretary Antonov commenced at once with his questioning. I had met this man on earlier occasions and I knew what a wily and bloodthirsty man he was. Later I shall relate some other experiences with him. The interrogation proceeded as follows:

Antonov: "Where have you been all this time?"

Grandpa: "I was fifteen days in village number 6, Kankrin, and four days in another village."

Antonov: "That is a lie. You were not there. You went to the city of X, where troops of our enemies are stationed. You were seen there. Witnesses who saw you there are in the next room and they are ready to testify against you."

Grandpa: "How can people say something like this, which is an obvious lie. I have never been to the city of X. I know where I have been, and you can send men to investigate about my whereabouts while I am in your custody. You will then see that these alleged witnesses and accusers are liars."

Antonov: "You have nothing but empty alibis. These men know you, they saw you there, and they know that you are our enemy."

However, the two men who had been ordered to fetch Grandpa Peters were not actually enemies of his, but friends, and they now commenced to speak on his behalf. They asked him, "Were you here at our headquarters after you returned from your flight?" Grandpa, "Yes, and Bat'ko Pravda told me to go home and to feel secure, for nothing would be done to me."

Whereupon one guard said, "When Bat'ko has told you to go home and to feel safe and nothing is going to happen to you, then that must be so. We suggest that you go home."

Turning to Secretary Antonov, they told him to be quiet and not to molest anybody, nor to mix in affairs which were somebody else's perogative.

That ended the interrogation. Grandpa was free and he hurried back to his home where the assembled people had prayerfully waited for the turn of events. How joyfully they greeted him and thanked God for having saved him once more. There was no question in my mind that Antonov had meant to kill Grandpa Peters during the absence of the bat'ko. Now thanks to these friends he had been saved from the bandits.

New Year's 1919

From this time on Bat'ko Pravda treated Mr. Peters in a very friendly way. The following episode illustrates this. As elsewhere in the world, people would gather on New Year's Eve to eat and drink and make music till midnight when everybody would go outside and there would be a good deal of shooting and whistling to welcome the arrival of the New Year.

We, as Christians, also would gather on New Year's Eve, but the purpose of our gathering was for Christian fellowship, for singing, for testimony, to read and hear the Word of the Lord, to search our own hearts and then to pray, while the church bells would ring in the New Year at midnight. This was the way Christians met the incoming year.

Now, on this last day of the year 1918, the Peters family went to rest quite early. All members had fallen asleep when suddenly, at about 11 o'clock, somebody was knocking at the window of Grandpa's bedroom. Upon his inquiry as to who was there and what was the occasion for this disturbance, the voice at the window identified himself as a guard from Bat'ko Pravda's headquarters. He had been sent by the chief to invite Mr. Peters to come to the headquarters to participate at the celebration of greeting the New Year. He was told that some other neighbors were already at the party. Furthermore, he assured Grandpa that there was nothing to fear for the bat'ko was in a happy mood.

Grandpa dressed and went with the guards to the headquarters. Six or seven other village residents were already there, several of whom were later murdered by these same bandits. Some of the Mennonites were musicians who had been requested to bring their instruments along to entertain the host. One can readily surmise how these men must have felt about this "request", and that they played with very little enthusiasm. However, it was a dangerous time and one was often compelled to do things for fear of frightful reprisals.

There was plenty of food on the table and large amounts of that evil-smelling and vile-tasting homebrew, which the bandits called samogonka, and which they consumed in vast quantity. Fortunately there was also coffee, tea and sugar, and just plain water. There was great pressure brought upon everybody to drink; however, Grandpa Peters begged to be excused from drinking anything and the chieftain relented in his case. The assembled crowd ate and drank until midnight. At the stroke of 12 o'clock Bat'ko Pravda held up his glass and made a short speech, stressing the fact that this was the time for the proletariat to assert its rights to rule and to act in any way it wished. Meanwhile, some of his troopers went outside to fire salvos in salute to the New Year, only to return and to continue to celebrate.

Grandpa was very tired and asked permission to be excused, and was permitted to go home. But the rest of the "invited" guests and the Makhnovtsy continued to celebrate until the wee hours of the morning.

Miracles

I call these memoires "Miracles of Grace and Judgment," for grace and judgment they were. This we had ample opportunity to observe and to experience. The fact that Mr. Peters was alive and back with his family, that some years later he was able to leave the country and to emigrate to Canada, was one of the great miracles of grace. On the other hand we also saw miracles of judgment, especially over the children of the ungodly, as we shall see below.

Our Canadian and American hymnals have a beautiful hymn, "God Leads His Dear Children Along," and in the chorus there are the words:

Some through the waters, some through the flood.

Some through the fire, but all through the Blood.

Some through great sorrow, but God gives a song,

In the night season and all the day long.

We surely experienced this, for we were like sheep left among the wolves, always in expectation of torture, suffering, persecution and death. And so at this time especially, did we learn to trust Jesus. There was another hymn which I liked so very much. It contains the words, "We have an anchor that keeps the soul steadfast and safe as the billows roll." Jesus is that anchor.

As was to be expected, instruction in our high school, as in all other schools was highly irregular. Someone in Canada asked me once what kind of salaries we were paid during those days. I have to confess that I do not remember whether we were paid at all at that time. During those months the problem of finding any kind of fuel to keep us warm often loomed as large as having something to eat.

Almost any piece of wood, including the fences between the school yard and the adjacent farms was used for the cooking of food, and for the heating of our house.

Our family stuck closely together. In addition to my wife, myself, and our three children, Margaret, Peter and Katherine, our maternity nurse, Miss Elizabeth Harder, it also included one of our high school teachers, Miss Helen Froese. We also frequently visited with Truda's parents, the Peters family, Grandma Toews and two of her daughters, Susan and Katherine, and their brother, Peter. Susan and Katherine were serving as operators of the local telephone station. Since the occupation of our village by Bat'ko Pravda, the telephone service was reserved for the exclusive use of himself and his staff. Our family also maintained intimate contact with the other two high school teachers, Henry P. Neufeld and Jacob J. Thiessen. Both were bachelors.

Singing and Romance

Despite all the inconveniences and frequent difficulties with the occupying bandits, somehow we managed to hold our group of singers together and we practiced as often as it was possible under these trying conditions. Of particular pleasure for all of the members of our choir was to see the friendship between Teacher J. Thiessen and Miss Froese blossom into romance. The marriage of Miss Fast and Mr. Neufeld was consumated while we still lived in Schoenfeld, while that of Miss Froese and Mr. Thiessen took place after we had moved away from Schoenfeld.

Among other members of our choir I should like to mention the two brothers, Bernhard and Gerhard Fast, and their cousin, Waldemar Thiessen. The frequent rehearsals afforded us much pleasure. We had little money, but this mattered hardly, for there was nothing to buy anyway. This meant that our womenfolk were more than busy with endless mending, ripping of old garments in attempts to make something wearable for their loved ones. Altogether we were so much at the mercy of the bandits that one had to be thankful for simply being alive.

I pointed out earlier that this bandit leader had requisitioned for his headquarters the farmstead of Mr. John Warkentin, including the nice home and all the outbuildings of this beautiful farm. In a corner to the rear of this property was a small cottage in which lived the widow Klein with her daughters, Anna and Sarah. When Pravda moved into the Warkentin home he ordered the two sisters to take over the housekeeping chores for the headquarters staff. All of us in Schoenfeld shared the mother's deep concern over the fate of her daughters. The son of our church custodian, David Mirau, was in love with Anna and wanted to marry her. The question was whether the bandit leader would permit Anna to get married and give up her share of the housekeeping duties at the headquarters. There was no way out of this dilemma but to approach the chief. After a good deal of hesitation they did ask him, and Pravda graciously gave his consent, but with the condition that he himself should give Anna in marriage.

CHAPTER 6

A Wedding, Blood and Death

This bandit chieftain directed that preparations be made for a big wedding. A large machine shed on the farmstead was to be the scene for the festivities which were to follow the wedding ceremony in our church. The shed was thoroughly cleaned and decorated as were the chairs and tables. A good deal of baking and cooking was done during the preceding week. Invitations were sent to all the inhabitants of Schoenfeld and vicinity.

To the best of my recollection, the wedding took place on January 13, 1919. Many people responded to the invitation and came to the church for this solemn event in so troublesome a time. Pravda kept his promise that he would take the bride and groom to the church in his own carriage, nicely decorated and drawn by a team of the finest horses. The coachman was in resplendent uniform. A large number of the bandits also attended but they heeded his injunction that none was to carry any arms whatsoever. Pastor Jacob L. Dyck, who some years earlier had performed our own marriage ceremony, officiated at this one. Strange as it may seem to the reader, the audience, though very restrained, seemed to be in a festive mood. Among those in the front rows was Grandpa Peters. Not far from him sat Bat'ko Pravda. After the singing of a hymn appropriate to the occasion, Rev. Dyck performed the wedding ceremony and concluded with a brief message to the newlyweds and the assembled people. Pravda seemed to be genuinely moved by the pastor's message and the congregation's singing, for one could see tears running down his cheeks. It is difficult to fathom what could be going through this bandit's heart and mind, a man who had committed innumerable murders and openly boasted about his acts of atrocity. And yet, here, the Lord seemingly had spoken to him and apparently moved him deeply.

After the conclusion of the ceremony at the church, the newlyweds, Pravda, and the guests went to the headquarters where a splendid repast was served them. There was music and plenty of samogon for anyone who wished to drink that vile stuff. Only his own men availed themselves of it. The whole meal was furnished at Pravda's expense, though one hardly needs to ask the questions as to how and where most of the stuff was gotten in the first instance.

There was, however, another side to the festivities which was in keeping with the Mennonite practice. Several weeks before the wedding we had asked the chieftain to permit our choir to sing several Russian hymns and that my colleague, Gerhard Doerksen, be allowed to present a short gospel message. To our surprise, and even greater satisfaction, Pravda gave his consent. Our choir had rehearsed several songs for this occasion. We had just finished our part of the program and were to be followed by Rev. Doerksen. But he had barely commenced speaking when we noticed a considerable disturbance outside. Its cause was soon revealed to us. In a neighboring village to Schoenfeld another gang of bandits had established its headquarters. It was simply another semi-autonomous component of Bat'ko Makhno's army. The name of its own leader was N. It was N. himself, accompanied by a small detachment of his men, who now entered the building and demanded that Rev. Doerksen's son, Gerhard, be delivered to him immediately. The charge, as was so often the case with these bandits, was very vague. He was supposed to have committed some kind of an act against members of his gang. May I add here that it was N. himself who sometime later admitted that the charges against this eighteen year old Christian youth had been unfounded.

This interruption put a hasty end to the religious portion of the wedding. A number of the members of our choir and others of the congregation left the shed where Pravda's men continued their festivities, and went into an adjacent room and began to pray. Rev. Doerksen was ordered to take N. and his men to his home to search, ostensibly, for incriminating evidence against the son. Several hours of rummaging through the house produced nothing along this line, but provided the searchers an excuse to help themselves to anything they liked. Before long we saw the gang getting ready to leave the Doerksen place. Young Gerhard had been placed in the wagon, surrounded by a number of men brandishing their pistols. His mother and sisters were standing close to the wagon. So was the father. The son tried to reassure them, imploring them not to cry, nor to despair, for though the bandits might take his body, they could not rob the Lord of his soul. "I am saved," he reassured them again and again.

Whenever I look at the picture of our school and the student body with Gerhard on it, I say thanks to the Lord for having had the privilege of knowing a student who stood so well the test to the end.

At the same time these bandits also arrested and took with them our volost secretary, David P. Dyck. The charges, as usual, were exceedingly vague—he was accused of having prepared against N. at some unspecified time an accusatory document. And so Dyck and Gerhard Doerksen were taken to N.'s headquarters in a neighboring village a short distance from Schoenfeld.

I am well-informed of what happened to these two men once they arrived at N.'s place, for several of the bandits who participated in the torturing, some years later became Christians, and testified and confessed to me what had transpired that evning. Gerhard was first forced to undress himself and was then repeatedly beaten into unconsciousness. Brought back to consciousness by pouring cold water over him, the torture was then repeated, until N. finally told his men "to take him out." This was the usual signal from the chief to execute the victim. Several men took Gerhard behind a straw stack and hacked him to pieces. There the father, my colleague, found the body the following day and buried him there. He could not bear to have anyone else, especially members of his family, see the terribly mutilated body of his son.

After the bandits disposed of the young man, they proceeded to beat the elderly David P. Dyck. He too was horribly beaten, but for reasons known only to themselves, the bandits, once their bloody lust had been satisfied, pushed Dyck out of the room into the cold night and allowed him to walk away. He collapsed into unconsciousness. Fortunately, somebody found him, took him to his house, cleaned and fed him and provided him with shelter until his kin could be informed about his whereabouts. It was months before Mr. Dyck was able to be up and around.

Such then was this fateful wedding day of Anna Klein and David Mirau. It had begun with the blessing of one bandit leader, and celebrated under his auspices with considerable fanfare as well as with some truly Christian practices of song and prayer, only to be terminated with horrible experiences that are difficult to relate even to this day. I do not know what eventually was the fate of this newly wedded couple. One can only hope that they were allowed to have some measure of happiness together.

It took some time after my former student Gerhard G. Doerksen was killed, but one day N. came to see the parents of Gerhard and told them that they made a mistake in killing their son. He apologized. Father Doerksen got up, shook hands with N. and kissed him. That certainly was not an easy task to do, but it is Christian to forgive and to be forgiven.

This was reported to me by Gerhard's brother Henry G. Doerksen of Winnipeg, Manitoba, Canada.

While the Tempest Still is High

It was pointed out earlier that there were several teacherages on our high school campus. In one of these lived the family of Peter Fast, including his two sons, Bernhard and Gerhard, and a nephew of the family, Waldemar Thiessen. They had felt very unsafe on their isolated estate, called Roppovo, and so had asked whether they might occupy one of the dwellings on our school grounds. We were happy to have them join our choir and Bible discussion group. Mr. Fast himself was in very poor health and needed the constant care and attention of Mrs. Fast and other members of the family.

A great tragedy was soon to befall this family. It was on a Sunday afternoon during the early part of February 1919 when I happened to notice the younger members of the Fast family driving into the school yard. In the sleigh were the two brothers, two of their sisters and their cousin, Waldemar Thiessen. While they were unhitching the horses and stabling them, I remarked to my wife that the young people must have had a pleasant ride and visit, for they all seemed to be in such good spirits.

It was only a short time later when I noticed another sleigh, occupied by five or six armed men, driving into the yard toward the house occupied by the Fast family. These men, armed to the teeth as was the Maknovtsy fashion, seemed to be in a great hurry. With deep apprehension I beheld them entering the Fast residence. I observed a good deal of commotion in the house, and about half an hour later several of the bandits drove off while the Fast sons and their cousin were taken away on foot by the remaining three Makhnovtsy.

During the preceding week our choir had been rehearsing a new Russian song which all of us liked greatly. The two Fast sons and their cousin were members of the choir. I knew all three of them well, but especially Gerhard since both of us were singing tenor. The English version of this song reads:

Rise ye children of salvation, all who cleave to Christ,
    the Head; Wake, arise! O mighty nation, Ere the foe on Zion tread.

A few days earlier before this Sunday event I had been talking to Waldemar Thiessen about our security in Christ Jesus by faith only. It seemed to me that Waldemar was as yet unable to grasp the whole truth of this.

And now these three young men were led away to the local head-quarters of the Makhnovtsy. Few who were taken there under arrest ever left that place alive. Goethe once wrote "Where men sing, there you may rest peacefully, for evil people have no songs." Unfortunately, this was not the case with the Makhnovtsy, for they sang lustily though they had no qualms at any time about shooting people, torturing them to death or cutting them down with their sharp sabers. Those of us who experienced these bandits' occupation during 1919 will undoubtedly never forget their favorite song, which in my own free translation reads as follows:

Red apple, little thing,
Rolling, whereabout?
In Makhno's hand you are
And will never get out.
Refrain: In Makhno's hand you are
And will never get out.

I felt terrible about seeing these young men being led away, and wished only that there were some way of interceding for them. However, one was so helpless in those days. I hastened to the Fast's house to find out what had happened. The entire house was in an indescribable mess. What the bandits had not found worthwhile taking along, they had thrown on the floors. The contents of drawers had been spilled all through the house and then they had dumped jars of fruit and preserves into heaps of cloth-ing, linens, and so forth. In one room I found the bed-ridden Mr. Fast, and close to him in an armchair sat Mrs. Fast, weeping bitterly. Truda had meanwhile joined me and we tried to comfort them with prayer and with the song, "Jesus, lover of my soul, let me to thy bosom fly while the nearer waters roll, while the tempest still is high."

Who can fathom the depth of the parents' sorrow? And yet they had fully surrendered themselves unto the will of the Lord, as Mrs. Fast kept on repeating the words, "Yes, Lord, if it is Thy way, then may this come over us. May we be chastened. May we suffer, only keep us near Thy bosom."

On Monday morning, on my way to school I had to pass the former Warkentin residence, now the bandits' headquarters. As Providence would have it, just at that very moment I observed a sleigh leaving the yard carrying several bandit guards and the three young men. It was the last time that I was to see them. As they passed me I noticed Waldemar looking toward me and shaking his head up and down. He could not speak to me but I felt then that he meant to let me know that he was in full agreement with what I had striven to make clear to him four days earlier, namely that he fully believed that Christ had died for him and thus had saved him.

Two days later, on Wednesday, four of the Makhnovtsy returned to the Fast home and arrested Mr. and Mrs. Fast, a twenty-year old daughter and an eleven-year old son. Mr. Fast was returned on Saturday with instructions to collect a substantial sum of money, upon receipt of which his two sons and nephew were to be freed. The ill and despairing father felt that it was really a useless effort for he did not believe that the young men were still alive. However, his son-in-law, my colleague Mr. Neufeld, went from house to house throughout Schoenfeld asking people to loan him whatever sums they could possibly spare.

On Sunday morning the bandits came back and hauled the father away. Days passed and there was no word about the fate of any of the arrested members of the Fast family. We tried to comfort the Neufelds, but words seemed to fail us. At Mrs. Neufeld's request I decided to go to the Makhnovtsy headquarters in hopes that I might possibly be able to find out whether any of these people were still living. At the headquarters I found Bat'ko Pravda's brother, Gregory, whom I had met before. After greeting me he inquired whether there was anything that he could do for me. I reminded him of the Fast family and a nephew of theirs, all of whom had been arrested by a group of Makhnovtsy from the village of Pokrovskoe, and that I and other friends of the family were anxious to find out what happened to them. He promised to telephone Pokrovskoe and find out. This he did. I listened to his inquiry and after a brief pause heard him say "Oh, you have killed them? I'm very pleased." Then he repeated these words to me, "They have killed them." The last phrase, "I'm very pleased" cut deep into my soul. This is an expression we often use when we make an acquaintance and in Russian we say, "Otshen priyatno"—in German, "Sehr angenehm"—and in plain English, "Very pleased." So this is how they felt about butchering our loved ones. Gregory said, "Otshen prijatno." I begged him to find out whether all seven had been killed. He obliged, and the reply was that five had been executed but there was no indication as to which two of the seven had been spared. We found out a few days later when the daughter and the youngest son returned to our village. The daughter had been terribly maltreated.

I don't think Gregory used the phrase, "Otshen prijatno" (I'm very pleased) when he was executed about a year or two later by the communists in Alexandrovsk.

Such tragedies were the order of the day in almost every Mennonite colony in our area which was situated in closest proximity to the huge village of Guliai Polie, the home of Nestor Makhno and of numerous of his followers. But they also happened in other single colonies and entire settlements as, for example, Chortitza and Sagradovka, for the whole countryside of several uiezds of the Ekaterinoslav and Tavrida guberniias was swarming with bandits.

God's Mysterious Ways

I call these events Miracles of Grace and Judgment. There was a judgment over us, and yet we still felt the hand of God's grace over and above us. The following illustration is a case in point. Many of our closest friends experienced the cruelest of torture and many of them met death, but we also knew that many of them held fast in their faith and they, with Paul, could say, "I have finished my course. I fought a good fight. I have kept the faith."

Let me relate here another event which seemed to me like a miracle of grace. This concerns a Mr. John Frank Martens who until quite recently had been the manager of a farm which belonged to P. Heidebrecht. For reasons known only to the bandits, they arrested Mr. Martens one day in early January of 1919. He was locked up in a small house which had been my living quarters when I first came to Schoenfeld as a high school teacher. It was a brick building close to the street and belonged to my wife's grandmother. Years back it had been the residence of my wife's parents, the B.J. Peters; on the other end it had housed my father-in-law's store. Now it was the guard house of the Makhnovtsy.

One cold morning shortly after the arrest of Mr. Martens, as I was enroute to school and was passing the small house currently being used by the Makhnovtsy as a jail, I suddenly heard my name called, not too loudly, but yet distinctly, "Teacher Schroeder." I halted and looked toward the small window of the cottage and there I beheld the face of Mr. Martens. He told me very hurriedly that tonight he was to be tried at the headquarters. Since he had grave doubts as to whether he would be freed, he begged me to go to the headquarters and ask the leader to allow the guards to take him to his home and to permit him to spend a few hours with his family. Furthermore, he would greatly appreciate it if I could arrange for one of the ministers of our church to come to the home and to help comfort and to console him and the family. In order not to attract the attention of the guards I did not linger, but hastily promised that I would do my best to help him, and hurried off to school.

At noon my colleague, Neufeld and I, while on the way home for lunch, met on the street two leading Makhnovtsy, both of whom I knew fairly well. One was named Khariton and the other one was Mit'ka, a brother of Bat'ko Pravdo. Both had the reputation in our village as being exceedingly dangerous men. They were walking in the middle of the street, while the two of us were on the sidewalk. They noticed us; we went over to them in the middle of the street and we greeted each other. Khariton immediately asked me whether I would come over to the head-quarters real soon and play the pump organ for them. I had done this once before on the occasion when I had to transact some business at that place. He said that he and his comrades had greatly enjoyed my playing on that occasion and that they would appreciate it if I could come in the near future for a repeat performance. It occurred to me at once that this was a God-sent moment for me to intercede for Mr. Martens. And so I said to Khariton, "I will gladly come and play the organ but I also have a request to make of you."

"Yes, what is it?" he inquired.

"Well," I said, "you have Martens under arrest, and I want to tell you that he is an innocent man. He is not a capitalist, but a laboring man. I do not believe that you want to kill innocent men."

"Of course not," said Khariton.

"Martens would like to go home to be with his family. Would you allow a guard to take him home and also permit a minister to be with him, perhaps Pastor Doerksen? Martens is to be tried tonight, and I hope that he will be found innocent."

"Yes," said Khariton, "I am in charge of the guards today, and I will make the arrangements."

"Thank you," I said. "I hope the best will come of this."

So we went our way. We did not talk to anyone else about this en-counter. But to our immediate immense relief, we found out the next day that not only had Khariton kept his word and saw to it that Martens was allowed to be home with his family, together with Pastor Doerksen, but also that last night he had been found innocent. Now he was free and at home.

There were two interesting sequels to that noon's meeting with Khariton and Mit'ka and Mr. Martens' freeing that evening. Here is the first one.

An Honest But Sad Confession

One evening some weeks later a Makhnovets came to visit me. He was an intelligent and obviously well-educated man. His name was Nebrat, which I felt certain was not his real name, but an assumed name. We had no fuel for our lamps so we sat in the dark room, close to the oven and conversed at length on a variety of subjects. I suggested that as an intelligent man he should turn to God, read the Bible and follow in the footsteps of Jesus Christ. To this advice he gave me an answer which I shall not forget as long as I live. These were his words:

"Do not try to change me with advice to read the Bible and to believe in God, or with anything of that kind of advice. We Makhnovtsy, as partisans and anarchists have only one program, only one desire and aim—to enjoy living off somebody else's property, to rob and to kill as we please. We will not change, and we will be a menace to others as long as we live. Nothing will change us, not the Bible, nor God, neither Hell or Heaven. We will live this way so long as possible. And when that is no longer possible we will commit suicide, and only when Mother Soft Earth has covered us, will we be harmless."

I was shocked to hear this kind of confession and I was glad that in the darkness of the room he could not see the expression on my face. Then he turned to another subject and observed that men at their headquarters listened to what I had to say. This surprised me, and knowing the fickleness of the bandits' opinions I asked him why he was saying this. Thereupon he reminded me of the arrest and trial of Martens, and pointed out that during the trial, when first Mit'ka Pravda had suggested that Martens should be given fifty lashes, and Comrade Antonov, the headquarters' secretary had recommended that Martens be shot, at that moment Bat'ko Pravda had produced a piece of paper and, with the words, "Listen to the words of Teacher Schroeder," had read what was written on that note. After its reading, Nebrat continued, all those present at the trial had agreed that Martens should be found innocent and be permitted to go.

I told Nebrat that I had never written any note or any paper about Martens and, therefore, had no idea what he was talking about. To this he repeated that my word did carry weight at the headquarters and that Martens had been set free because of what I had written on that piece of paper. This perplexed me, but the subject of our conversation was changed, and I never said a word to anybody about this conversation with Nebrat.

And here is the second sequel to that street encounter in early 1919 with

Mit'ka and Khariton and the brief discussion about the plight of Mr.
Martens. This incident took place about a month or so later. One day
when I returned from school, Truda informed me that Petro had been by
and had asked that we come to his house that afternoon to participate in
celebrating the christening of their baby. Petro Polikarpov, that was this
man's name, was a Makhnovets and as such claimed to be an anarchist.
As mentioned earlier in this story he was the husband of Alexandra, or
Sashka, as we usually called her. She had been a maid at Grandma
Toews' house for a considerable number of years.

We felt that we had no choice but to go. So we hitched up our horse,
Cossack, and drove to the village where the Polikarpovs lived. It was only
a few miles distant from Schoenfeld. You should have seen the sight
when we arrived at their place. A sizeable crowd had gathered for this
occasion. We were greeted with much enthusiasm. A number of the menfolk were already under the influence of *samogon*, that obnoxious concoc-
tion of a home made drink. Several men rushed up to unhitch our horse
and promised to take excellent care of him.

We were invited into the house and asked to sit down at the table laden
with plenty of food, including a savory borshch with goose meat in it. A
jolly time seemed to be had by all, most especially by the Makhnovtsy
who were by now pretty heavily under the influence of drink. And who,
do you suppose, was sitting to the right of me? None other than Khariton.
He was in a particularly good mood, and in typical Slavic exhuberance
insisted time and again upon embracing and kissing me, and to assure me
that no man would ever dare to harm me because, as he said, "We love
you very much." Fortunately, the men, when finally satiated with food
and drink, went outside to relieve themselves and to have their smokes.
Only a group of women, sober and respectful, remained in the room and
it was to them I dared at this moment to expound the Word of God. This
was in early March of 1919. Later I shall quote to you from a letter which
I received several years later when we already lived in Canada, in which
one of the women present that day related the great influence my talk had
had upon them.

Khariton suddenly returned and asked me to come along with him, for
he wanted to have a private conversation with me. It can easily be imagined what feeling took hold of me at this moment. All too many people
amongst my acquaintances had had tragic experiences as a result of such
encounters. But what choice was there for me but to comply? He led me to
a secluded part in the barn and said, "You remember how in January we
met on the street of Schoenfeld and you told me of Martens and that he

was an innocent man?"

"Yes, I responded, "that I remember well. What of it?"

"Well," he said, "I went into the guard house, sat down at the table and wrote down all the words you had said. And when the crucial moment came, as Antonov demanded that Martens be executed and commenced to read the death verdict, I quickly pushed the slip of paper on which I had jotted down your words, to Bat'ko Pravda, and asked him to quickly read it. This he did, and the rest you know."

And so, I found out what effect my words with Khariton had had that noon in early January. I had taken quite a chance for it could have meant death for me. However, it was the guiding hand of our Lord and God who performed that miracle and saved the life of Mr. Martens.

CHAPTER 7

Darker and Deeper

A Letter from Russia

This letter is dated March 23, 1925, and comes from Lubimovka, the home of Bat'ko Pravda and of a number of other bandits of the Makhno era. It is the village in which I tried in 1919 to testify for the Lord Jesus Christ. Before my family and I left Russia I asked a younger brother in Christ, Jacob Friesen from our mutual home village, Rosental, to go to Lubimovka and visit these newly converted former bandits, and bring them the message of salvation. And here is his letter.

Dear Brother in Christ:

Your letter brought us great joy. The letter was received when I was absent from the village. For the brethren here it was a real holiday. The brethren asked me to give you the picture, and to write you about the joy that they received through your letter. Brother Peter Polikarpov was quite busy with some necessary farm work; and in his home there was a visiting relative belonging to the Greek Orthodox Church. But when your letter arrived, Brother Polikarpov left the work and he left also his visitor; and a number of brethren came together and they listened when the letter was read to the whole church and all are very grateful to the Lord and thankful to you there in America.

This letter, as the pidgeon of Noah, brought the olive leaf that is testimony that on the other side of the ocean are hearts who are warmed by the love of Christ and joyfully beat for Christ and us. You, Brother Schroeder, perhaps remember when you were at the Polikarpov's home when they celebrated the birth of their daughter, Vera, and the christening of Vera.

You, at that time, spoke the word of God to some in the Polikarpov home. There was also the aunt of Alexandra, by the name of Darochka, who always loved you so much for speaking the word of God to them. Sister Alexandra says if you have forgotten this woman Darochka, perhaps your wife, Truda, will remember her. Now Sister Alexandra is asking you that you may pray for them, that God may give her and others much wisdom to speak to the hungry and thirsty souls. The father of Alexandra, Savely Evtushenko, is a godless man, but Alexandra is asking you that you may pray for him also. Alexandra is also asking you to write about all your relatives. Then she went on enumerating the names of many which we will skip.

You write further that reality often seems to you as a dream and a dream seems like reality. With many of us here it is the same. Brother Peter Polikarpov says that he often seems to see you coming somewhere, and he is expecting you that you should come somewhere.

We will be so glad when you send us a photo of yourself and your family. Sister Sashka often remembers the time when you at Schoenfeld at Christmas time would have special meetings and how you would sing and have a joy in Christ. Now she is much grieved that she at that time did not know the joy of fellowship with the Lord that she has now, but she is so glad that she has this fellowship with the Lord now. She often suffers physically, but her heart is full of joy in the spiritual life. Our meeting place is getting too small, and we have to think about building a larger building for our church services. Sister Sashka is asking me to send best greetings to Sister Anna, Mariia, from all of us here.

Awaiting the reply from you and a meeting with you, if not here, then in the presence of the Savior Lord Jesus Christ. I am your Brother J. Friesen, and the Polikarpov's send greetings.

Looting and Shooting

Here in Canada and in the United States the farmers have a hay rack to haul hay and straw. In Russia we too had a hay rack, but it looked quite different. We called it a *Leiterwagen,* literally translated it means a ladder wagon. It had an extended under-carriage on both sides on which were mounted ladders, about four feet high and about fifteen feet long, placed at a slightly sloping angle. They served essentially the same purpose during the threshing season as the hay rack on a Canadian or American farm. After the close of the harvest season the ladders were dismounted, the under-carriage shortened, and then the wagon would be used for the usual farm work for the rest of the season.

The Makhnovtsy found a different usage for these ladder wagons. On almost any day during January and February of 1919 we would see them leaving the headquarters, drawn by a team of two to three horses, and loaded with several heavily armed Makhnovtsy. From Schoenfeld they would fan out in all directions into neighboring Mennonite and Lutheran colonies on plundering expeditions. In late afternoon or evening they would return, with the wagons heavily laden with every possible kind of loot. All too frequently such looting expeditions would be accompanied by executions of individual colonists, or in massacres of entire families, and even entire villages. And the bandits then might ask one, "Do you know so-and-so in village N? We entered him as expense!" (that is, they had shot him).

Lukashka

One of Bat'ko Pravda's assistants was a young man who went by the name of Lukashka, which is the Russian diminutive for Luke. Lukashka was of small stature, and a man who yearned to display his vanity through wearing flashy clothes, riding a spirited mount or using a fine carriage driven by a liveried coachman and drawn by a span of beautiful horses. Lukashka found it indispensable to show his authority by being armed to the teeth at all times, including the carrying of a *vintovka* (army rifle), a *nagan* (short, stub-nosed revolver), a saber, a handgrenade or two dangling from his belt and in his hand the dreaded *nagaika* (Cossack-type of whip).

Lukashka was quite a sight to behold, especially when he wore his favorite *Tuzhurka* (suit coat) made of velvet. In the living rooms of the prosperous or the more pretentious Mennonite farm homes, the table, often of oval form, was frequently covered by a velvet table cloth of vivid color. The brigands had a decided preference for a suit coat of this material, and as soon as one of them could lay his hands on one of them, or had found a piece of drapery of similar material, he would demand the name and place of residence of the village seamstress. In Schoenfeld a maiden by the name of Neta Riesen had the reputation of being an excellent representative of this trade, and soon she would be compelled to fashion a *tuzhurka* of the military type which during World War I was commonly called a "French jacket." Lukashka was inordinately proud of his jacket, and how he would strut when he accompanied Pravda on his foraging and plundering expeditions in Schoenfeld's environs, or in visits to different homes in our village.

I recall an incident of this nature. To the best of my recollection it took place in February, 1919. Pravda and his headquarters staff had decided to hold a party. Such an affair invariably posed the danger of ending in a drunken brawl and shooting affray amongst their own members. Hence Pravda had made it a rule that on the occasion of a party all personnel, himself included, had to surrender their weapons to Lukashka. The latter was under standing orders to lock the surrendered weapons in the wardrobe of an adjoining room.

Soon the usual and predictable turn of events took place. After considerable quantities of their homebrew—*samogon*—had been consumed, the inevitable fracas ensued. In accordance, too, with his usual practice, Pravda, when the brawling threatened to get completely out of hand, would resort to his accustomed method of restoring discipline. This consisted in ordering the unruly person or persons to lie down on the floor and receive a good whipping from Pravda himself. The recipients of this form of humiliation and punishment naturally resented it, but it was a rare individual who would dare to protest openly. On this particular occasion, as I was told by one of the men present, it was Pravda's brother, Mit'ka who stood up and challenged the chief, by demanding to know who he thought he was to arrogate to himself the authority to inflict such pain and indignity upon one of his own subordinates. "Do you think that you are Tsar Nicholas, that you can beat and mistreat us the way you do?" he wanted to know. The challenge infuriated Pravda and he told his brother to take his leave immediately if he did not wish to be shot. Mit'ka's retort was, "You have no weapon with which to shoot. You are nothing but a mean man to treat us in such manner," and walked out. Pravda called Lukashka and ordered him to bring his revolver. The latter's protestations were of no avail, he had to obey his master's orders.

Mit'ka returned a short time later. Observing Pravda sitting on the davenport behind the table laden with all kinds of food and drinks, he commenced to taunt the chief by likening him to a little tsar. Pravda ordered him to hush up and take himself from the room if he did not wish to be killed immediately. Mit'ka once more accused him of being a bully and that, moreover, he had no gun to carry out his threat. Without further ado, Pravda raised his weapon and fired it point-blank into the face of his brother. Mit'ka dropped dead to the floor.

The carousing gang was stunned momentarily, then commenced to protest loudly, telling Pravda that his deed would be reported to Makhno in Guliai Polie. Upon receipt of the news, Makhno directed another one of his sub-chiefs, Naumenko, to proceed with a strong force of his men to Schoenfeld and bring Pravda to his headquarters for interrogation. Resistance being futile, the culprit surrendered without offering force. What transpired at the meeting of these well-known leaders and cut-throats is not known to me. However, when shortly afterwards I happened to meet Pravda, he told me that Makhno had authorized him to punish, even execute, any partisan who failed to obey his orders.

Mit'ka was buried in the village of Liubimovka, which was located about four miles south of Schoenfeld, with a good deal of fanfare. From eyewitness accounts of the funeral I heard that Pravda had shown much contrition over his deed, wailing loudly and repeatedly, "My dear brother, Mit'ka, why have I shot you? Why have I killed you?"

And yet not very long after this event he told me at a casual encounter that, "If I had ten more brothers like Mit'ka who would disobey me, I would shoot them all."

Events of the Spring and Summer of 1919

The spring and summer months afforded Schoenfeld some respite from almost daily experiences of brigand raids of pillage and extortion, generally accompanied by torture and wanton murder of many of its inhabitants. The first period of unrestrained plunderous expeditions by the Makhnovtsy on the east bank of the Dnieper within a radius of about 80 to 200 miles from their "capital," Guliai Polie, a period which had commenced with the retreat of the occupying forces of the Central Powers in November 1918, and the almost simultaneous and utter collapse of whatever authority and armed force the Petliura government had ever possessed in the Ekaterinoslav guberniia, had slackened off considerably by early March 1919 when the Soviet government had pretty well reasserted its control throughout most of the area of this guberniia and of the continental portions of the Tavrida guberniia. The heartland of the Makhnovshchina was at this time confined roughly to the district from Zalivnoe in the north, to Pologi—Orekhov in the south, and from about Kamyshevatka and Zherebets in the west, to slightly beyond Chistopolie and Turkenovka in the east. Guliai Polie, the home of Nestor Makhno and of a number of his followers, was situated virtually in the center of this area.

Schoenfeld and a number of other Mennonite colonies, numerous individual estates and a number of estate sized farms owned and operated by groups of closely related families were scattered throughout this lair of the Makhnovshchina. As pointed out before, there was scarcely a Mennonite home in this district which during the four month period had not suffered heavy property losses, while many had paid a terrible price in human lives.

Upon its return, the Soviet government either found it temporarily advantageous, or saw itself compelled to maintain a *modus vivendi* with Makhno and other bat'kos of the numerous brigand movements throughout Southern Russia. It was a particularly uneasy alliance with Makhno who was by far the most talented, popular and powerful leader among all the Robin Hoods of the civil war era. To remain master of the political and military situation in the areas here under consideration, the Bolsheviks had to allow the Makhnovtsy a certain degree of freedom of action in and around Guliai Polie and to carry out occasional pillaging raids into the settlements of the district which was mainly inhabited by Mennonites and smaller numbers of Lutherans and Catholics. For the most part, however, the government sought, and on the whole did succeed, in maintaining control of the situation through its political police, the Cheka, and the Red Army. To provision its own agencies and to feed the urban population, the government resorted to frequent forced contributions of grain and other food products from the landed proprietors who so far had managed to hold on to varying portions of their former land holdings, and from that class of the peasantry which later was to become known as *kulaks*.*

The agrarian revolution in the Black Sea littoral, the region which since the days of Catherine II was called New Russia, had by spring of 1918, to all intents and purposes, become an accomplished fact. Although the German occupation and its stooge, the Hetman government, had temporarily undone it, their collapse had almost immediately led to its restoration throughout the south. Recognizing this fact and accommodating itself to it, the Bolshevik government at this time had neither the power, the time, nor the inclination to undo the *fait accompli* through the introduction of a forced collectivization policy. Hence, it contented itself temporarily by holding out inducements to farmers to group themselves into fairly loose farm associations, called *artel*. Bearing in mind the political and military situation then existing throughout the South of Russia, this agrarian policy achieved a modicum of success.

I shall touch briefly on the situation in which we and other Mennonites of Schoenfeld and its surrounding areas found ourselves during the spring and summer of 1919. The terror instituted by Makhno and his followers during the preceding months had considerably reduced the Mennonite population in our district. Many people had been murdered, sizable numbers had fled to the more populous Mennonite areas to the

*the Russian word for fist

south of us, namely the Molochnaia settlement with its more than fifty villages, while others, of necessity, stayed behind on their farms or in their businesses. Of the latter, many perhaps remained in their abodes because of their expectation that somehow a more stable government might come into being in the not too distant future. No one knew whence and how such an eventuality could or would take place, but many of these people placed enough credence in the frequently circulated rumors that the Red government in Moscow was on the verge of collapse, or that the counter-revolutionary forces which were converging from various directions along the periphery of the old tsarist empire—the so-called White Armies under this or that one-time Tsarist general, with English, French, Japanese or American support—were making rapid progress from the Crimean Peninsula, the Don Territory, or the Kuban, or from Polish or Rumanian territory and ere long would reach our vicinity.

On the other hand, some of us who remained in place were not as sanguine in our hopes or expectations, but did so out of necessity—and for most varied reasons—decided to make the best of the slightly improved situation in our immediate vicinity. Spring was upon us. Everywhere there were signs of a new birth of life, in the yard, the garden, and in the field. Numerous migratory birds were returning, and who amongst us that grew up on the steppes of Southern Russia does not recall the thrill of hearing the meadow lark in the morning? Or who of us was not enthralled with the song of the nightingale during the evening hours and during the night and had not, in such moments, experienced a feeling of peace from the cares and toils of the day? We trusted God and hoped for better days to come.

The farmers who had remained in their homes and still had some draft animals in their possession and also owned some grain, potatoes, and seeds of various vegetables, commenced to plow and to plant. So did we school teachers, for no matter how bad the situation was in our region, instruction in the elementary and secondary schools in the Mennonite villages was never discontinued unless the fighting between various contending factions of the civil war was right upon us and the schools were right in line of the firing.

The payment of teachers' salaries was a very uncertain thing at this time. The Mennonites had always maintained their own schools at their own expense. The Bolshevik government had taken them away and we teachers were now supposed to derive our compensation entirely from the district, guberniia or national government. But all too frequently there was no civil government to be found, and we depended for our sustenance

entirely upon what the local village community or individual farmers
were willing or able to contribute to supplement whatever we ourselves
were able to raise in the way of produce. In many places the teachers
depended upon their livelihood almost entirely from bartering in the
neighboring city's market place, selling of their possessions what was
deemed disposable, or what they felt that somehow they could get along
without. We were fortunate if we could get some food items in exchange,
for the currencies in circulation represented a kaleidoscopic picture of
largely worthless pieces of tattered paper, of varying sizes and shapes and
of incredible denomination. Some were of the Tsarist era; others were
kerenkii (issued in 1917 by the Provisional government); still others were
chervontsy (issued by different Ukrainian "governments" in 1918); there
were also absolutely worthless pieces of paper issued at one time or
another during these chaotic days by different cities and finally, of course,
there was Soviet money.

Hence whatever remuneration we teachers received came preferably in
the form of any kind of grain or other produce, and in assisting us in
plowing a piece of land on which we could do our own sowing and planting. This we did with potatoes, watermelons, pumpkins, or perhaps a
small patch of millet. Vegetables were almost invariably planted at one's
own residence or at the teacherage.

I still had a horse of my own from way back. He still bore the proud
name which once upon a time I had bestowed upon him, namely Cossack. There was nothing of the "kossakisch" or "kosatskii" left about
him, for he had reached the venerable age of twenty-one years. Yet he was
a really valuable possession for he could still pull my little and rather
decrepit wagon, called *sharaban* (gig), to take me places as need be. Occasionally, I loaned him to relatives or friends who also had only one horse
left, to assist them in plowing, or hauling of one thing or another. Altogether, with the help of neighboring farmers I succeeded in planting a sizable patch with potatoes, pumpkins, and watermelons. I should stress at
this place that watermelons were for us at this time more than a delec-
table, to a Russian Mennonite an almost indispensable item on his table,
piece of food during the summer and fall, but also for pickling, while the
syrup we made out of the juice was about the only sweetening available to
most of us at that time.

I also still possessed two very good milch cows, several pigs and a flock
of chickens. Altogether, the outlook for my family in the spring of 1919,
as far as food was concerned, was not bad, providing that we would be
allowed to reap and keep for ourselves the things we possessed and the

crops we hoped to harvest in the summer and autumn. This picture
looked still brighter when one remembers that most of the "governments" which then ruled over us usually considered the teacher as a member of the laboring class and; therefore, was entitled to exemption from
various kinds of exactions, requisitions, "contributions", etc. Unfortunately, except for the Bolsheviks who usually tried to live up to this practice, the followers of the various bat'kos did not believe or observe it.

The situation for the farmers in our area was quite different. Those
who had not fled to the Molochnaia during the reign of terror in late 1918
and early 1919 faced a hard decision in the spring of this year. Should
they take a chance and stay and attend to their farming business, with the
limited means left to them and with the hope that they might be able to
harvest what they had sown and planted? Was it worth risking the lives of
themselves and of those dear to them when there was no guarantee that
raids from Guliai Polie and other nests of bandits might not be resumed
at almost any time, and apparently without fear of reprisal from the
Soviet authorities? In early May, for example, several farmers in our vicinity were murdered by Makhnovtsy. Among them was a Mr. Jacob
Heidebrecht, a friend of ours who suffered such a fate. For some reason
the raiders also killed a hired maid on this farm. Truda and I took Mrs.
Heidebrecht and a very young son to live with us for awhile, since it was
too dangerous for them to remain on the farm. She still had several horses, and before leaving the farm asked me to take one of them, a very nice
looking young mare called Galka, for my own use. Our family became
greatly attached to it.

Not only farmers, but also former owners of business or industrial
properties, suffered at this time a similar fate to that of Mr. Heidebrecht.
Thus on May 2 Mr. Jacob Isaak Dyck, formerly a flour mill owner, was
brutally murdered by a group of Makhnovtsy. Events like this prompted a
slow but steady attrition of people from Schoenfeld.

Some of our farmers and several business and professional people
thought they might possibly have a better chance of saving their lives and
securing for themselves a livelihood by joining a cooperative type of farm
organization, called *artel*. This was greatly favored by the Bolshevik
authorities at this time and constituted, in the main, a pooling by its
members of their livestock, farm machinery, implement and produce, and
sharing all the work in common. However, each member would possess
his own home or residence and all the household belongings, and continue to reside in it.

Peasants from neighboring villages to Schoenfeld were particularly eager to move into farms and homes which had been abandoned by their owners and organize artel's. For example, around early April an artel of somewhat disparate, but quite congenial members was organized in our village. The once-beautiful Warkentin homestead, in which Bat'ko Pravda had had his headquarters for several months, was vacated by the brigand leader when the Bolshevik government re-established its control in our guberniia. I am not certain whether Pravda left these comfortable quarters of his own volition or whether he had found it more politic to remove himself to perhaps a safer place in or near Guliai Polie. At any rate, the very nice and commodious brick buildings of this once well equipped and beautiful farm across the street from my in-laws, the B.J. Peters', was vacant once more. But only for a short time, for soon we noticed several peasant families moving into it. Much to our relief these were people whom we knew quite well, namely Savelii and Maria Evtushenko and their daughter and son-in-law, Mikhail Peresypkin. Before long they were joined by Peter Polikarpov who was also well known to us.

Soon after their arrival these three families decided to establish an artel, which my father-in-law and Henry Doerksen, a close friend of mine, joined soon after its organization. Subsequently a few other peasants, former hired farm hands in Schoenfeld, joined up, among them Arkhipus, one-time hired man of Frank Rempel, another friend of mine. According to some reminiscences sent to me by Henry Doerksen, the artel functioned smoothly and successfully, and in the summer and autumn harvested abundantly as the result of its labors. For most of its Mennonite members, unfortunately, their labors had been in vain. The return toward the close of September of Bat'ko Makhno with many thousands of his armed followers to Guliai Polie, after their successful breakthrough at Uman of the White Army detachments which had encircled them, unleashed a new wave of murderous assaults upon those Mennonites who had not yet sought safety in flight to the Molochnaia or other large settlements of their co-religionists. The end of Schoenfeld was near, for its fate was now sealed forever. Soon there would be only ruins, with most buildings burned or torn down and every brick and other structural materials-in short, everything that could be hauled away—taken to one or other of the villages which were the home base of the Makhnovshchina.

Our First "Elections" Under Communism

But let me relate some other experiences we had during the spring and summer of 1919. One of these related to the first district elections under Soviet rule in which we were ordered to "participate". The balloting was designed to fill all the positions of our volost (district) administration. Its seat was located in the village of Zalivnoe, located within relatively few miles from our Schoenfeld. I happened to be one of the group of electors sent to cast our vote at the scheduled elections. I recall that enroute thither we debated amongst ourselves for whom we might possibly cast our vote. That concern turned out to be premature, for when we got to Zalivnoe we found a large assemblage of delegates from other villages in the yard of the volost building, surrounded by a sizable detachment of Red Army troops. The meeting was opened by its chairman—a man I knew—N. His opening remarks left no doubt about what was in store for us in case we did not act in accordance with what was expected of us. His introductory remarks were, "We know who you are. We know what some of you are planning. We know your sentiments. You see those Red Guards behind you? You make one false move and they will take care of you."

After several more remarks and further threats, accompanied by the vilest of curses, he proclaimed, "We are now ready to proceed with the election of officers. The following are the names of the candidates given to us by our head office in Alexandrovsk." With that he commenced to read a list of names—comrade so-and-so is named for such and such a position. No one was asked to second the nomination, or whether other candidates were to be nominated. The only question asked of the assembled delegates was, "Who is against this candidate? Just raise your hand," which statement was followed by a string of further cursing. Of course no one raised a hand in opposition. As far as my fellow-delegates and I were concerned, I can only say that we kept our hands down as firmly as possible. With no one voicing a "nay" to the reeling off of names, he directed himself to the recording secretary, in the case of each office to be filled, with the words, "Write into the minutes that Comrade [whatever his name may have been] was unanimously elected [Chairman, Executive Secretary, and so forth]". Thus ended our first participation in an election under our new system of government.

Aside from occasional Makhnovtsy raids upon our village and other Mennonite settlements in our vicinity, and endless decrees issued by various local levels of Soviet officialdom, life during the spring of 1919 was bearable though no one knew how long this comparative calm would last. Instruction in both the elementary and the high school continued on what for those days could pass for a fairly normal schedule.

Still, there continued to be a good deal of uneasiness amongst our Mennonite people in Schoenfeld and its surroundings. In school one noticed from time to time that children of certain families suddenly ceased to attend, and upon inquiry one heard that they had quietly disposed of such possessions as could still be sold and had moved to the Molochnaia. This was bound to have a contageous affect and, in fact, more and more people were leaving. Among these were Miss Helen Froese, one of our teachers who had been living with us in our home for some time, and the Abraham J. Dyck family, who also had lived for a while in one of the buildings on the high school campus. Another family, Herman C. Enns, a neighbor of ours, also left. Gradually these were followed by a goodly number of other friends and acquaintances, from either Schoenfeld or its immediate vicinity. Everyone sold what could not be easily taken along, and few of the families knew beforehand in which of the Molochnaia villages they might find a place of refuge.

Upon request of my brother, John, who was living in Rosental in the Old Colony, I purchased two good milch cows for him. An acquaintance of his from Rosental, Jacob Lawrence Loschitz, was sent to fetch those two animals. Knowing that one man would have much difficulty in driving home with two cows tied to the wagon, I decided to help him with this task. It was a distance of some sixty miles and I found it quite a tedious job. However, it gave me an opportunity to briefly visit with my parents and other members in the family before returning to Schoenfeld.

Realizing that the time might soon come when it might well nigh be impossible for my family and myself to remain in our present home, I began to give serious consideration to moving elsewhere, but the question was, where to? Briefly I considered the Molochnaia settlement where in one of its villages I had heard of the availability of a teaching position. I went there to look over the situation but did not find it to my liking. And so Truda and I decided to remain where we were. Fortunately for us, her parents had also resolved to stay, as did also an especially dear friend of mine and my colleague, Mr. Gerhard Doerksen. Several other families we knew well also resolved to stay. With these relatives and friends we often met for prayer, Bible reading and singing, all of which were of great comfort to all of us.

Our resolve to remain where we had lived for a good many years, as was undoubtedly also the case with similar decisions by some of the other families, was perhaps bolstered, if not motivated, by increasing evidence coming from the south and east of our area that a change in the political situation might take place in the not too distance future. Rumors that components of Denikin's army were advancing from the Crimea and the Kuban and Don Regions reached us with increasing frequency.

This, in fact, did take place in early June of 1919. The counter-revolutionary forces, often also called the Volunteer Army, under the overall command of General Denikin did indeed advance northward out of the Crimea and the Caucasus, gradually gathering momentum and forcing quite a rapid retreat of the Red Army and its temporary ally, Nestor Makhno's superbly mounted cavalry and highly mobile infantry units, which were transported on the well-known spring wagons called *tachanki,* confiscated from the Mennonite and German colonists in the Ekaterinoslav and Tavrida guberniias.

Shortly before Denikin's units reached Schoenfeld, our village received an unexpected visit from Nestor Makhno with a substantial retinue of his followers. We had, of course, no definite idea whether this visit possibly presaged a retreat of his before the advancing enemy from the south, or whether it was occasioned by a conflict within his own ranks or with the Bolsheviks. As it turned out, it was of short duration. He established his headquarters at my wife's parents' home. Mother Peters prepared a good dinner for the well-known and feared bat'ko and several of his chieftains. She invited us to have dinner with the self-invited guests. I cannot say that we relished the affair but I must say that on this occasion we found Makhno a very friendly man, and we had a rather nice visit with him. Apparently all of his companions had been ordered to be on their good behavior for no one was harmed, nor was anything pilfered during their stay in the village. However, on leaving, some of his other retinue had spotted several horses in the village pasture, and had taken a particular liking for my horse, Galka, which, as pointed out earlier, I had been given by the widow Heidebrecht. And what these brigands liked, they took. Galka had been taken. As soon as I got word of this I rushed to Bat'ko Pravda who now had his headquarters in a different village. My plea for his assistance in recovering my precious possession was answered in the affirmative. And sure enough he kept his word, for Galka was soon returned to me.

For nearly four months the Denikin forces managed to maintain a shaky control over most of Southern Russia. Yet the general's regime was never able to set up a viable civil administration, nor did it succeed in arousing popular support among the urban inhabitants. It is not strange, perhaps, that the Mennonites and other land owners and people of industrial and commercial properties, (all or most of which they had lost during the preceding years of revolution and civil war), had welcomed the advance of the Volunteer Army, hoping that it would establish a constitutional monarchy or a Democratic Republic with all the forms of a private property, private enterprise and religious and political liberties. By August; however, it became obvious to all but the most politically naive and of hopelessly reactionary views, that Denikin and his chief associates, because of personal incompetence, lack of political savvy, and for reasons of domestic chaos and external affairs over neither of which they had any control, could not possibly come up with a program that conceivably might appeal to broad masses of the Russian people and enlist their support, or devise a provisional form of government capable of administering the affairs of State.

It is so trite a statement to stress the saying that "hope springs eternal," and yet without some hope for better days to come, we surely could not have survived during those days. Young people still got married in the spring and summer seasons. Among these nuptial events I recall particularly the wedding of Henry Mirau and Sarah Klein on July 11, 1919. The bridegroom was the son of our church custodian, and the bride, Sarah, was a daughter of the Widow Klein who lived in a small cottage on the Warkentin farmstead where, as I pointed out earlier in this story, Bat'ko Pravda had established his headquarters in the late fall of 1918. The reader may recall our concern at the time over the fact that the widow's two daughters, Sarah and Anna, were compelled to keep house and cook for Pravda and his staff. I also commented earlier on the wedding of January 19 of that year, of the bridegroom's brother, David, to the bride's sister, Anna. But God protected these young women, for no harm was ever done to them by the bandits while they were under duress to work for Pravda.

CHAPTER 8

Growing Apprehensions

As the summer progressed, new apprehensions over the future commenced to occupy the minds of many of our people. The maid, Tina Knelsen, who had been with our family for about two years, decided that she wished to go back to Rosental to be with her parents. Much as we would miss her, we did not attempt to persuade her to stay with us since more and more we also were leaning toward the idea that it might be safer for us if we left Schoenfeld and moved to Rosental where my parents and other members of my family lived. It would have been most difficult for her to reach her parents' home since, at that time, direct public transportation in the direction of Rosental was, to all intents and purposes, non-existent. Therefore, I decided to take her there in my *sharaban*, confident that my twenty-one year old Cossack would make it there and back. To the best of my recollection it was August 18 when we embarked upon our journey, a distance of about sixty miles. We arrived safely, much to our relief and that of our relatives. However, I spent only one day with my parents, since I was especially concerned with making arrangements for one of the several buildings on the parental farmstead for my family to move into should we decide to leave Schoenfeld. My mind was pretty well made up by now that all signs seemed to be pointing to an early collapse of Denikin's forces, the comeback of the Mahknovtsy to their home base, and the horrors which their return would undoubtedly spell for all Mennonites anywhere in the environs of Guliai Polie.

Our family's home was located on a very large lot. Beside the old farm house, with its auxiliary buildings, which now was occupied by my brother John and his family—for some years now he had taken over the operation and management of the farm—there were two other buildings on the lot. One was a relatively new brick building in which my parents and my youngest sister, Lena lived. Then toward the back of the lot there was a small cottage which father had built some years ago and which was presently vacant. It consisted of a single room and a kitchen, and though crowded, Truda, the children and I would be able to live in it quite comfortably. Moreover, its smallness had a decided advantage in case Rosental should again be occupied by the Makhnovtsy or other partisans, anarchists, or whatever other name one wished to call them. All of them had a most pronounced preference for quartering themselves in the largest buildings they could find. Its very unpretentiousness would also be a deterent to endless searches and pilfering expeditions by the bandits, or what they liked to call *posharit'*, that is, "rummaging."

I returned to Schoenfeld on August 20. Very tragic news awaited me upon my return. Truda told me at once that during my absence four Mennonites from our district had been murdered in the village of Zherebets, located about twenty miles from us. It was the sadder to hear because the men had embarked upon a very hazardous, if not foolhardy enterprise, considering the conditions of the time and the disposition of so many peasants of that area toward the Mennonite landowners.

Here in brief is what had taken place while I was in Rosental. During the preceding period of the Makhnovshchina, peasants throughout the Guliai Polie region, as in other areas, had plundered the Mennonite farms and businesses at will, appropriating much of their land and seizing anything they could lay their hands on and take with them. This was particularly true with farm machinery and implements, clothing and furniture and other household goods. Most vulnerable to "liberation;" however, were horses and livestock.

The inhabitants of the village of Zherebets had been notorious for their thieving propensities, or what they preferred to call "plundering the plunderers." Many a farmer in our vicinity had lost choice horses and fine cattle to them. Now, with a counter-revolutionary government presumably in control of affairs in our region, six Mennonite men from around Schoenfeld and vicinity decided that now was a propitious time to get even with the Zherebets expropriators, and hence they drove there to demand a return of their horses. The group included Peter Neufeld, a good friend of mine, two brothers, Gerhard and Jonn Pankratz, Henry W. Schroeder, Henry G. Schroeder (who are no relation to my family), and a certain Friesen, whose first name I do not recollect. The six men apparently knew exactly to which peasants' homes they wished to go and make their demands. However, scarcely had they driven into the first yard when they were met by a volley of shots from several men who must somehow have gotten word of their approach. Neufeld and Henry W. Schroeder were fatally shot as they alighted from the wagon. The two Pankratz brothers who had also stepped from the wagon attempted to find safety in a nearby corn field but were soon found and brutally slain. Only Friesen and the other Schroeder, who had stayed on the wagon, had managed to turn their team around and had driven off as fast as their horses could run, escaping with their lives.

I can scarcely find words to express the shock I experienced when I heard of the killing of these four men. Not long afterwards I had a long conversation with Henry G. Shroeder and got some details of the affair and how they had been surprised when they drove into that peasant's yard. He and Friesen had also been targets of several shots, but he was aware of only one bullet having hit Friesen and that had been deflected by a pack of cards which he had carried in the front pocket of his jacket. Friesen boasted several times that, "Those devils couldn't get me." These words shocked me. I felt very strongly that all of us had better learn the lesson to depend in all things on our Lord and God who is able to save us to the utter most. I made a very earnest plea to Schroeder that if he valued his life he had better flee to a place where he would not be a marked man. He refused to heed my advice. It was just about two months to the date after this escape that he was murdered.

The families of the murdered men were at a loss as to how to recover their bodies. I do not remember how those of the Pankratz brothers and of Henry W. Schroeder were returned, except to recall that those of the brothers were badly decomposed upon their return. I am not sure whether this was also true with Schroeder's body. However, all three were buried without a formal funeral.

Neufeld's body was recovered in a rather strange and perhaps in a somewhat unique manner. I presume that it was at someone's suggestion that his mother decided to hire the mother of Bat'ko Pravda to try to get her son's body. She agreed to it and did succeed in returning it to Schoenfeld. I vividly recall the events of the funeral of this friend of mine.

What a tragic end for this attempt at the recovery of lost property. It is pointless to condemn the actions of these men, for all of us are so attached to earthly possessions that we will commit all kinds of rash deeds to get back what once we owned, or to get even with the people who have dared to injure us. And yet, one can scarcely repress the thought that these men ought to have remembered how some of our people in 1918, during the German occupation of our area, had resorted to similar action against peasants who, prior to April of that year, had seized either their land, farm machinery, livestock, and other things and how, with German help, had recovered some of their possessions, only to have experienced terrible revenge, all too often having ended in their being murdered at the hands of the same peasants in the late fall of 1918 after the retreat of the German armies.

Our Move to Rosental

The August tragedy of the families involved hastened our resolve to leave Schoenfeld as soon as we could get our affairs settled. We managed to hire several men with teams and *Leiterwagen* ("ladder wagons") to help us move our belongings. Fortunately, I was able without too much difficulty to hire two reliable men with the requisite means of transport. With the help of relatives and friends who were not yet willing to flee—among them were Truda's parents and my colleague, Gerhard Doerksen and family, the Mirau's and the John Marten's families—the packing and loading was expeditiously accomplished. In early September we took off for Rosental where we arrived without mishap. Among some of our prized possessions we had taken along was my piano and Galka, the beautiful black mare which Mrs. Heidebrecht had given to me earlier that year.

In anticipation that the Makhnovtsy, or some other brigands, would undoubtedly sooner or later plunder the high school and destroy its buildings—as indeed happened not so many months after our departure—I took with me a number of books from the library and some chemistry and physics apparatus, items which I thought the Chortitza high school might use to good advantage. It is needless, perhaps, to add that during the fall of 1919 when the Makhnovtsy were held to the Chortitza area by the retreating White Army and the advancing Red Army; from late September to the end of December 1919, we lost everything that we had salvaged from Schoenfeld, and more.

Before leaving Schoenfeld, I had talked and pleaded with a number of peasant acquaintances in the neighboring villages, most of whom were strongly infected by the "spirit of Makhnovism", not to destroy the schools and other buildings, but to use them for the purposes for which they had been erected. Unfortunately, this is not what they did. On the contrary, scarcely a month or two later everything was in ruins. What could not be torn down and hauled to the neighboring peasant villages was burned. Schoenfeld, or taking its literal translation "Beautiful Field", had ceased to exist.

With the welcoming hand of my family it took little time for us to get settled in our new home. It was small but adequate under the conditions of the time in which we lived, and relatives and friends assisted in every way to make life comfortable for Truda, the children, and myself. Since it was getting close to the end of harvest time, there was no dearth of field work on the family farm in which I could be of help. There were potatoes to be dug, and watermelons and pumpkins to be picked and hauled home. Then there was the fall plowing to be done to prepare the soil for spring planting. A hired boy, aged about fourteen or fifteen, named Nicolai, helped me with this chore by driving the span of four horses while I guided the plow.

One day while engaged in this work in a field near the village we suddenly became aware of the fact that something disturbing was taking place. I was not certain of its cause or nature but I sensed that something was wrong, and as a precautionary measure we stopped plowing, hitched the horses to the wagon and drove into a valley nearby. I halted at a pond which in summer time was the chief watering place for the community's cattle and horses, and decided to await further developments. Not so very much later my father came looking for us, bringing the information that a troup of partisans, or anarchists, as we usually labelled them in accordance with their own chiefs' preferences, was in our village and was demanding a large *kontributsiia* (contribution) of money. *Kontributsii* were the favorite form of extortion used by the Bolsheviks (partisans and just plain ordinary bandits), a practice which was almost invariably accompanied by the seizure of prominent laymen or preachers as hostages. Father told us to wait here until we received word that the armed men had left, lest they also take our last horses away. It was late at night when at last we got word that it was safe to drive home.

The Makhnovtsy are Back

My apprehension that the White Army's days were numbered and that the Bolsheviks, or more likely the Makhnovtsy, would soon be back materialized a few days later. Nicolas, or Kolia, as we usually called him, and I were in the field plowing. The village of Rosental was situated in a deep and broad valley, but its arable land was located on a rather high plateau, affording an unobstructed view of the almost limitless steppe to the north, west, and south. To the west from where we were plowing, at not very great a distance from us, were the tracks of a very important railroad.

Leading from a westerly direction past Rosental and Chortitza toward Einlage Kichkas, it crossed the Dnieper on the strategically most significant bridge between Ekaterinoslav in the north and Nikopol in the south, a distance of about 110 miles.

All at once we heard artillery fire, and looking toward the railroad tracks we noticed first one armored train and then another one. The distance between them was not exceptionally great and as they got closer it became obvious that they were engaged in battle with each other. Kolia jumped from the horse he was riding and cried, "Uncle, I am scared. I am afraid." My response to him was that I too was scared. We ceased plowing, quickly hitched the horses to the wagon and drove homeward. As we approached the first windmill at the outskirts of Rosental, I inquired of the miller whether he knew what was going on and whether it was safe to drive further. But he professed not to know anything unusual taking place in the vicinity.

In the morning as we left for the field, I had still observed some White Army soldiers marching down the street. Now I wondered whether a change had already taken place in our political situation. We drove down the steep hill into the village but no messenger met us. Even as we rounded the sharp corner on the main street and proceeded straightforward over the bridge across the "Jordan Stream", as the Mennonites called the *Kantsirskaia Creek*, we still could not see any armed men anywhere. Only as we were within about three houses from our place did we encounter a troup of mounted men among whom I at once recognized Bat'ko Makhno. I greeted them as they passed by us. We drove on without being molested by these men. However, a few minutes later, as I was about to make a right turn into our yard, another mounted Makhnovets rode up to us, levelled his gun at us and ordered us to jump off the wagon and be quick with removing the plow and our other belongings. I did as I was ordered, and without further ado several other Makhnovtsy, who meanwhile had joined the mounted one, got on the wagon and drove off. I was so startled at the quickness with which we had lost our precious possession of four horses and the wagon that I stood there, speechless, hardly knowing what to do. But as I looked after the departing men I suddenly noticed that Makhno and his immediate entourage, apparently having realized that they had failed to turn left onto the street which led to the Dnieper and thence to the river bridge, had turned around and were coming back in my direction.

By now I had recovered somewhat from the shock of the encounter and the loss just sustained, and I decided on the spur of the moment to take a chance on appealing personally to the bat'ko. So I went straight toward him and said, "Comrade Makhno, you know me. You have been to our place in Schoenfeld. I am a teacher. Just now I returned from plowing a field for my relatives. Your men have just taken my horses and wagon. You know that I am a teacher, a laboring man, not a capitalist. Couldn't I have my horses back?" He ordered the men to return my possession and rode on. But these followers of his refused to obey his order, they merely untied the two outside horses, gave them to me and hurriedly drove off with the other two and the wagon. One of the horses seized belonged to my brother John, the other was my highly prized Galka. Such was my introduction to a new visit by the Makhnovtsy.

The civil war since early 1918 had made most of us familiar with a number of practices by the various participants of this fratricidal struggle. For example, the levying of *Kontributsii* with or without all sorts of pretexts whatsoever; familiarizing us with the infinite variety of word usages, such as the simple form of address, the inquiry, request or demand, and above all the threats, to which the word *Khoziain* ("owner" or "proprietor", "manager" or "supervisor" of a home, a farm, a business, a yard, or any other piece of property) could be applied. The word *khoziain* took on a particularly sinister meaning, an ominous connotation, or bore direct consequences when used by the Makhnovtsy or other brigands. Even now, more than fifty years later, I still experience a momentary shudder when someone unexpectedly addresses me by this word, even though I know that it is in fun. I am sure that very many of our elderly Russian Mennonites who went through that period of terror have the same reaction.

During those days of endless horror no one had a desire to be the *khoziain* of a residence, a farm or business, because he was the one whom the bandits inevitably demanded to see first and to whom all their demands would be addressed, which in almost every instance were accompanied by cursing and dire threats, often followed by shooting. And if the khoziain had the temerity to ask the men whether they had a search warrant ("A prikaz ob obyske imeietie?") that most likely would earn him some heavy blows from the butt of the gun or perhaps even a bullet.

As indicated earlier, my brother John had taken over the family farm and; therefore, he was the khoziain at our place of three residences. However, brother John had been a marked man to the Makhnovtsy almost from the start of their current occupation of Rosental. He had to flee to save his life. With his departure the role of "owner" of our farm with its several buildings had unavoidably devolved upon me.

What a physically enervating and soul draining experience this business of being the owner entailed. Often I was so desperately tired during either the day or the night from facing the endless demands and meeting the incessant cursing and threatening, that I would scarcely have the energy to go inside the house to rest, but simply plopped down on one of the two benches, which were to be found on the front porch of just about every Mennonite farm home in Southern Russia. During the summer and fall months this was a comfortable place to rest, for almost invariably it was surrounded by large shade trees. An added advantage of resting here was that occasionally one might succeed in answering the bandits' querries satisfactorily without their entering the premises or, what was by far more important, occasionally one succeeded in delaying their entry sufficiently long enough to enable one or the other of the threatened members of the family, especially the womenfolk, to escape and hide somewhere.

However, it was not only the members of one's own family that the *khoziain* of a household during those terror filled months might be called upon to protect or to pay for, but the bandits might also often hold him accountable for neighbors or acquaintances, or at least demand that he supply them with all kinds of information about other people. There were times when one was under compulsion to accompany man hunting bandits to the house of an acquaintance or a neighbor where the bandits thought they might encounter resistance—a most unlikely event under the conditions of the time—or where the occupants had fled and "white guardists" might be hiding and effect an ambush.

Thus one night I was ordered to accompany a group of these men to the neighbor of ours across the street. There lived the Elder of our church, Isaak G. Dyck, the best known and most influential clergyman in the Old Colony. He, his wife, and one unmarried daughter lived in this house at the time. The elder's life had repeatedly been in danger, and at this time he and the wife and daughter were in hiding in the home of the local high school's art teacher, Henry J. Dyck. The latter's residence was located over a rather steep hill behind the elder's orchard. A low fence with a gate separated the two residences.

The Makhnovtsy who insisted upon my accompanying them to the minister's home claimed that they knew the preacher had joined the counter-revolutionary armies in order to bless and to pray for their victory over the partisans. That, however, would be in vain, for they were bound to find him and kill him. There was nothing for me to do but to accompany them. When we got to the front door and found it locked, I was told to call to the people inside, telling them to open the door at once. I called several times, though I knew that the house was deserted. Thereupon the bandits insisted that we try the back door. This too was locked. However, one of the bandits noticed that the window to one of the rooms was open. I was ordered to approach it and to call inside. When this produced no results I was told to crawl through the window into the house and to open the back door from the inside. This I did, whereupon they came in and commenced systematically to search the place, to no avail. There was nobody inside. They followed me outside, and just as we emerged from the house several men took note of a path and a series of steps leading up the hill into the orchard and thence through a gate to the residence of the art teacher. They demanded, "Where does this path lead?" My instant response, and I am sure the Lord gave it to me, was, "It leads only into the orchard."

The bandits seemed to be satisfied with my answer and followed me back to my home. They entered the house, and when they noticed the piano they demanded to know if I could play the instrument. When I answered in the affirmative I was asked to play something for them. This I did, and somewhat later they wanted to know whether I knew their favorite song _Yablochko_, a song to which I have made reference at an earlier place in this story. I played it for them several times, much to their delight and pleasure. Perhaps the Lord used even this to quiet them down and make them forget about the elder across the street.

Next morning I went to see an uncle of mine, Mr. John Klassen, where lived a cousin of mine who was married to Elder Dyck's daughter, Helen. I apprised her of my experiences of the preceding day of the great danger her father and family faced, and that she had better tell them of the urgency to find a safer hiding place. May I interject here that Reverend Dyck, during these terrible months and earlier in the year, had many narrow and, what seemed to me, miraculous escapes from the hands of the marauders. Death in 1929 undoubtedly saved him from an equally terrible fate, either exile to the Arctic region of Russia this side of the Urals or to Siberia during the collectivization later that year.

When the armed and highly mobile hordes of Makhnovtsy arrived unexpectedly in Chortitza on September 21, 1919, approximately half of the force under Bat'ko Makhno's leadership paused only briefly and then raced at full speed toward the Einlage-Kichkas bridge before the White Guardists could destroy it. They crossed it and pushed as fast as possible toward Guliai Polie. They were followed a few days later by more units, leaving only several hundred of their men behind on the right bank of the Dnieper. In very short order the followers of other bat'kos, as if sprung out of the ground, joined them in their pillaging, plundering and murdering expeditions throughout the sixteen villages of the Old Colony.

When the spearhead of the Makhnovtsy got to the Dnieper River on September 21, it found the bridge guarded by a handful of White Guardists. These men were Mennonite youths mostly from Chortitza and Rosental, who in the summer of 1919 when units of the Volunteer Army reached this area, had, after considerable pressure from a recruiting team in which at least one Mennonite White Guardist from the Molochnaia participated, agreed to enlist, but only for guard duty at some strategic point. The bridge across the river was the only strategically valuable position in our area and several of these young men were assigned to guard it.

The Makhnovtsy took the men completely by surprise and easily disposed of them. All but one were seized and thrown over the railing into the river, a height of 147 feet. The one exception was made with Hans Andres of Rosental, who was given the choice of either jumping voluntarily off the bridge or being thrown over the railing by his captors. Andres, a very good swimmer, opted for the first choice, providing he was allowed to crawl over the railing and to jump from a place of his own choosing. The wish was granted and Hans, after getting over the railing, lowered himself as far as possible on the framework of the bridge and jumped. Miraculously he survived the jump but did not regain consciousness until the current had carried him a great distance down the river. He eventually managed to swim to the left bank of the river, almost opposite the Chortitza Island, where he met a fisherman who agreed to take him in his boat and bring him to our side of the Dnieper. He succeeded in getting back to Rosental where friends were able to hide him safely during the more than two months the Makhnovtsy continued to occupy our village.

The arrival of the Makhnovtsy in Chortitza and its environs with hurricane-like force and speed, and their immediate resumption of wholesale plunder, torture and murder, had dealt the Mennonite population a stunning blow from which a recovery seemed all but impossible. However, because of the incredibly swift crossing of the river which the main force of these bandits was able to effect, and the complete inability of the few White Army troops left behind by the Denikin high command to guard its rear, the onrushing tide of this elemental force could not be stemmed from heading straight for Guliai Polie. This left Chortitza and adjacent districts on the right bank of the Dnieper, and Alexandrovsk with a number of peasant villages and a considerable number of small Mennonite hamlets and knutors in its vicinity on the left bank, under a relatively small occupying force for a few weeks and thus afforded us at least a brief spell of relief from continuous terror.

The machinery of local government which the Denikintsy had established during the summer months in our area had at best been a rather fragile instrument for administering such civil affairs as the military had left to it. It collapsed immediately under our new occupying forces. The former local officials had either fled or were in hiding, if they had been fortunate enough to escape slaughter at the hands of the brigands. The latter had no interest in establishing any form of formal government on the ruins of the old; their main concern was to maintain a state of anarchy as long as possible. It was the workers of the factories and mills in Alexandrovsk and Chortitza, and in a few of the other Mennonite villages in the district, who decided to take the initiative in forming new soviets at the village, city, and district levels in order to restore a semblance of order and to meet the most essential needs of the urban population.

The author, 10 years old in 1900, was the pet of his lady teacher Natalia Victorovna Karpinskaia, for whom she had to have this photo taken, and who would treat him with hot chocolate and other sweets when he would have to stay in after classes.

G.P. Schroeder, 1912, at the age of 22 years.

The authors parents, Maria and Peter J. Schroeder, in 1912. They were married December 4, 1875.

The graduating class at the Ekaterinoslav Teachers' Institute writing the final exams, in the Spring, 1913. At left is the author.

"First Graduation of Ekaterinoslav Teachers' Institute 1913". At top: Director N. P. Runovsky. Second row: professors and staff. Third row, third from left: G. P. Schroeder. Fourth row, right, is author's friend, Andreas Vogt.

Brick building belonging to grandma Toews. At the front end was the apartment of teacher Schroeder in 1913 and 1914. Some students, along with uncle Peter Toews, are standing in front of the house in 1914. In the fall of 1918 the makhnovtsy made this building their guardhouse, with a prison on the front end. This is the place where John F. Martens was kept in prison.

G. P. Schroeder horseback on his "Zabavnik" in the fall, 1913.

The main building of the Schoenfeld Central High School in 1914. This school was destroyed in the years 1922 and 1923.

B. J. Peters' business place. Peters was the representative of International Harvester Company, selling McCormack binders and engines. In the front building at the left end were the living quarters and the right end a grocery and yard goods store. The roofs were made of sheet iron and the walls of brick. The house and store were equipped with steam heating and a telephone in the office. Across the street from this building S. Pravda had his headquarters.

Truda Peters and G. P. Schroeder just prior to their marriage.

An invitation in Russian to the wedding of Gertrude Peters and Gerhard Schroeder, May 27, 1914.

The B. J. Peters' in Canada, 1925.

CHAPTER 9

My New Position—Volost Secretary

New Elections

The order to hold district elections in the Chortitza volost and in its component villages, although nominally initiated by the workers of Chortitza-Rosental, came actually from the workers' soviet in Alexandrovsk, and it was carried out under the supervision of its representatives. On the day of the elections in Chortitza-Rosental I, like undoubtedly most of its citizenry, was not sure whether I should go from our home to the teachers' seminary in Chortitza where the balloting was supposed to take place. Although I was by profession a teacher, thus automatically belonging to the laboring class and; therefore, *ipso facto* having the right to participate in the electoral process, I was still dubious about the advisability of availing myself of this right at this particular moment. Had I actually been the *khoziain* of our farm and not merely its currently *pro forma* possessor, I would not have faced any dilemma whatsoever, for then I would have been axiomatically excluded as a former capitalist exploiter of the laboring men.

My reluctance to participate was resolved by my father, who insisted that I should go to the meeting lest our entire household be considered and dealt with as belonging to the counter-revolutionary group of inhabitants. So I went. The auditorium of the seminary was completely filled. The audience was largely composed of men, although there was also a considerable number of women. The meeting was chaired by a local laborer, Kovaliev, by trade a carpenter. The balloting was preceded by the inevitable round of speeches in which our present state of liberation from the yoke of the exploiters was accorded its usual praise. This was followed by extolling our fortunate position whereby the workers once more were able to elect their own government.

When the election was about completed, and several men from Rosental had been chosen, I suddenly heard one of the local factory workers call my name. This greatly surprised me for I had been absent from my home village for so many years, first in college, then teaching, followed by three years of service in the Red Cross during World War I, and two more years of teaching in Schoenfeld after my discharge from the service in 1917, that I assumed very few people knew me. When my name was called, someone in the audience inquired, "Who is Comrade Schroeder?" In response, Chairman Kovaliev, who lived not very far from us and remembered me, called, "Comrade Schroeder, will you please rise?" When I did so, he continued, "This is Comrade Schroeder. He is a teacher and a dependable man." That seemed to be a sufficient recommendation, because I was forthwith elected by unanimous vote to the district soviet. Our volost, or district, it may be recalled, at the time consisted of sixteen villages whose population until the fall of 1917 was composed of approximately 95% Mennonites. The balance were Lutherans, Greek Orthodox, and a few Catholics and Old Believers. Two years later the accretion of non-Mennonite inhabitants had wrought appreciable changes in the district population, primarily in those villages like Chortitza-Rosental, Einlage and a few others which had factories and mills.

One of the immediate tasks of the elected members was to organize as the district's executive committee and to elect its chairman. A series of balloting always resulted in my election to the chairmanship, a position which I resolutely refused to accept. I was at a loss of what to do, and so at last I resorted to a private conversation with one of the other members of the newly elected executive committee. It was Jacov Lavrentii Loshitskii. The reader may possibly recall him under his former name, Jacob Lawrence Loschitz. He was the man whom several months earlier I had helped to drive two cows to Rosental which I had purchased in Schoenfeld for my brother John. He had meanwhile "Russified" his name. I endeavored to persuade him to accept the chairmanship, which at first he refused to do on the ground of his inadequate educational background. However, he was flattered that I had shown such confidence in him and when I offered him a deal, namely that if he would accept the chairmanship I would agree to become his secretary, it was tempting enough for him to accept. Thus, I became the volost secretary.

There were exceedingly valid reasons for my reluctance to accept the chairmanship of the district's executive committee, and why I, in sheer desperation, contrived a plan which limited the scope of my responsibilities to those of its secretarial post. Here, in brief, was the situation. By mid-October the political conditions in our part of the Ekaterinoslav guberniia were taking on a new turn, one decidedly against us. This change-in-being not only threatened our whole economy with total ruin, but placed our very survival in greatest jeopardy.

As the reader will recall, we had been under the occupation of the Makhnovtsy since September 21; however, as pointed out also, the major contingents of this force had departed almost at once for their homes in the Guliai Polie region. Now, as the Red Army was driving Denikin's armies back toward the Black Sea littoral, more and more of these troops were speedily retreating through the Ekaterinoslav guberniia in the direction of the Crimean Peninsula and the Don Region. Their main routes of retreat, once these troops had crossed to the left bank of the Dnieper at either Ekaterinoslav or Einlage-Kichkas, led directly through the heartland of the Makhnovshchina. Their numbers now were sufficient to have crushed whatever resistance Makhno and his hordes could have put up. To save his armed force from such a blow, Makhno hastily withdrew them back to the right bank of the Dnieper at the Einlage bridge, where they positioned themselves in an area roughly from Ekaterinoslav in the north, to about Belenkoe in the south, and extending about thirty to forty miles westward from the Dnieper River. Here they remained loosely encircled by the steadily retreating Denikintsy to the east, on the left bank of the Dnieper, and to the west by the slowly advancing Red Army units heading from the north in the direction of Nicolaev-Kherson and Odessa, from about mid-October to the last days of December 1919. In the encircled area, the Makhnovtsy made the two Mennonite settlements, the Chortitza and the Nikolaipol volosts, with the very numerous Mennonite khutors and hamlets between and around them, their headquarters and their chief bases of operation. It is difficult to obtain exact statistics on the size of Makhno's strongly armed forces at this time, but it is generally estimated that it consisted of from 6,000 to 10,000 men.

The Old Colony and the other Mennonite inhabited places in this area thus experienced the fury and the horrors of a strongly reinforced Makhnovshchina for an additional ten weeks.

Camels Instead of Horses

The immediate consequences of the return of Makhno's brigands to the Chortitza area was their resumption, in increased tempo and scope, of pillaging and terrorization of the populace. The experiences of every farm and every other household throughout the volost were much the same as those we suffered in our home. We were at once relieved of all our horses, except for one small crippled one. In place of the lost draft power we were given a pair of camels which the bandits undoubtedly had "liberated" from some estate in the southern portions of the Tavrida guberniia, the only region in these parts of the country where such animals could occasionally be found on a private estate. In a way, we could consider ourselves distinctly fortunate that we had received at least a measure of compensation for the lost horses since this enabled us to a degree to continue the various chores which still had to be done during the autumn months, hauling watermelons and pumpkins from the field, plowing, and other odd jobs.

It was assuredly not an easy or pleasant task to handle and to hitch the camels to the wagon or the plow, for they might spit on you and be quite stubborn to a novice such as I, in handling them. And what a peculiar noise they emitted most of the time! This; however, was not without some advantages to me who was working with them most of the time. In the first place, not a single horse in our village had ever been exposed to their kind of a sound, or noise, and so all vehicular traffic on the street or on the road would get out of my way whenever or wherever I was driving them.

I recall one such incident vividly, one that was not without some amusing aspects. On this particular occasion I was driving along our main street in the direction of Rosental's major portions of arable land. The street rose quite steeply as one approached the outskirts of Rosental. This section of the street we called *haumboaj* ("hem-hill" or "brake-hill") because loaded vehicles descending the hill had to be "hemmed" or "braked", which was done by means of tying a board to the rear of the wagon and on which someone would stand during the descent to help "brake" the vehicle. As my camels were slowly moving up the hill, a farmer was coming down with a load of pumpkins. As soon as his horse caught sight of my animals and heard their strange noise, it started to buck and pull to the extreme sides of the street, first to the left and then to the right, to avoid my camels. Meanwhile pumpkins commenced to fall off the wagon and came bouncing down the hill all around my team and wagon. The farmer had my sympathy in his predicament in not being able to handle his horse, but I could scarcely suppress my amusement over the rolling and bouncing pumpkins.

Later, when our crippled horse had improved considerably, and with the aid of another horse we had meanwhile been able to buy, the camels proved to be a valuable asset indeed, for we managed to do a considerable amount of plowing during late October and early November. Needless to add, that long before the Makhnovtsy's departure from Chortitza in late December, they had relieved us of the camels as well as the two horses.

We suffered a similar fate with clothing and food. Any piece of clothing that had not been buried in the ground or hidden deep in straw stacks prior to the arrival of the bandits was irretrievably lost. The only manner in which people succeeded in keeping some of their better apparel was by covering it with patches of odds and ends of old pieces of materials and wear it day-in and day-out.

Eventually we fared just as badly with food. Toward the tail-end of the Makhnovshchina the food supplies of almost all farmers were nearing the vanishing point. And if occasionally we had a decent meal it was because we gradually were reduced to eating what the bandits who stayed in our homes had stolen from peasants of the neighborhood, who so far had largely escaped either pillaging by the bandits or having them quartered in their homes. More will be said below about the desperate plight in which we were left at the turn of the year when the Red Army finally forced the Makhnovtsy out of the Chortitza area.

Trying to Save Human Lives

Now let me return to some of the trials and tribulations I experienced during these months as a result of my position as volost secretary. Early on the morning following my election I went to the volost building. I found the place open and noticed that Mr. Nesterenko, the custodian, was just about finished with his daily cleaning job. A roaring fire was going in the built-into-the-wall *pech* (oven), a feature so characteristic of all our Mennonite buildings at the time.

I decided to look around some of the office rooms in which I was henceforth to work, God only knowing for how long and under what conditions this was to take place. The officials who had functioned here during Denikin's short regime—in many cases these had been the same persons who had been employed here for years prior to the advent of the Bolshevik regime—had gone into hiding or had fled on September 21, 1919 as soon as the advance cavalry detachments of Makhno had entered Chortitza.

Now as I went from room to room I noticed papers strewn over desks and the floors, mute evidence that some of the bandits had thoroughly rummaged around, obviously more interested in finding money than in

the contents of papers and record books. As I looked over some of the
papers I realized at once how fortunate it had been for some people,
whose names I immediately recognized, that most of these bandits had
been illiterates. Had they been able to read the contents of some of the
papers whose subjects dealt with transactions that had taken place during
the preceding months under Denikin's government, the evidence would
undoubtedly have incriminated a number of well-known Mennonite
leaders. Even though these men, among whom I noticed the names of
many of our neighbors and acquaintances from Rosental and Chortitza,
including the signature of my brother John, had merely carried out
orders of the previous government and had met its requisitions of food,
clothing, grains, etc. under compulsion, all of them would have been in
mortal danger had their names become known to these trigger-happy
brigands.

I realized at once that these papers must be destroyed, but the question
was how to do this as expeditiously as possible. Nesterenko, the janitor, a
pleasant and naive fellow, had obviously not realized the significance of
many of the papers lying on desks and floors, some of which he had
picked off the floor and stacked on desks. And all at once a thought
flashed through my mind, why not tell Nesterenko that he had done a
very good job for the day and that he might as well go to his quarters
situated at a short distance from the headquarters building to spend some
time with his family. To my indescribable relief the janitor was greatly
pleased with my suggestion and hastened to take himself home. I now felt
myself exceedingly fortunate that I had come at such an early hour to the
office building, for it was quite unlikely that the other officials might
show up within an hour or two. That would give me enough time to dispose of a very considerable number of potentially dangerous papers in the
furiously burning fire of the oven. I proceeded with great haste to throw
into the fire arm-fulls of papers of the last summer's administration, and
felt so grateful that none of my new colleagues had shown up at an early
hour, and that my action perhaps might have been a contributing factor
in saving several people from a dire fate, horrible flogging and other
forms of torture or immediate execution.

During the initial weeks of my new job in the volost, when the
Makhnovtsy were not as yet prevented from reaching their homeland in
and around Guliai Polie, and while their stay in the Old Colony was still
not an uninterrupted day-in and day-out affair of horror, we often
received visits from various officials and leaders of a variety of political
views of the Left from the nearby city of Alexandrovsk. At times it was

well nigh impossible to know whether the visitors were Makhnovtsy, the followers of other bat'kos, or whether they were Bolsheviks, Anarchists or even Mensheviks, as some of them professed to be. I distinctly recall one such incident that surely had me puzzled for some time. On this particular occasion, while a heavily attended session was taking place in the meeting hall, I was attending to my work in one of the offices. After awhile one of the visitors from Alexandrovsk came into my room and observed, "I understand that you are one of the members of the executive committee and the volost secretary." Having received my affirmative reply, he continued, "You must know that each change of government is usually accompanied with unnecessary bloodshed. In many instances this is brought about through the finding of incriminating pieces of paper by the new governing officials, a fact which only incites them to take revenge against members of the preceding wielders of power. I would advise you to destroy all such papers which could incriminate some people no longer able to defend themselves."

I assured the visitor that I was cognizant of such dangers and that I would heed his advise. Afterwards, I wondered for quite some time whether this man had been merely pretending an affiliation with the Anarchists or Bolsheviks, but that in reality he might have been a former member of the Denikin forces, or perhaps had even been a one-time tsarist official. However that may be, whenever possible in subsequent days I surely made every effort to follow his advice.

I remarked earlier that I had found my brother John's name on some of the papers dating back to days of the White Army's occupation of our area in the summer of 1919. He had been in hiding since the arrival of the first Makhnovtsy in Rosental. I managed to keep in touch with him and made every effort to assure him that to the best of my ability I had taken care of all papers in the volost archive which linked his name to the preceding government.

The closing days of October marked a distinct worsening of our situation in the Chortitza settlement and in the surrounding countryside, especially to the north of it toward the city of Ekaterinoslav. The White Armies were relentlessly pushed by the Red Army toward the Crimea. In the course of their retreat they forced the Makhnovtsy out of the heartland of their base of operation, the Guliai Polie district, and to seek safety on the right bank of the Dnieper in a region roughly from the southern boundary of the Chortitza volost and north to about fifteen miles beyond the Mennonite Nicolaipol settlement, and stretching some twenty-five to thirty miles westward from the Dnieper River. The area of their continued occupation through the months of November and December of 1919 was largely Mennonite inhabited, containing, as the bandits assumed, virtually inexhaustible resources of every kind to satisfy their lust for plunder. This area was inhabited almost exclusively by people unarmed and defenseless upon whom they could wreak their hatred with absolute impunity.

During these seemingly endless weeks most of us felt as if the days and nights of horror would never end. My post as secretary of the volost often required my staying in the office late into the evening, or even throughout the night, listening to unreasonable demands from the bandits for food, clothing, horses, and whatever else suited their fancy, trying to scale down their harshest demands, while endeavoring to meet those which were negotiable, and at the same time struggling to keep my composure while being subjected to verbal abuse of the foulest language accompanied by threats of the seizure of hostages and their summary execution if the demands were not met forthwith.

In reality, these threats were minor in comparison to the apprehensions one constantly had for members of one's family at home, who were always subject to beatings, extended torture or murder, and rape of the womenfolk. Scarcely a day went by without reports reaching one of such experiences in the homes of friends, relatives, acquaintances or neighbors, not only in Chortitza-Rosental, but throughout the Old Colony. Communications between the different villages of the volost were difficult to maintain since every single one of them was under Makhnovtsy occupation. However, occasionally a farmer-teamster, who was conscripted to transport them from neighboring or more distantly situated villages to their headquarters in Chortitza, would bring the news of villainous acts perpetrated in his community.

The Massacre of Eichenfeld—Dubovka

One of the most gruesome of these Makhnovtsy deeds was The Massacre in Eichenfeld-Dubovka, October 26, 1919. Eichenfeld was one of the villages in Jazykovo settlement, a daughter colony of the Chortitza settlement founded in 1869-70. Its five villages, Nikolaifeld (Nicolaipol), Adelsheim (Dolinovka), Hochfeld (Morozovo), Franzfeld (Varvarovka), Eichenfeld (Dubovka), and a number of hamlets (Petersdorf, Reinfeld, Paulsheim, Friedensdorf, and numerous individual estates) comprised the Mennonite volost of Nicolaipol. It was situated about seventeen to twenty miles to the north of Chortitza and about thirty-forty miles from the city of Ekaterinoslav. With rare exceptions, the Mennonite estates in this, as in almost every area throughout the Ekaterinoslav and Tavrida guberniias, had been seized by neighboring peasants since the late fall of 1917, their buildings often burned or torn down and hauled away, the livestock and every piece of movable property plundered, and the owners, who had not succeeded in prior escape, murdered. Some of the surviving owners had returned to their former homes for brief months in 1918 during the German occupation of the Ukraine, and for even shorter periods during Denikin's control of the area in the summer of 1919. The hamlets, though repeatedly subjected to plundering raids from gangs of bandits and neighboring peasants, frequently accompanied by the murder of some of the farmers during the period from October 1917 to the fall of 1919, had generally managed somehow to survive. Now, during the months of October and November of this year they were all wiped out. The pattern of destruction usually took the same course. A detachment of Makhnovtsy, or a gang under the leadership of a local bat'ko, would stage a raid upon the hamlet, commence to plunder and kill all male members who had not succeeded in hiding in orchards or fields, often including women also, and then threaten to return the next day to finish their bloody business. Usually this sufficed to cause the survivors to flee to one of the nearby larger Mennonite villages, whereupon the bandits would inform neighboring peasant villages to complete the job of plunder and destruction.

The five villages in the volost had also experienced numerous raids and some slayings of its inhabitants, but not to the same extent as the hamlets, nor in such mass numbers. Now their hour had come. The immediate excuse used by the Makhnovtsy was that the young men of the villages had during 1918-1919 formed self-defense units, heavily armed by the retreating German forces in the autumn of 1918 and by the Denikintsy in 1919, and had during both periods forced numerous peasants to return their pilfered goods, especially horses and livestock, and had also executed several of their leaders. Basically some of the charges of alleged deeds perpetrated by certain members of the self-defense units were true, though the executed men in the volost headquarters in Nicolaipol had not been Makhnovtsy, but members of another one of those "governments" which during the fall of 1918 and the spring of 1919 succeeded each other in kaleidoscopic fashion and frequently with startling speed.

It was almost invariably standard procedure for each of these swiftly changing administrations to use acts of individuals or of groups of citizens taken by them in self-defense against deeds of terror perpetrated by one of its predecessors, as an excuse to revenge "the fallen comrades" by seizing hostages, collecting stores of food, clothing and other goods, and imposing heavy fines upon the entire population of the village, usually followed by new acts of atrocity against the helpless people. Makhno's men were particularly apt at this form of exacting tribute and inflicting punishment. Except for the dreaded Cheka, no other military or para-military group was feared thoughout the South of Russia as much as Makhno and his followers, for none could even remotely compare with them in fiendishness of venting hatred against real or fancied enemies and in giving free reign to their carnal instincts and their lust for plunder.

Throughout most of the Nicolaipol district it seemed to be generally believed that the leader, or leaders, of the self-defense unit which had led the raid upon the volost headquarters which ended in the slaying of three officials, had been residents of Dubovka. Furthermore, there seems to be little doubt that the Makhnovtsy were well acquainted with the facts of the incident, and that they knew the identity of the men allegedly involved in it. Moreover, Dubovka, or Eichenfeld, was a very prosperous Mennonite colony, thus constituting a highly desirable prize for looting by Makhno's men and then to be turned over for wholesale plunder to some of the neighboring peasant villages.

But whatever the cause, the general populace of the object of revenge was to pay a terrible price on Saturday, October 26, 1919. The day before, toward evening, the small number of Makhnovtsy stationed in the village was considerably augmented by the arrival of new units. After spending a rather quiet night the bandits about noon on Saturday commenced their systematic slaughter of every male inhabitant above the age of sixteen on whom they were able to lay their hands during the course of the daylight hours. Apparently with the intent not to alert the whole population of the massacre in progress, gangs of the bandits proceeded from house to house to carry out their gruesome deed, generally hacking the adult and teenage males to death with their sabers. More than half of the seventy-six victims of this slaughter met their death in this manner. Hence, when the wife or other female member of one household went to a neighbor's house to inform its occupants of the tragedy that had befallen her beloved ones, she was at once confronted with tales and sights of a similar fate in the house visited.

Tent Missionaries

Eichenfeld's victims included seventy-one males and five women. Among the slain were six non-residents, all members of a group of so-called tent missionaries. The group had been formed in Moscow shortly after the March Revolution of 1917 by several Mennonite servicemen under the leadership of a J.J. Dyck. The provisional government's decree of complete religious freedom, including the right for anyone to carry on evangelistic propaganda, had shorn the Orthodox Church of its monopoly in this sphere of religious activity. Dyck and his men were highly successful in their efforts to carry the Gospel to the ordinary folk in the street, peasants, workers and soldiers. After the Bolshevik's seizure of power, Dyck and followers shifted their activity to cities, towns and villages in Southern Russia and carried it out with remarkable success despite the aggravated situation everywhere brought on by the civil war.

In the late summer of 1919 Dyck with a score or so of assistants, including not only Mennonites but also converts to his cause from other denominations and churches, including some prominent men from the membership of the Greek Orthodox Faith, and even a former Jewish woman, had come to the Nicolaipol district to carry on evangelistic work among both Mennonite churches, the old established one, the so-called *Kirchliche Gemeinde*, as well as the Brueder Gemeinde, or the Brethren Church. During these fateful late October days the group had divided itself into smaller parties to carry out their missionary work in the different villages of the district. Fate had placed three Mennonites, J.J. Dyck, the group's leader, and Miss Liese Huebert, both from the Molochnaia settlement, and John Schellenberg from nearby Reinfeld, and three non-Mennonites, O. Jushkevich from Riga, J. Golitsyn from Mogilev, and Miss Regina Rosenberg from Konotop, on this day of tragedy in Eichenfeld. They happened to be in the midst of conducting an evangelistic meeting in the village school building when the bandits commenced their grizzly act of senseless killing. All were taken to a nearby farmer's barn and slain.

The other villages and hamlets of the district also suffered many fatalities on this October day of terror and slaughter, but they were minor in comparison to those of Eichenfeld. Hochfeld had suffered fifteen killed, Varvarovka and Nicolaipol three each, Friedensdorf one, and Petersdorf three. Approximately twenty-five more were killed in this area during the last days of October and the early days of November.

The reader can easily surmise the feelings of our people in Chortitza-Rosental or, for that matter, in most other Mennonite colonies of the Chortitza volost, when the news from the Nicolaipol district reached us. Ever so many of our citizenry had close relatives or friends among the martyred people, and even though acts of terror, beatings, other forms of torture, and not infrequent killings of innocent persons, were the order of the day in and around Chortitza; our volost had not experienced mass slaughter.

S. Pravda in Rosental

One morning during these bleak and despairing autumn days, I happened to be standing in front of a window of our home facing the main street of Rosental. Preoccupied with thoughts about problems at the office and the incessant danger facing all of our people throughout the Chortitza volost, I was sort of aimlessly staring at what was going on across the street from us in the yard of the Mennonite elder Isaak Dyck. I knew that he and his wife and the one daughter living with them had left their home to seek safety elsewhere, and that to the best of my knowledge the place was empty. And yet as I was standing there deeply troubled about our present helpless situation, I suddenly realized that a group of Makhnovtsy were obviously in the process of moving into the residence across the street. As I followed their activity more closely I began to see a number of familiar faces, those of friends, or should I rather say, acquaintances, from my Schoenfeld days during the preceding winter and spring months. Among them were Bat'ko Pravda, Naumenko, and a number of others from the village of Liubimovka. I decided to go over and meet them and in some sort of way to welcome them by pointing out where my family and I lived. The reader may recall that I had had an extensive acquaintanceship with this particular bat'ko and some of his henchmen, a relationship which on some crucial occasions had redounded to the advantage of my family, friends, and other acquaintances.

And so I went to the Dyck home to meet this motley assortment of comrades. The upshot of the meeting was that Pravda and his staff decided to make their headquarters on my father's homestead, namely in the building in which my parents and my sister Lena lived. The move meant that they had to give up two rooms to the self-invited guests. It can scarcely be said that neither I, or any other member of our extended family living in the several buildings of the parental homestead, were particularly happy with this decision of my "friends." On the other hand, had Pravda and his murderous staff-companions not moved in, others of the Makhno bands would have done so, for not a single house, except that of the poorest cottager, in Rosental-Chortitza was free of them during practically the entire period of October through December of 1919. There was no assurance that these others might not have been much worse than what we had now.

One of the more important flunkies on Pravda's staff was Nicolai

Ermolovsky, who was generally called by the diminutive of his name, Kol'ka. This lad came from the village of Zherebets, another one of those peasant villages near Schoenfeld which, like Guliai Polie and Liubimovka, was the home of a number of Makhno's most zealous, plundering and murderous followers. Kol'ka had his wife, Anna, and a very young child with him. His spouse was usually addressed as Comrade Anna. He was a nice-looking lad, of friendly disposition and seemingly very decent behaviour, at least to us. Hence we got along with him rather well. It was; however, not so long before I found out what a devilishly fiendish individual he really was when citizens of our village were brought to Pravda for interrogation. For example, one day several bandits brought Cornelius Pauls, a neighbor of ours who lived just around the corner from us, for investigation, and while we did not witness the act of brutality, it was heart-rending to be aware of what was taking place in the rooms which the chief bandit and his companions occupied.

Another such incident which I recall distinctly took place one late afternoon to the rear of our yard. Frost had followed days of rainy weather, and now the low places in the backyard were ice covered. I happened to watch ours and some neighboring children having great fun sliding on the ice. As I followed their diversion I noticed Kol'ka Ermolovsky leading a young man from Chortitza to our straw stack. His name was Heese. Kol'ka was soon joined by several other bandits. Young Heese was ordered to lie face down on the straw, and this was followed immediately by cruel beating from every one of his tormentors. In the usual course of procedure by the Makhnovtsy, an order to lie face down on the straw almost invariably meant execution by being shot in the rear of the head. The children, apparently sensing that something terrible was about to take place, had run away as soon as they saw Kol'ka and his victim heading for the straw stack. I too went away quickly, knowing that I could not possibly save this young man. However, hours later I did find out that Heese had not been executed, though his subsequent fate is unknown to me.

One night I had a lengthy conversation with Pravda about my teaching days and life in general in Schoenfeld, including some of the events when he and his followers had occupied the village earlier this year. Kol'ka was present and listened to our conversation and exchange of experiences of those days. All of a sudden he asked whether I knew Peter Neufeld, or rather Pet'ka Neufeld, as he, in Russian fashion, preferred to use the diminutive of Peter. My reply was that I had known him very well indeed, that Peter was dead. Kol'ka averred that he was aware of this fact, and then asked, "Do you know who shot him to death?"

"No", I said, "I have no idea who did it."

"I killed him," he said. "You know how he and several other Mennonites came to our village to demand the return of their horses. A number of us, knowing that they were coming, had gathered in a house to which we expected them to come, and therefore held our guns in readiness. As soon as they drove into the yard and came to a halt, we dashed outside and commenced blasting away at them. Those who had gotten off the wagon started to run in various directions hoping to save their lives by flight into the field. I pursued Pet'ka Neufeld who tried desperately to get away from me. I kept up my fire and finally hit him in one leg, shattering the knee. He could no longer run, and so I caught up with him. As I approached him, he commenced to cry and to plead for his life, telling me that I could keep his horses and take all his possessions, if only I would not kill him. I told him that he was a fool, for he no longer possessed anything to give me. All that he and other Mennonites possessed now belonged to us, and what I now wanted of him was his soul. With that I fired a shot through his head. And that is how I killed Pet'ka Neufeld."

Later in this account I will relate to you how this man, Kol'ka, came to his own end.

Such were some of the experiences I had during those days and nights at home while during most days I was still trying to attend to my duties as volost secretary, all the while worrying what might be transpiring at home to my family and to the meager possessions still left to us. As one may easily surmise, even with a chieftain like Pravda having quartered himself on the premises of my parents, little was safe in their home or ours. Thus, one day, as I came home for lunch from duties elsewhere in the village, I decided to first of all check in the stable to see whether our precious camels were still there. They were gone, and when I hastened into the house to tell Truda about their disappearance, she told me that only a few minutes ago several bandits had led them away in the direction of Chortitza.

I forgot all about lunch and hastened after the "liberators" of our last draft animals. As soon as I rounded the sharp corner on the main street not far from our home I caught a glimpse of the man with the animals. It was the height of my luck that day that just about the same moment I beheld Pravda's carriage and beautiful span of horses coming in my direction with the chief and some of his staff members in it. I was close enough to the carriage to hear him call to the men who were leading my camels away as to where they were taking the animals. The reply was that they were merely going to try them out and see whether these beasts could pull a wagon. Pravda's order was to immediately return them to the place from which they had taken the camels. Without further ado they were turned over to me.

Once more, as luck would have it, I surely had profited from my acquaintance with this crippled bandit chieftain. However, like everything else in those days, my fortune in this respect ere long ran out. It was not much later when another group of brigands took them away from us.

CHAPTER 10

Epidemic of Typhus

By about the middle of November, the Makhnovtsy inflicted another tragic experience upon almost the entire population of all the villages in the Old Colony. This was the epidemic of typhus, a plague which during the next several months claimed hundreds of victims in our immediate area. In some of the Mennonite villages almost every single inhabitant contracted the illness, with the mortality rate in some of them rising as high as 30% to 40% of the population. The disease was spread wholesale by the lice-infected bandits, who themselves died like flies in the hastily improvised hospitals—perhaps one should say mortuaries—which the leadership of the bandits compelled our citizenry to establish and man in several of the local school buildings in Rosental-Chortitza.

Medical facilities throughout the volost had been entirely inadequate ever since the October Revolution of 1917. Now there was scarcely any to be had for the civilian population, for the one or two doctors left in Chortitza were unable to meet even the most elementary needs of the population; their time being directed under the threat of death to be given to the bandits. The civilian population's lack of clothing, especially underwear, and the generally unsanitary condition under which it was compelled to lead its existence, made a struggle against the disease well nigh impossible. Each day demanded its victims, and fortunate were the survivors in a family if they, with the help of neighbors or nearby relatives, managed to muster enough strength to dig a grave and somehow get the corpse to the cemetery for burial. Funeral sermons and services were a thing of the past. So, generally, were coffins, and the surviving members considered themselves fortunate if they still had some kind of a sheet in which to wrap the body of the deceased. It also was very common that when the corpse was with much difficulty removed to the cemetery, one found that someone else had already placed a corpse into the grave.

One day, I received word that a very dear friend of mine, Mr. Andreas Vogt, a teacher in the local high school, had succumbed to typhus. Our friendship was of longstanding, dating back to our attendance in college in the city of Ekaterinoslav several years before World War I. Upon completion of that part of our education I had taken a position in the Schoenfeld high school and Vogt in a Mennonite village elsewhere. Now, after service in the war, he had become a teacher in the Chortitza high school, while I had gone back to my position in Schoenfeld. Having recently returned to my home village, Rosental, our friendship had been resumed. Since the Vogts lived in one of the teachers' residences on the high school campus, a place I had to pass daily in going to and from my work in the volost office, we saw each other quite frequently during these dark days. I was deeply saddened to hear the news of his passing, and enroute to the office I stopped by their residence to offer Mrs. Vogt my deeply felt sympathies in her bereavement. She told me that with great difficulty she had succeeded in finding someone to dig the grave, but she was totally at a loss as to how she could get the corpse to the cemetery and get it buried.

How could I help her at this trying hour? I thought much about it during the hours of my work at the office but could not find anyone among the people of whom I made inquiry who still possessed a horse or who had the strength to respond favorably to my appeals for help. On the way home in the late afternoon I resolved to ask Bat'ko Pravda for assistance in this matter. All through the months of our acquaintanceship he had insisted that as a teacher I was a member of the working class, the same class to which he had belonged all his life—actually he had spent years as an ordinary beggar in the Mennonite colonies and hamlets around Schoenfeld and; therefore, we were comrades. Hence, when at any time I needed help, I should come to him. And so upon returning home, I addressed myself to him as follows, "Comrade Pravda, a dear friend of mine, also a teacher by the name of Andreas Vogt—you would have called him Andrei Vogt—has died of typhus. His wife has no way of taking the body of her beloved husband to the cemetery. I have been unable to find anyone who could do this for the bereaved woman. Can you help me?"

I wish you could have seen Pravda preening himself and hastening to assume the pose and play the role of a benevolent autocrat. Orders were issued at once by him to one of his drivers to harness a team and forthwith to drive to the Vogt residence on the high school campus and take the corpse of Comrade Schroeder's friend to the cemetery.

As the reader knows, every Mennonite home throughout the Old Colony was during these months subjected to never-ending house searches, allegedly for weapons, but usually ending up with the bandits taking anything they liked, irrespective of what it was and whether they had any need for the object or item of clothing, utensils, etc. Valuables such as jewelry, watches, gold and silver coins, if they had not been buried deep in the ground, of course, had been the first objects of which we had been deprived during the early days of the Makhnovtsy occupation. Although such searches could and did take place at any hour of the day, preference, however, was usually given by these brigands to the hours of darkness. If the *khoziain* of the house had the temerity, before responding to the pounding on the door and demands to open it at once, to inquire whether the party demanding entry had a search warrant, the response elicited was prone to be a shouting "nagan, vot tebe nash prikaz ob obyske" ("The revolver, that's our search warrant for you."), invariably accompanied by a flood of the vilest cursing, of a kind which they themselves labelled as *dvukh-etazhnyie* words (two-story high cursing).

Only the homes of the poorest cottagers or the village herdsman were ordinarily immune from such molestations and terror. For the remainder of our citizenry these kinds of raids had gradually reduced us to a state of near starvation and ragged clothing.

However fear-inspiring all of these daily and nightly "rummaging" (*posharit*, as they were wont to reply to an owner's question as to the purpose of the particular party's searches) enterprizes were for the occupants of the house; the most frightful of these experiences were those conducted by the so-called *kontr-razvedka* (counter-intelligence) units of the Makhnovtsy. The self-professed mission of these units was "to ferret out counter-revolution" against the Makhno movement. Factors which at the time might have caused a citizen to be labelled as a counter-revolutionary could have been almost anything: having held an office during Tsarist days or during the recent brief period of Denikin's occupation of the area; use of assistance of the German-Austrian forces during their 1918 occupation of the Ukraine to help recover seized land, livestock, and other goods from neighboring peasants; having personally belonged to the self-defense (Selbstschutz) units which a number of Mennonite villages had set up during 1918-1919; or having had an immediate or remote member of one's family involved with that organization; or simply having been accused by some local sympathizer of theirs of having caused him injury or in some way aggrieved him.

These "ferreting out" house searches were invariably accompanied by torture of the suspected or accused individual, often extending to other members of the family involved, or the taking of hostages. I recall one particular such incident which had fateful consequences even after the bandits had been driven out by the Red Army around New Year's, 1920. This happened to persons in Rosental whom I knew well. The particular person first involved in this incident, whom I shall merely identify by the letters "M.W.", was not personally accused of having been a counter-revolutionary at any time of his life, but as a person who allegedly possessed knowledge of all people in our village who had either been members of the White Army, or had weapons and ammunition in their possession. They arrested M.W., after a merciless beating, and in fear of imminent execution, finally gave his torturers the names of three citizens. I do not know whether these men, according to M.W.'s revelation of their names to the interrogators, were supposed to have been members of the Deni-kintsy, or were supposed to have weapons in their possession. Under whichever charge they were seized makes really little difference, for all three were subjected to diabolical treatment. Two of the men were brothers whose parents lived in the southern part of Rosental. The third man, an older man, a former proprietor of a flour mill in Chortitza, was named Peters. Despite the merciless beating they underwent, the torturers were unable to wring from them either a confession of having belonged to the White Army, or to find any weapons they allegedly owned. Peters succumbed to the terrible wound inflicted upon him shortly after his release. I did not see either of the three men after their ordeal, but in the spring of 1920, when I had started teaching in the Chortitza high school, one of Peters' daughters, in a composition for one of my classes related that her father, when he finally was released and permitted to go home, was found to have undergone such brutal beatings that the flesh on many parts of his body had been literally torn from the bones.

The morning after M.W. had given the names of these men to his tor-mentors, he came to me as volost secretary, pleading with tears in his eyes. He had done a terrible wrong. He had been in such excruciating pain and fear that he had not realized what he was doing, and begged discon-solately for me to do something to save them from further harm. Techni-cally, there was nothing that anyone of us in the volost administration could have done for the men, either at the time of their arrest or after-wards. Fortunately the two brothers, younger men, eventually recovered from their horrible ordeal.

Months later, in the spring of 1920, I happened to hear several men talking about this tragic event and disclosing their intent of avenging the deed. There was no doubt in my mind that this meant death for M.W. I judged it to be too dangerous for me to personally warn M.W. of the dangers he might be facing. However, I told M.W.'s nephew to inform his uncle of an act of retribution that was in store for him, and that he had better disappear as quickly as possible. Although the nephew apprized him of his dangers M.W. refused to heed the warning and some weeks later he was found slain. The devil had the reigns in his hands, danger loomed all around us, and no one knew what ills might next befall us.

As the weeks of the Makhno occupation of our area dragged on, it became next to impossible to meet the almost daily new demands for livestock, horses, food, fodder, transportation, clothing, and so forth. When these could not be filled the house searches were intensified. These were so thorough that no matter how deeply in the ground one had buried a few precious pieces of clothing, or hidden them behind walls, or under false floors and ceilings, the bandits seldom failed to locate them. It seemed as if the devil was leading them to the place of hiding and told them, "Comrade, here is the place to dig, to probe, to pry, to smell. Dig, brother, dig."

My Life on a Silk Thread

Experience had taught me, as it had everyone else in our area, that attempts at hiding things from these brigands were not only futile but could often lead to special torturing of the proprietor on whose premises buried objects were found. Still, one day I decided that it was not safe at all to have the few pieces of good clothing which we still possessed remaining in the wardrobe of our living room. Even with one of the big chieftains quartered in my parents' house there was no assurance that anything his men, or the followers of another one of the sub-bat'kos with which Makhno's army abounded, would respect the authority of Pravda, or Makhno himself. So I took the chance and buried a sack of clothing deep under a pile of hay in the hayloft. Not so much to my surprise, but to my great worry, the seemingly inevitable thing which almost always happened to us in those days took place. Some of Pravda's own men, on a "digging" spree, found the goods and reported their discovery to him. In no time I was called before the chief to answer for my deed of not trusting him, a fellow member of the laboring class and my friend.

I must mention here that when Pravda and his staff moved from the Dyck residence across the street to my parent's home, three of the lower ranking members of his staff had quartered themselves in the small cottage which my family and I occupied. They were Michael Peresypkin, whom the reader may recall from earlier pages of my story, Feoder (or Fed'ka) Borzenko and a young man whom I knew only by his first name, Grishka. They all came from Liubimovka. Michael, or Mishka, as we usually called him, was a very decent man who always tried to help my family and me. This time, too, when I was called before Pravda, he came along to defend me, knowing that in cases where Pravda felt himself insulted because his position of power and his word had not been trusted, he could, and most likely would take terrible revenge upon the mistrusting party. I too feared that it could well mean life or death for me, for he held the gun in his hand when I entered the room. Mishka tried to defend me, while I was endeavoring to explain my action by explaining to "Comrade Sen'ka", as I addressed him this time in an attempt to mollify him by appealing to our common "labor" background and past friendships, that I had hidden the clothing not out of fear of his own men, but of others. When he kept insisting, "but you did hide things from me, and why did you do it?", I told him that during his absence in the past week a group of men from another party had searched our home and had taken a number of objects which to us were of considerable value and which he, Pravda, and his staff members had always indicated were ours to keep. When he still seemed to doubt my explanation I added that I could readily give the names of the men who had perpetrated the act last week but that I preferred not to do so at this time.

Now Pravda was really angry at whoever had dared in his absence to come to the house where he had established his headquarters, to search its premises and to rob its proprietors. As on similar occasions in the past, he soon learned the names of the men involved, who happened to be people from our village. It took only a short time before the guilty men were brought to the headquarters and administered such a whipping that they found sitting down on a bench or chair a very painful experience.

The Power of the Gospel

As had been my practice in Schoenfeld during the preceding winter and spring, when an opportunity presented itself, during these fall and winter days I would try on occasion to discuss the gospel of Jesus Christ with some of these hardened souls and try to convince them of the dire need of salvation in Christ Jesus. It was Mishka in particular with whom I loved to converse. He was an intelligent and well read man, but I felt that he had read too many of Tolstoy's spiritual writings. Christ, in Tolstoy's view, had been a good man, and to follow in his footsteps was indeed a praiseworthy thing. But he was not the Son of God. This was also Mishka's difficulty, a problem which I earnestly tried to explain to him. Thus, one winter evening Mishka and I were sitting in the little kitchen of our cottage and discoursing on various subjects. A heavy rain was falling and there was a good deal of shooting taking place throughout Rosental. We heard horses galloping up and down the main street, accompanied by much cursing and shouting by their riders. Both of us were at a loss as to the cause of the noisy commotion taking place on the street.

But then, since the front between the Whites and the Makhnovtsy was only a few miles distant from us, the Dnieper separating the enemies, rifle firing and artillery shelling were not really novel events for us, we continued our discussion in the unlit kitchen. All of a sudden Mishka asked me, "What is the confession of your Mennonite faith?" Here I answered him very precisely, "My dear friend Mishka, the matter of your salvation is so very simple. If only you would look at Calvary and see the three crosses and the crucified Jesus. In your spirit look at the one cross and behold Jesus and believe that he was crucified for you, for the remission of your sins and for the salvation of your soul. That very moment when you do this, you are saved."

I had no idea as to what was going on in his heart, but years later I received word that he was miraculously saved. Further on in these reminiscences I will bring translations of several letters I received from some of his associates with the Makhnovtsy who also were saved. I am sure that it was my pointing out to him to look to the cross at Calvary, however much he resisted the advice at the time, that had much to do with his eventually finding Jesus Christ.

With the passage of time our food resources were nearing the vanishing point. There were no stores in which we could buy any edibles to replenish our larder and, as mentioned earlier, gradually we were reduced to such a state that we almost literally depended for survival upon what food supplies the bandits quartered in our homes brought in from the equally dwindling food stocks of our Mennonite farmers. Toward the end of their occupation such supplies came largely from the bandits' requisitioning trips to neighboring peasant villages. Mishka was particularly helpful and at times he himself would prepare an especially tasty meal, including a very tasty borshch.

The health of our people was also rapidly deteriorating. Undernourished, with will power drained by constant fear and anxiety, poorly dressed and day-in and day-out exposure to live infestations from the bandits to a degree that defies description, more and more people succumbed to the typhoid fever epidemic. Most of the citizenry had no change of underwear and it was a common practice for members of a family to take turns undressing in the morning or evening trying to keep warm under such covers as the family still possessed, while the other members wrapped the clothing in rags or paper and placed the packages on the grates of the moderately hot oven in attempts to disinfect the apparel. At the same time the rest of the family, hovering close to the oven, would be busily engaged in killing lice along the seams of other items of clothing either by crushing the innumerable vermin between the nails of the thumbs or by systematically whacking the seams with a small hammer to the accompanying crackle of the bloodfilled suckers. The nightly delousing of the head was a scene which reminded one constantly of similar performances by monkeys in a zoo's cage.

Truda in Danger

Throughout its duration the reign of the Makhnovtsy posed for every Mennonite inhabitant never ending mental anguish and constant threat of physical danger. Only the poorest tenant laborer or the small cottager could ordinarily regard himself as being immune to searches of his premises and seizure of his property. Even rarer, he was in danger of receiving physical maltreatment. And while scarcely any other male from his early teen years to ripe age was safe from whipping or torture, usually on the slightest of pretexes or for no reason whatsoever except to satisfy the bandits' dislike, or their lust for violence, young and middleaged women faced the constant threat of molestation, and not infrequently of being raped by a number of these brutish men.

There were a number of cases in several of the villages where the husband was tied to the bed in which his wife was subjected to mass raping by the very men quartered in his house, and where the victim of this bestial outrage would have to wait on these same men by preparing meals for them at any hour of the day or night. There was rarely an escape in flight from such frightful experiences since the entire Old Colony was under the occupation of these brigands. The only warranty against exposure by a woman to such fearful maltreatment was on those rare occasions when one or several of the bandits who still had a conscience might warn the head of a household as to the danger facing his wife, daughter, sister or mother in the coming night.

I am in the position of relating such a case from personal experience.

As the reader knows, my family had to provide sleeping accomodations in our small kitchen to three Makhnovtsy. These three were not vicious men themselves, at least not to us, for they had joined Makhno's hordes for the freedom to pillage. As a matter of fact, on several occasions they were our veritable lifesavers.

Thus, one day Mishka and his two companions came to me and warned me that my wife was in grave danger during the coming evening from Bat'ko Pravda. They had heard him boast about his designs upon Truda. Having imparted this intelligence to me they told of their chief's mode of procedure in such fiendish designs of his.

He would go to the house of the intended victim accompanied by one of his henchmen carrying an ample supply of food and homebrew. He would announce to the *khozian* that he wished to show him that not all Makhnovtsy should be feared as robbers and murderers. On the contrary, there were many good people among them. To demonstrate to the head of the household that his family had nothing to fear from him, he had come with food and drink to show his good will toward him and his family.

Mishka and our other two tenants and boarders then gave me the names of several homes in Rosental where Pravda had given "evidence of his good intentions." After the advancing Red Army on January 1, 1920 freed us from this scourge, it was reported that there had been about 100 cases of rape in Chortitza and Rosental.

The reader can well surmise my feelings after having received this information. Mishka, Grishka and Fed'ka assured me that they would do everything in their power to thwart Pravda's scheme. But the question that still haunted me was, could I trust their word? I could neither tell Truda of the dangers ahead, nor advise her to seek safety in another home in the neighborhood, for every one of these was filled with equally evil men. How I prayed that evening, and how I implored God to help me trust the assurances of these men that they would stay with us in the cottage, come what may.

As the day drew to a close and darkness fell upon us, I told Truda in an off-hand manner that several of Pravda's men had mentioned to me during the course of the day that their chief planned to visit us this evening. Furthermore, I added, this visit was unpredictable as to the length of its duration and she should go to bed, taking the children with her. This she did right after supper. I remained in the kitchen conversing with Mishka and the other two men. It was not long after Truda's retirement that I heard Pravda's stumping ascent on the stoops of the porch, and a moment later he entered accompanied by another man carrying food and samogon. The kitchen was so small that it could hold very little furniture—a table, a bench and a chair or two. Mishka had appropriated the bench and had, in fact, already bedded himself down for the night. The only sleeping facilities we had for the two companions of his was a mattress which during the day was kept in our bedroom and at night placed on the floor of the kitchen. Grishka and Fed'ka were sitting on it as Pravda entered. I occupied the only chair available, but I did not think it necessary to offer it to Pravda, for his short legs made it more comfortable for him to sit on the mattress. This he proceeded to do.

Almost immediately the bandit chief asked, "Where is Borisovna?" This meant Truda who, as the daughter of Bernhard Peters (in Russian this would read Boris Peters) was often addressed as Truda Borisovna. My response to this inquiry was to inform him that she had retired for the night because she was not feeling well and was in fact already asleep, as were our three children. His retort, "I don't want Borisovna to be sick. I want her to be healthy, and I wish to cure her. You call her right away to come and join us."

I went into the bedroom and told my wife that Pravda demanded her presence, but advised her to be real slow in responding to his invitation. I knew Pravda would commence at once with drinking, and I hoped the more he consumed of that evil tasting homebrew the deeper his inebriated condition would get and, therefore, the less of it would be left for us to join him in toasting "our friendship". Mishka dished out the meat and the other food and placed the bread on the table. It fortunately fell to my lot to pour the drinks. For Pravda I had selected a large glass, and for Truda and myself two ordinary cups. Mishka had already poured himself a glassful while Grishka and Fed'ka had gone into our bedroom, stretched themselves on the floor and continued observing our doings through the open door to the kitchen.

As the evening progressed, I kept on filling Pravda's glass with lots of alcohol and very little water, and then did the reverse with the cups for the two of us. I could do this without arousing the suspicion of the chief, not only because of his sitting on the mattress and the top of the table thus being above the level of his eyes, but also because of the very poor lighting in the kitchen. My doings, however, had not escaped the two people watching us from our bedroom, and when once I happened to be standing very close to them one of them whispered to me, "Why do you keep on eating and yet you hardly touch any liquor?"

Pravda, frustrated at the lack of any progress he was making in getting us drunk, at last demanded that Mishka and the other two men leave us and go somewhere else. This they refused, with Mishka as the spokesman, insisting that the cottage was their quarters which they would not leave. Moreover, because of the lateness of the hour he felt it was time for Pravda to go to the big house and to retire for the night. This advice at first evoked only a string of cusswords and threats, but to no avail, since Mishka and the other two persisted in their refusal to depart. So, at last, Pravda consented to leave; however, since even in sober condition he had great difficulty in walking by himself, he demanded that Mishka guide him to his quarters. But before the two managed to get out of the kitchen, Grishka and Fed'ka hurriedly returned to the kitchen and filled their containers with the chief's liquor. What a relief it was for my wife and myself when at last Mishka and Pravda had left the cottage. We thanked God in our hearts that the terrible ordeal we had been facing had finally come to an end.

When Mishka returned he was convulsed with laughter and called our attention to the back of his coat which was absolutely covered with mud. To our inquiry as to the reasons for his unabashed mirth and the cause of his muddy coat, he replied that he had played quite a trick on Pravda by leading him not along the walk to the front house, but through the deep mud in the farmyard, and that the chief had been so angry that he had let go of his hand, then with both of his hands had grabbed mud and flung it at his back.

We were most thankful to these three men for having stayed with us during this trying ordeal. Fortunately, never again did we undergo another similarly unpleasant encounter with Pravda.

Trifon

Among the Makhnovtsy was a man whom earlier in the year we had encountered in Schoenfeld and were now to encounter in Rosental, and with whom we had an occasional pleasant but more often unpleasant contact, one Trifon, whom I mentioned much earlier in this story. He had at one time held the post of some kind of commissar in Schoenfeld. Now he too was staying on my father's premises, except that he had taken quarters in the old house in which my brother John and family had lived.

If he was proficient in anything, it was swearing. It seemed as if he could hardly say a single sentence without a stream of swear words. Like all his comrades he was infested with lice, and in his uncouth manner one could observe his grabbing some lice from his neck and throwing them to the floor. To a question as to why he did not kill them would come the reply, "Oh no, let them live. We shall see who lives longer, they or I." He could be decent on occasion but more often than not he enjoyed displaying the most unpleasant side of his character.

I would now and then try to talk with him about spiritual matters, but I was unable to make any impact upon him. An aquaintance of ours from the village Zalivnoe, Mrs. Kuklenko, a deeply devoted Christian, had on earlier occasions warned Trifon by telling him that God was watching him and that he would not escape being held accountable for the many atrocities he was committing. "God will meet you one day," she kept on telllng him, "and you will meet God." "What kind of God? There is no God," Trifon would reply. Sister Kuklenko persisted in her warnings to him that God's punishment was inescapable. Still, neither her admonishings at that time nor my present advice had any affect upon him.

Another character of some notoriety whom I remembered from my Schoenfeld time, and whom I unexpectedly encountered one very late evening in Rosental, was a brother of Nestor Makhno.

Savely Makhno

As volost secretary I was often called to Mennonite homes in Rosental and in Chortitza to help straighten out difficulties between the home-owner and the bandits living on the premises. At times, the conflict could be a matter of simple misunderstanding between the owner and the "guest". On other occasions, it might be an issue of serious threats and where a terribly frightened member of the household would come to my office, or reach me at home at night, imploring that I come with him and intercede on behalf of the person threatened.

Thus one night a well-known retired farmer of Rosental, formerly an influential person throughout the Old Colony, Johann Penner, came to the cottage and begged me to come with him as speedily as possible to ward off some dire threats being made to his wife, the former widow Franz Janzen, and her son and daughters. He had married the widow Janzen not so long ago.

Due to strict curfew which the bandits imposed upon the civilian population, it was dangerous for us to be stopped on the street by one of their sentries. Fortunately, as district secretary I was each day given the code words and responses established for the particular night, so we managed to get to the Penner residence without difficulties. When I followed Penner into the house and into the living room, the room was occupied by some sort of leader; I was surprised to see that it was none other than Bat'ko Makhno's eldest brother, Savely Makhno. I remembered having seen him in Schoenfeld in the machine shop of my father-in-law, B.J.

Peters. However, I was not certain whether he had ever met me.

After inquiring into the causes of the difficulties which had arisen between his men and the owners of the residence, and listening for awhile to his arguments and explanations about the rightness of his men, I told him of my teaching years in Schoenfeld, that I was the son-in-law of B.J. Peters, and that I had known and still knew a number of people from Guliai Polie, Liubimivka, Zherebets, Zalivnoe and other villages in that area. Savely soon adopted a more conciliatory, and even friendly attitude. He stressed that he knew Mr. Peters well, and his other son-in-law, Julius Rempel. Also that at one time he had worked in Rempel's machine shop. This recognition of mutual acquaintances of pre-civil war days helped to allay the flared tempers of Savely and some of his men who stood around and listened to our conversation. Whatever had provoked their threatening behaviour, I now no longer recall, but at any rate the tempers of the Makhnovtsy had cooled noticeably. Therefore, it seemed perfectly safe for the Penner family, at least as far as I was able to assess the situation, so I decided to go home.

During my conversation with Savely that evening, I happened to ask him at one stage of our meeting whether it was true that Nestor had been a teacher in the earlier years, a story to this effect having been widely circulated at this time. To this came the disparaging reply, "What kind of a teacher could he have been? He was an ordinary worker, painting roofs and doing other kinds of manual work."

As our conversation went on I observed some interesting transactions taking place between Savely and a number of men allegedly under his command. Earlier, upon arriving at the Penner farmyard, I had noticed a wagon near the front of the house, with a big metal barrel on it, the kind in which liquor used to be transported in Southern Russia prior to the Revolution. On the basis of my observations and experiences with the Makhnovtsy there was no doubt that these men, before leaving some particular areas in the Southern part of the Tavrida guberniia, had "liberated" the barrel from a distillery and had filled it with vodka.

Sure enough, ere long several men came to Savely and asked permission to fill the containers which they held in their hands from the barrel on the wagon. That was granted. Other men came into the living room and asked for money. These requests, too, were met without any hesitation. Savely appeared to be amply supplied with all kinds of money issued since the spring of 1917 by the various governments which had held sway in Russia at one time or another during the past several years. All of these currencies had, of course, greatly depreciated in their face value, but I was intrigued to observe that the men appeared to prefer the twenty and forty rubel notes issued by the Provisional government under Kerensky. These notes were commonly called *Kerenky*. Savely had big sheaves of these notes and as requests were being made he would take a pair of shears and scissor off the amount asked for.

With this observation strongly imprinted on my mind, I took leave and went home, marvelling all the way at the wonderful grace of God and the miracles He continued to perform, here to see and to experience, if only we kept an open eye and continued our faith in Him.

The Typhus Epidemic and its Tolls

As has been indicated before, many of the bandits who occupied our homes throughout the Chortitza district during the last three months of 1919, either arrived there seriously ill with several types of typhoid fever or contracted it from their comrades after they got there and then, due to their heavy infestation with lice, commenced to spread the disease to the civilian population.

The bandits usually were covered with lice. Their generally dark clothing was so full of lice that one could see them crawling on the collar, the sleeves and around the pocket flaps. Most of the men had no conception of personal hygiene, and often had little desire to fight the vermin. Small wonder that our Mennonite people, hard as they tried, soon faced a serious problem of how to combat them, a fight which, despite heroic efforts was made so exceedingly difficult because our people had hardly any change of clothing left to them.

I had been fortunate enough to escape the disease for a number of weeks but I finally succumbed to it toward the close of the year. This put an end to my work in the district office. For about two weeks I was so ill that I was convinced that my days were numbered. The two doctors of our district hospital, Theodore Hottmann and David Hamm, occasionally managed to steal a few minutes from their forced attendance to sick and wounded Makhnovtsy for a rare visit to some Mennonite homes. Dr. Hamm came to see me on several occasions and told my wife and my father that there was little, if any, chance that I would pull through. I myself was so firmly of the opinion that my end was fast approaching that I wished to say farewell to my immediate relatives and friends. How clearly I remember those moments when many of the people dear to me came to my bed in the big house where I had been moved after I became seriously sick. I had the feeling of complete ease and lacked any anxiety of the impending departure, this despite the young wife and the almost infant children I would leave behind. I had only one thought—I would go home to my Heavenly Father and my Saviour, the Lord Jesus Christ.

But my father would sit at my bedside and try to cheer me up, reminding me of my family I had to provide for, of my own youth, and then insist that I must wish to live and thus to keep up the fight for life. Because of his age (68), he kept on repeating that it was he who would die in my place. And as fate would have it, it was indeed he who succumbed to this illness some six or seven weeks later, in February of 1920, while I did recover.

Death was everywhere. There were very few homes in our village or in the other Mennonite communities in the district which did not experience a loss of one, and occasionally several of its members. The death ratio among males was especially high, just about two to one for each female. There were, to be sure, two hospitals in Chortitza-Rosental, one a Mennonite District Hospital, and the other one, until the fall of 1917, had been maintained by the rural Zemstvo institutions. However, both of them, with their depleted staffs and minute supply of medicine, were unable to really do anything for the Mennonite people. As Dr. Hamm pointed out, "When I would arise in the morning and look into the yard of the hospital there would be as many as thirty *oboianki* [these were a type of spring wagon used extensively by many Mennonite farmers for Sunday or visiting purposes] all filled with bandits waiting for me to attend to them, usually accompanied with direct threats of punishment, even death on the spot, if I did not at once do something for them." Even if the doctor was ready and willing to admit the bandits, or a Mennonite, to the hospital, there was slight chance that this would be of any assistance to the patient, for the Makhnovtsy had already plundered them of medicine, beds and blankets, etc. When Dr. Hamm complained personally to the biggest bat'ko usually found in the Chortitza-Rosental area, Bat'ko Pravda, about these depredations, the latter simply replied, "Go to your *burzhuis* (bourgeois) and plunder them. Your capitalists have lots of things." It was useless to tell him that there were no capitalists left after his men—and others like them before—had robbed and plundered our district for endless weeks.

Definite statistics as to how many inhabitants in our seventeen villages were ill with typhoid fever during the winter of 1919-1920 are not currently available to me. The percentage of sick people varied from sixty to seventy percent in the smaller villages. In the larger villages such as Chortitza, Rosental, Osterwick, Neuendorf, Einlage, and Nieder Chortitza, the figure was eighty-five and ninety per cent because throughout the period of occupation these had the largest number of bandits quartered in them. The epidemic consisted of three different types of typhoid fever. Speaking very generally, all three types, though varying in certain detailed aspects, were characterized by protracted periods of very high fever, prolonged spells of delirium, the spread of a red rash over the entire body, and marked by extreme prostration. The disease was spread mainly through the lice from the bandits to the civilian population and was greatly aided and abetted by the inability of the people to generally observe even elementary methods of hygiene. Malnutrition, from which the civilian Mennonite population suffered so severely, but not the Makhnovtsy, especially during the latter part of November and throughout December, had left few people with the strength to resist the epidemic.

The most prevalent type of illness at this time was the so-called *typhus exanthunaticus,* or spot typhus. It was marked by red spots showing up over the entire body, loss of appetite, severe headache, high temperature, difficulty in breathing, and was often accompanied by swelling of the spleen. The crisis in this type usually took place between the twelfth and seventeenth days of illness.

The second type was called abdominal typhus. It lasted longer than spot typhus, the duration varying from four to five weeks. It affected particularly the intestines and the bowels and the patient had to be particularly careful with the type and amount of food intake during the period of recovery.

Lastly, there was the *vosvratnyi tif,* i.e., the repeat or "returning" type of typhus. In this the period of recuperation was four or five weeks, marked by alternating stages of recovery and renewed illness. Heart ailment in each case of these illnesses greatly increased the incident of death.

I do not possess accurate statistical data as to the number of people who died of these epidemics during the winter of 1919-1920 throughout the Chortitza volost. I do recall that for most of the colonies the figure given at the time ranged from around ten to twenty per cent of the Mennonite inhabitants. For Chortitza, Rosental, Osterwick, Neuendorf, and Nieder Chortitza I have seen the estimates of death during the months in question as having been approximately 175, 180, 75, 150, and 94 respectively.

The deaths among the Makhnovtsky were much more numerous. They died like flies, not because of malnutrition but because of the filth in which they lived (even though the Mennonite homeowners were constantly forced to clean up after them) and because of the terribly dissolute life they led. Until shortly before Christmas their authorities had made efforts to establish some improvised hospital facilities for their

The family of Peter J. Schroeder, June, 1914. Center: Peter and Maria Schroeder. Left: Gerhard's brother-in-law Jacob Kasdorf, his wife Anna, and their children. Jacob perished in slave labor under the communists in 1937. Anna died in 1936. In the center, standing: Gerhard and Truda, just married, Gerhard's sisters Mary, Katherine and Helen. Right: brothers John and Peter and their families.

Truda's family in 1906. Center: Bernhard J. and Margareta Peters. Standing left to right: Willy, Katherine, Margareta, and Truda. Front row left to right: Anna, Hans, Mika, and Susan.

Schoenfeld High School, 1914. Teachers in front row, left to right: Henry D. Neufeld, shot by the makhnovtsy in 1919; Jacob J. Dyck, went to Canada. Peter P. Sawatzky, Principal, later tortured to death by the communists; and G. P. Schroeder.

A teachers' conference in Schoenfeld, June, 1914. Front row left to right: teacher A. Isaak; unknown; G. P. Schroeder; John P. Dyck, member of the board of directors; P. P. Sawatzky, principal of our high school; inspector of schools Maidachenko, who in 1915 closed our school; H. Wiens, Oberschulze (chief) of the Schoenfeld Volost, unknown; teacher Koop; teacher, unknown. Second row left to right: sixth from the left, teacher Jacob J. Dyck; teacher Henry D. Neufeld; teacher Heinrichs; teacher, unknown; and teacher Jacob F. Toews. Third row, third from left, teacher C. C. Peters and teacher Nickel. The others are unknown.

The last students and the last teachers of the Schoenfeld Central High School, Spring, 1919. In the front row left to right: teacher Jacob J. Tiessen, students Anna Heidebrecht and Agatha Wiens, teachers Helene Tiessen (nee Froese) Henry P. Neufeld and G. P. Schroeder, with daughter Margaret standing in front of him.

Money used under Tzar Nicholas II.

Money used under Alexander Kerensky, 1917.

Money issued by the Ukrainian Republic, about 1918.

Front

Reverse

Nestor Makhno was born in Southern Russia on October 27, 1889. At the age of sixteen years he was taking part in political affairs. In 1908, he was sentenced to death by hanging for participation in acts of terror. This sentence was later commuted to life. When the revolution started in 1917, he was set free and started organizing against any form of government, especially in the years 1918-1921. When the communists gained the upper hand, he fled to France, where he died in 1934.

Before WWI, one ruble was worth 50¢ in American money. But by the end of 1921, with the communists in power, 50,000 rubles (above) would buy less than two pounds of butter. By 1923, one pound of butter had soared to 10,000,000 rubles. It took 180,000,000 rubles to buy one American dollar. Inflation knows no boundaries when governments turn on the printing presses and counterfeit their own currency. This cannot happen when a country's currency is backed by gold.

The freight train with about 750 emigrants from Chortitza, July 3, 1923 at the railroad station in Alexandrovsk-Zaporoshie. In the front are four teachers from the Chortitza Central High School: J. J. Klassen, D. H. Epp, John P. Klassen, and G. P. Schroeder.

This is the document that took us across the border from Russia to Canada in 1923. At the bottom is our landing card in Quebec.

own sick. The Chortitza boys' high school and the Rosental girls' high school had been converted to hospitals of sorts, but the facilities provided consisted in the main of the classrooms and assembly halls having been cleared of the furniture and straw having been spread on the floors on which the sick were bedded down. Both schools were equipped with a system of hot water heating and the rooms were kept exceptionally warm. Therefore, as soon as the vehicles loaded with their sick men arrived at the schools—they were brought there not only from Chortitza and Rosental, but also from other Mennonite villages—the patients were undressed in an effort to delouse their clothing, and were then left to lie on the straw, usually stripped to the waist. The men were so full of lice that one could see them crawling over the entire body. Medical help? There was none, although the local Mennonite doctors would occasionally manage to drop in for a few minutes of administering some aid.

Since the Makhnovtsy themselves refused to take care of their own ill men, the students from the local boys' high school, the teachers seminary, and such other young people as the bandits were able to conscript and compel to report to these hospitals, were usually the only attendants to look after the sick. Each of these "orderlies" was assigned to a classroom which, on the average, held about thirty patients. As a rule few of the young men managed to serve a shift of more than a few days before they too came down with the disease. The number of Makhnovtsy who died shortly after having been brought to the hospital was so large that the wagon, or wagons, which had delivered the ill almost invariable left the school grounds with a load of dead men. In private homes the death rate among the Makhnovtsy was just about as high, and toward the closing days of the occupation the bandits did not even bother to pick up the bodies of their deceased comrades. They were to be found in their quarters, in the stables or lying on the street.

During the last weeks of December the Mennonites had (if that were possible) even greater difficulties in burying their dead. There were cases where one or both deceased parents were for days lying in the same bed with their sick children until some relative or acquaintance happened to have the strength to visit homes where none of its inhabitants had been seen about for days. Only with serious difficulty did most families manage to dig a grave for their deceased members. Equally serious was the problem of how to get the corpse to the cemetery located on top of a steep grade in Rosental. Since draft animals were all but non-existent, the usual mode of conveyence was to tie the corpse to a handsleigh, which one or two people then might succeed in pulling to the cemetery. Once having reached the grave, it was not at all an uncommon sight to find that someone else had already placed a corpse in it. Nor was it unusual for people to beg of a neighbor, friend or relative, not to fill the grave with dirt, for they expected to have to bury one of their own members within a day or two.

Such then, were the conditions which prevailed throughout the Old Colony, conditions from which hardly a single home in all the villages had managed to escape

While I was still very ill, my sister Marie's husband, Abraham D. Kroeger, died of typhus. They lived not far from us and while my parents and Truda insisted that they had told me of his passing, I have no recollection whatsoever of the event. About the same time a daughter of brother John and his wife, Anna, died of the same illness. My brother Peter was also critically ill but he did eventually recover. A similar situation prevailed in the house of my sister and her husband, Jacob Kasdorf. Here, too, a member of the family was ill with typhus but only the father-in-law, J. D. Kasdorf died. And when I was barely on the road to recovery my wife Truda came down with abdominal typhus. In 1919, of all the members of our extended family, only father and mother did not succumb to this illness.

A Change in the Political Situation

Shortly before Christmas it became apparent that a change in the political situation was approaching. The Makhnovtsy were getting more restless by the day, more unnerved, and at the same time more difficult to put up with as the holidays were upon us, though it is certain that few people were thinking about the approaching Christmas. The rumble of the artillery fire became more audible from the north and the west, but we were not certain whose forces were advancing toward the Chortitza area. For several months we had had no communications with either Ekaterinoslav to the north of us, or with Alexandrovsk just a few miles across the Dnieper River.

On December 25th, large units of the bandits commenced to move out from Chortitza, Rosental, Neuendorf, Osterwick and other villages. Their exodus, accompanied by more beating and looting of the little that most families had left of clothing, bedding and underwear, continued during the last five days of December. On New Year's Eve we learned what had compelled the Makhnovtsy to move on. It was the advance of the Red Army, slowly but relentlessly pushing the White Army which sought to escape from encirclement and annihilation by retreating to the Crimean

Peninsula. With the almost total defeat of the White Army in sight, the leadership of the Red Army had no further need of the covert or open support from Makhno's brigands. And Makhno realized that his game was up, that he and his men were also facing annihilation, so they therefore sought to flee in the direction of Guliai Polie, the heartland and the backbone of what had sustained his marauding bands for several years.

On New Year's Day all of the Chortitza district was freed from the scourge of thousands of free booters, murderers, thieves, and just ordinary peasants who had gone along for the ride of what seemed to be the easiest way to looting with abandon, and to revenge themselves for the centuries of abuse and exploitation they had suffered from government official and landlord, irrespective of the fact that they were taking out their hatred on people who, with very few exceptions, had had nothing to do with their ill fortunes of the past.

It is safe to say that never before or after, had the surviving Mennonites been so glad to see soldiers with the red five-pointed star emblem on their caps.

For several months we now were able to enjoy peace and relative order. Although the new troops also had recourse to quartering themselves in our homes and occasionally resorted to requisitioning of very scarce items, there was no looting, beating and torturing of people. The new authorities also made every effort to root out banditism; they helped with the burial of the dead Makhnovsty and the many killed and starved horses which were to be found along streets, in farmyards and along roads. Above all, the new masters did try to render assistance with cleaning up the indescribable filthy conditions the bandits had left in many homes, schools and other public buildings, as well as to bring in some medical assistance.

During the entire course of the Makhno occupation of our area, we had been completely cut off from contact with other Mennonite centers, the nearby Schoenwiese for example, which now for about a decade had been part of the city of Alexandrovsk, but above all we had had no communication with the very large Mennonite center, the Molochnaia settlement. We suspected, but above all we hoped, that it had been spared the ravages and killings of those bands from Guliai Polie, located at such a short distance from its northernmost colonies. Nor had we any idea what might have taken place in such settlements as Memrik, Ignatievo, and Zagradovka, all of which had once been very prosperous and beautiful colonies. Now, with our encirclement lifted, we found out that some of these so-called daughter colonies, while not having to endure so prolonged an occupation as the Old Colony, the massacre in one of them, Zagradovka, dwarfed anything we had suffered in the Old Colony, Eichenfeld-Dubovka excepted, for on November 29, 1919 units of the Makhnovtsy, with help from neighboring peasants, had murdered 192 men, women, and children in addition to carrying out terrible looting and the burning of a very large number of homes and farm buildings.

CHAPTER 11

God Performs Miracles

Help from the Molochnaia

We now had peace of a sort in the Chortitza volost, but the future looked very dark for all of us. Food for almost every single family was a critical issue. Nor was there an end to the typhus epidemic, as more people, who had escaped it during the late autumn weeks of 1919 and the early days of 1920, came down with one or the other types of the disease. And what were we to do with the hundreds of children who had been orphaned through either the natural death of their parents or through murder? And what were we to plant in our gardens and to sow in our fields, since seed grains and vegetables were had by few families and individuals? In addition, there were scarcely any horses to be found on any farm, except for some crippled and sick animals which the bandits had left behind.

Soon we were to learn that we had not been forsaken by God and by our brethren in the Molochnaia settlement. The Denikin regime and forces had been in control of this area since the early summer of 1919 and it was not forced to surrender this territory until the early days of the new year. These brethren; therefore, had ample supplies of all essentials to sustain life. As soon as they received word of our plight they embarked upon a large scale program of bringing relief to the hungry and ill co-religionists throughout the Chortitza district. With tacit as well as open approval of the newly established Soviet authorities throughout the southern regions of Russia, these Mennonites succeeded in transporting large amounts of food, clothing, medical supplies, and personnel to Chortitza and environs, which helped to save thousands of our people from starvation and also helped to stem the tide of the typhus epidemic.

More than that, seed grains, vegetable seeds, potatoes, etc., were also distributed on a large scale in time for the spring planting. Finally, hundreds of orphans were taken to the Molochnaia for adoption or for placement in foster homes. Few of them could have been cared for by their relatives in their home villages and it is highly doubtful whether many of them would have survived the hard times of the next year or two. Even though there seemed fair prospects that most of us would be able to make a go of it, what with help from the Molochnaia brethren, with the end of the the civil war and the utter defeat of Wrangel's White Army in the fall of 1920, and prospects that the Soviet government now might be disposed to make various concessions which would make a rebuilding of the shattered economy possible, little did we know that as far as sheer physical survival was concerned, we would face even greater tragedies than any of us had endured so far. That of course came with the total crop failure of 1921 and the resultant famine of unequalled scope and proportion in a country which had seen terrible famines before in its long history.

Help for Our Family

In this our pitiful situation, with danger and suffering from all sides, suddenly there came a ray of hope in the form of temporary help from a source we had not expected. Early in January 1920 my father-in-law, B.J. Peters, his two daughters, Greta and Anna, along with Mr. Wansiedler whom we have mentioned before as coachman—"kutscher"—came to Rosental to help us. They were taking a big risk facing many dangers day and night. But they came, and this fact alone had its positive affect. Greta and Anna had received documents that they were going to help as nurses in the typhoid stricken area. They brought us many things we needed badly. Covering a distance of approximately fifty-five miles from Schoenfeld to Rosental they had seen many dead horses at the roadside. Crossing the Dnieper River on a sleigh was quite a unique experience for them.

At this time I already was able to walk around the house and could help others. Truda, my dear wife, and her brother, Hans Peters, who was about 14 years of age at this time, were slowly recovering but still unable to walk. My two sisters in our house were also bedridden. Our three children Margaret, 5, Peter, 3, and Katherine, 1, were not sick but much neglected in many things. My mother and father were still able to help us but the task often was beyond human capability. Grandpa Peters in his memoirs has written about this:

The first thing we did was to clean the house. We put clean linen on the beds, aired the rooms and saw to it that the sick got the necessary attention. Because some of the sick had recuperated enough to help themselves and also were able now to help others that were still sick in their beds, it was decided that we should not stay here too long at this time, but rather take the children Margaret, Peter, and Katie along to Schoenfeld. This was done, because the other sick, our son Hans, our daughter Truda and her husband, G. P. Schroeder, were still too weak and sick to travel in the cold air a distance of about 55 miles. It was decided that somebody from Schoenfeld would come back in about two weeks and bring the Schroeders and our son Hans along, too. The used laundry was put into sacks and the children placed in the sleigh, and, after two days of helping in Rosental, we started on our way back to Schoenfeld.

On their way back to Schoenfeld they met with many difficulties and dangers; they could have lost their lives, if it had not been for the kindness and extreme hospitality of a Russian "mushik"—a peasant—who along with his wife and their sons, sheltered them, gave them good food to eat and protected them against some intruders who, late in the night or very early in the morning, came into the house to find out who these outside visitors were. They were drunk and there were indications that they would cause our travelers a lot of trouble, and perhaps even kill them. But they were protected by these kind peasants, and I wanted my family to remember this in later years. Grandpa Peters wrote about this:

In the morning our host excused himself for the disturbance in the night by these unpleasant intruders; the lady of the house served us a nice breakfast. The two horses were brought out by these two young sons of our hosts. The two horses were well fed and cleaned. All our belongings were placed back into the sleigh, so we drove home to Schoenfeld. Here we were joyfully received. The children by their grandma Peters were taken into the warm bathroom, their hair was clipped short and they all received a good bath and all conveniences they had missed for such a long period of time because of the illness of their parents. Clean clothing was brought into the room and the children were dressed in entirely different clothes.

In the dining room the table was covered with the nicest meal, and we could see how these dear children really enjoyed all the attention and the good meal they were given. Their faces brightened up. Their eyes were sparkling. Then, when they were put into a clean warm bed, it didn't take long when they fell asleep. These three little ones soon became stronger after all those horrible experiences in Rosental.

My Father's Departure

Soon after our helping visitors from Schoenfeld along with our three little children had left us, my father became very ill with a severe case of typhus. I personally always felt very close to my father but in this case we all felt our utter frustration. There was very little that we could do but pray, and this we did. But no medicine was obtainable and the doctors were helpless. I would sit at his bedside, trying to be of some help. The rest of the family were still bedridden except my mother, who by this time was at the end of her physical strength, too. I myself was pretty weak, but I spent all of my time helping the sick in our home.

It was February 11th or 12th when I noticed that the hour of Father's departure was at hand. I called on all the sick members of our family in their beds to pray. They did this but they were unable to come and help. Only mother came to see her dear husband once more. When the hour came there were tears, there were prayers, there was excitement. I saw Father once more lifting up his hands; he waved and then he was gone. Several days before his departure he prayed that the Lord should take his soul home and he asked me to write to our relatives in Canada in case of his departure, also to help mother and sisters.

We had to prepare for the funeral but what could we do? There was no lumber at the lumber yard to construct a coffin. Under the direction and instruction of my brother John some men climbed up into the hayloft, and there underneath the roof were some boards which held the rafters together; some of these boards were torn off and somebody built a very primitive coffin for our dear father. We had to pay 400 rubles for the coffin and 1200 rubles for digging a grave. I stood there near the lifeless, motionless body of my father and shed my tears. No longer would I be able to have fellowship with him or get advice from him. He was saved and now had gone home to be with Christ Jesus in all eternity.

Peter John Penner, teacher of our Chortitza Central School and pastor of the Mennonite Church was asked to officiate at the funeral. He had been a personal friend and schoolmate of my father. We all loved him very much.

I do not remember much of the details of the funeral but I remember that he mentioned that the crown of the home and of the family had fallen. In normal times there would have been hundreds of friends, neighbors and relatives. There would have been a meal for all invited partakers along with the famous Mennonite Zwieback and coffee. There were hardly twenty people present. We were still so weak. Truda fainted during the service. In our hearts we thanked God that my father had died a natural death and not a victim of the bandits.

It was at the end of February 1920 when we once more came to Schoenfeld as visitors for a brief period of time. Jacob Andres, a good friend of ours took us across the Dnieper River to Zaporoshje, at that time called Alexandrovsk, to the village Schoenwiese. Here at the K. Janzen's we usually had our lodging, sometimes meals, too, in the good, olden days, and here we were supposed to meet with Truda's brother, Gerhard Peters, who had come to take us the remaining forty miles to Schoenfeld.

At the Janzen's we met an unexpected difficulty. They were afraid of the contagion of typhoid fever and would not permit us to enter their house. They brought us some hot coffee into the barn but we were tired and hungry and could not rest nor eat a decent meal. When we finally reached Schoenfeld we were exhausted. We drove into the familiar village, into the familiar yard of our parents, the B.J. Peters. We received the warmest welcome from our three children Margaret, Peter and Katie. It was all so cordial, so pleasant; it was quiet and peaceful. A very delicious supper was prepared for us. The room assigned to us was very cozy; was I dreaming or was this really happening to us? This sudden change, plus the strenuous trip from Rosental to Schoenfeld was too much for me. I began to cry like a little baby. I did not want to eat. Here I must give you a passage from father B.J. Peter's memoirs:

We were all very anxious to see them in Schoenfeld, but when they arrived what did we see? We could not withhold our tears, nor could anybody stop the tears of our children, the Schroeders' and Hans'. They looked like people that had come out of the grave. Their eyes, their cheeks, their whole body showed the horrible experiences they had passed through. Without hair, (on account of lice) almost lifeless bodies, they were lifted from the sleigh and carried into the bathroom. They were given each a good warm bath, clean underwear and then they were taken into the warm living room, coffee was served, so they would have a chance to gain strength. Their three children by this time looked quite different than several weeks ago; the parents wondered and couldn't seem to take their eyes off the healthy children. All their laundry and clothing was buried in the ground in the orchard for disinfection. Later it was taken out and made useable again. Hans and Truda soon recuperated. The good nourishment, the big nice apples from our own orchard, plus all the extras they received here soon made them healthy and strong, only our son-in-law Schroeder, who was almost back to normal health, suffered a relapse and was very sick for a long period of time in Schoenfeld.

The clock in the room where I rested had to be stopped because I always saw fire in it. In the corner near my bed was a walking cane which had to be taken away because I was just about ready to use it in defense against the bandits, who were always near somewhere threatening to kill us all. I heard them knocking at the door and jumped out of bed; what I was going to do, nobody knew. As soon as I had jumped out of the bed I collapsed and had to be put back into bed. Somebody had to watch me day and night and this took quite a period of time. At my request they gathered one evening in the adjoining room and under the leadership of pastor G.H. Doerksen, they had a special prayer meeting for me. I could hear them pray. This seemingly was the only positive factor in my recuperation, besides all the loving care from everybody. It took weeks, but slowly I was gaining strength and I was able to walk around, when Truda escorted me to some of the neighboring places, to grandma Toews, uncle Peter and the aunts Susanna and Tina. We began singing Gospel songs. We all realized that this was the last accord. Soon, soon, we all would have to abandon this place.

Salt

Salt may seem to the reader to be a cheap and insignificant commodity, but when there is none you begin to miss it more than many other things of this world. Yes, we had been without salt for a period of time. I found out that in the Co-op at Lubimovka, about four miles south of Schoenfeld, they were selling salt in very limited quantities to a customer. So one day I walked the four miles to Lubimovka, which name in English could be Lovedale, for this is what the name indicates. There were bandits in this village but very little love.

Here at the Co-op I met several of the familiar makhnovtzy and had a friendly chat with some of them. I already had purchased my share of salt—and what salt it was! Years back I had thrown it to the cattle. Now it was precious and valuable. Among the men I spotted Khariton, and when he saw me he greeted me in a friendly manner and asked me what I had in the small bag. Salt, salt (in Russian "solj") of course. "Wait a minute," he said, "would you like to have a few more pounds of salt? You may buy my share because we have plenty in our home." Anybody could easily figure this out. The bandits and gangsters in Russia at this time were faring quite well. I accepted his offer of a few pounds of salt, thinking not only about the physical salt but about the spiritual salt. Mark 9:50 states: "Ye are the salt of the earth—have salt in yourselves." Inwardly I rejoiced that this rough makhnovetz had offered me physical salt, and I was just awaiting that moment when I would be able to repay him with much better salt.

Our Last Days in Schoenfeld

During our brief stay in Schoenfeld we had a chance to visit with our friends and relatives and regain our health and strength. There was absolutely no question in our minds that the remaining few families would have to leave soon. At this time most of the buildings were still intact and in fairly good condition but we all realized that this was only a lull before the storm.

At this time I also had an opportunity to visit with some of the makhnovtzy, trying my best to influence them with the Gospel of Jesus Christ. I walked to Zalivnoe to visit Trifon and I also visited with Michael Peresypkin and Peter Polikarpov and others.

For a time there seemed to be a chance for our parents to sell their property to the Co-op in Lubimovka. They were taking a waiting attitude; but all this waiting was in vain, as we will see later.

Spring in Rosental—1920

The time had come to drive back to Rosental in April. Again we were taken to Schoenwiese and from there to Rosental. Here we moved into the house with my mother and my two sisters Lena and Tina. Lena was unmarried. During our absence Tina's husband, Hans Andres, had died of typhus. She had a little baby girl named Erica, her joy, hope and comfort. Grief and pain prevailed in so many places. When you wanted to comfort people you did not know where to start and where to end. Injustice, cruelty, sickness and death surrounded us on all sides. Two of my sisters, Mary and Katherine, now were widows, after a marriage of less than two years. Mary, Mrs. Abraham Kroeger, (son of the clock maker) had a son named Ernie, and Katherine had a daughter, Erica. My mother never was very strong physically but she was always up and around, and just to have her with us gave us comfort. In 1926 she was able to come to Canada and died in Morris, Manitoba at the age of almost 96 years—in 1951.

I was missing my dear, dear father. The following poem which many years later I found somewhere, expresses my thoughts and emotions of that time.

MY DEAR OLD DAD

On your cheeks the lines of care
Your eyes have lost their radiance rare,
And dimness shades the lustre there,
It makes me sad,
To see you wave and bend at last,
A storm-subdued and withered mast
Wrecked by the tempest of the past—
My dear old dad.
Long since the dawn has passed away,
The mid-day sun has shed its ray,
And night is closing on the day,
It seems too bad,
That such a perfect work of clay
Should blossom only for a day
And end in pitiful decay—
My dear old dad.
O, God! Let nothing part us now!
To serve his every whim, please tell me how,
In humble supplication, thus I bow
With only this to add!
That in return for all his love of me
Staunch and faithful to the last I'll be,
He shall not end in lonely misery—
My dear old Dad.

With the departure of my father I was facing new obligations and new difficulties. There was no fuel, no wood or straw to make a fire. In every yard, quite a distance from the house, was the so-called "Backofen", i.e., baking oven built up from bricks. These ovens were heated by straw, which was very hard to get. I had to haul it in a bundle on my back about two blocks, and we considered ourselves fortunate to get this wet straw, which we had to dry before we could make any use of it.

It was spring and the fields should be plowed; a new crop was supposed to be planted, but there were just a few horses left and almost no grain for seeding the fields. The cow and horse manure, piled up in the backyard, was heavily mixed with grain which the bandits had wasted while feeding their horses. The chickens found enough grain in the manure but we had no grain for our own use. My brother John was the farmer of our property, but he was facing the greatest difficulties to cultivate and seed the 113 acres of arable land. Each of the thirty-five farms of our village had its difficulties.

My mother, Maria Schroeder (nee Klassen), decided to divide some of father's personal belongings among us children. I would like to mention here just one item, and that is the big Kroeger wall clock, which is wound up by a brass chain. Among all the grandchildren at this time there was only one grandson with the name Peter, at that time only three years old. Mother decided that our son Peter should have this clock, which at the beginning of this century was bought for 15 rubles—or about $7.50. This clock is now at our son's home here in Lodi, California.

The Last Letter from Schoenfeld

This letter was dated April 27, 1920, which means it was written only a few weeks after we left Schoenfeld. It was delivered to us by a man who came from Schoenfeld. There was no chance to send a letter by mail. It was written by Truda's sister, Susie B. Peters:

Dear Loved Ones!

To write a letter on an empty stomach is not very pleasant, but first of all I got up pretty late and secondly we are very much in a hurry, because we have definitely decided to move, only we don't know what day it will be.

In the night from Friday to Saturday we had "visitors", and such visitors I would not wish for any of you to have. Sister Anna awoke from a sharp noise, perhaps a shot, and heard the awful barking of the dogs. When we went to the windows we saw the whole surprise: In the middle of the yard we saw a man standing; we saw somebody lighting the lamps in the front building. Then they came towards this building, into the machineshop. The door was opened, the wagon was pushed out. From there they went upstairs where they found Greta and mother in the hay. They had found Wolja (Waldemar Rempel) before this, where we kept the corn straw. They didn't find papa. Here Greta had kept all of her's and the children's winter underwear, Wolja's furcoat and the children's dresses; all these things were put into the wagon. Just the previous day we had brought all the sacks with bedding downstairs, because we had hoped to be able to sell the house. All these belongings also were taken, plus three mattresses, two quilts, four of Greta's pillows and of ours three pillows, Hans' overcoat and many other things, which we don't even know. The drawers of papa's desk were pulled out and the contents put into the ready sacks, of which we had plenty.

Then everything was loaded on the wagon, our horses were hitched to the wagon, and one of the men mounted on Penner's horse.* So they went! But first they fired about 15 shots into the air, just to scare us more than we already were.

At our house they were just about half an hour. They used quite a sly trick to do their dirty work. First they went to the volost (county) building, the David P. Dyck's. They were knocking at the door for quite awhile threatening them, but the doors were securely locked, also the inside board shutters of the windows. They dared not to break the windows at D.P. Dyck's home. From there they proceeded to the shoemaker D. Mierau's house. They lifted out the kitchen window and robbed them of everything in clothing, laundry, footwear, etc. The Mieraus have retained only the clothing they had on their bodies. They also gave a severe beating to D. Mierau. Both the Mieraus were forced to go with them to the neighboring houses.

When they came to our house, they ordered D. Mierau to call our papa. When papa recognized a familiar voice, he responded. Then D. Mierau said: Here are soldiers, open the door. But at this time the other bandits were already at the other side of the house, knocking at the windows. When nobody opened they said to D.M.: Lead us to the kitchen window; there we will get in. First they fired several shots through the window, then they forced Mrs. Mierau to slip through the window into the house and open the door. From then on they proceeded as I already have written.

The Lubimovka Co-op, exploiting the newly developed situation, has changed its attitude about buying our property. At the A. Rempel's (formerly Gerhard Neufeld) the destructive work is going on. They have taken off half of the metal roofing. All of the remaining residents of Schoenfeld have received orders from the bandits to vacate the place, because they are planning to destroy this village. The Doerksens, Mieraus and Lammerts for the night always come over to our place, 34 persons altogether in one building. Should the bandits come again, we have decided not to open.

The same night the bandits were also at the Doerksen's door, but they refused to open. There is positive evidence that familiar men have done this work.

On the Schoenfelder line no Mennonites have been left; only the few of us here in the village of Schoenfeld. All residents from Schoenbrunn have moved to the Molotshnaia colony. Well, my letter is getting long inspite of my hurry. Greetings, Susa.

* My horse "Cossak" was taken.

They had several unpleasant visitors after this and mostly in the night. The Peters family packed all the belongings still left in their possession, hired several teams of horses with big vehicles and waited to move the next day.

The same night another bunch of bandits came, fired shots through the windows, demanding entrance into the house. Three of the Peters daughters fled through the window towards the creek and hid in the bush, where they remained till the morning, almost without clothing on a cold night. Four bandits entered the house and demanded a big sum of money which father Peters did not have. They took whatever pleased their eyes. They must have been without horses, else they would have taken more.

The three daughters came from their hiding place in the morning, and they all waited for the teams to come and move south towards the Molotshnaia colony. But these tricky men appeared only at 4:00 p.m. when it would be too late to drive a longer distance away from the bandit infested place. The Peters family had no choice; with heavy hearts they loaded everything into the wagons and drove off into the very dark future. Goodbye, thou our nice, beautiful Schoenfeld, garden, buildings . . . everything. What will happen? O, God lead and protect us!

For the night they stopped at a big Russian village; they drove into a big yard with a sizable house. There were several drunk men standing nearby. They saw in the newly arrived people a good occasion to rob and to steal, perhaps with the approval of the teamsters. They actually took from the wagons, all they desired, and it was a miracle that they did not kill all of the Peters family. Three or four times during the night they opened the door of the room where the Peters' were resting, not sleeping but rather praying for God's protection. The next morning they drove on south and arrived at the city where one of the teamsters dumped everything from his wagon and drove back. The other man with his team took the Peters' to the next German village and from there also returned back to Lubimovka. Only through the mercy of God and the kind help of some people in this village did they manage to drive on to the village Lichtfelde, Molotshnaia, where father Peters' sister and her husband, Jacob Wall lived. Quite a few people already were occupying this house but the Peters family was given food and shelter, so there were now twenty-five people living in this house. In the meantime, we in Rosental knew only that the family had left Schoenfeld. The anxious question in our hearts and minds now was: have they been able to reach a safer place, or have they all fallen victims of brutal men somewhere on the road? It was abso-lutely impossible to receive or to send any message by mail. The only thing we could do was to pray and wait.

CHAPTER 12

Deeper And Higher Spiritual Values

Those of us who have seen our villages in Southern Russia in the spring, will understand what is on my mind right now. Even at this time, in the spring of 1920, everyone was trying his very best to keep things in fairly good order. The fences around our beautiful orchards were still there, at least in many places, though at some places the wooden fences had been used up for fuel during the cold winter months. But now it was warm. The fruit trees were again loaded with plenty of fruit; the accacia trees were covered with beautiful white blossoms, spreading a very pleasant sweet aroma and attracting multitudes of bees. The farmers had done their best to put in as much of a new crop as possible. We again had planted a sizable piece of land with watermelons, potatoes and sweet sugar melons. I have never tasted sugar melons as good as we had in Southern Russia.

Our three children were full of life and would happily play in the yard with other children of the neighborhood. Only occasionally, when some of those men with long hair, pistols, handgrenades etc., came into our yard, they would hide and be quiet. It is a strange thing that after so many years now in our beloved and beautiful America and Canada we have to see men with long hair. It would not bother me if they would not, through their speech and general behaviour, show some of the inclinations similar to what we saw in Russia. I hope the reader will forgive me, but my thoughts always go back to some Russian proverbs or idioms of speech. One Russian proverb says: "Volos dlieny, no um korotok.", i.e., "Long hair but short brains." But we love you all, short or long hair.

While we had periods of a more quiet life, I felt the urge of deeper thinking, reading, and meditating. Even my mother noticed this and asked why I would sit for hours and hours and read. It is good for all of us from time to time to take inventory of what we are, what we have, and what we believe.

Church history shows us how from time to time new groups of believers, Christians, have come up, started a new work, a new church, a new denomination, following the principles shown to us in the book of Acts of the Apostles as closely as humanly possible. As time passes on, the fire seems to be losing its original heat, the zeal of the Christians grows weaker and weaker, the leaders of the church are permitting compromises with the world, the standard of the Church of Jesus Christ is being lowered and soon even outsiders notice the lukewarmness of the church. Many of the so-called Fundamentalists of our time still have the form of Godliness but they are denying the power thereof.

We had seen this and noticed it in Schoenfeld and found the same situation in Rosental-Chortitza. There were dear people who had a sincere longing for a deeper spiritual life; many Christians realized that they needed more spiritual food. In our Mennonite Church we had only one service a week on Sunday morning; no Sunday night service, no midweek Bible study and prayer meetings. To fill this need, Bible study and prayer meetings were held in private homes. The Herman Borm bookstore no longer was in operation, so we rented this empty storeroom and held services, separate from the Mennonite church. The leader of this group was my cousin Abram Klassen, with his brother, Peter Klassen (now living in Paraguay) assisting him in various ways.

There was a small group of Christians who called themselves the Mennonite Brethren who conducted their services in a private home, with John Harder as their leader. The feeling amongst the members of our group was that the group, at that time was more concerned about keeping certain biblical forms, but had lost the real zeal to be in the center of the will of Christ and win souls for Christ. Whether or not this was true I dare not say, because I really did not know.

In retrospect of so many years it seems to me, in our group we were not so much concerned about the form or modus of baptism, though we were baptizing by immersion only, but about a complete surrender to the Lord Jesus Christ. As Menno Simons had derived his convictions from the Holy Bible, we were determined to keep the same principles, emphasizing the *Birth from Above* (John 3:3,5) before baptism, and the subsequent church membership.

During the winter months, due to the unrest and to the typhoid epidemic, we held no services but in the spring of 1920 the meetings were again conducted as regularly as possible, even though sometimes this would lead into difficult problems, persecution, jail, etc.

Because we strongly believed in the unity of all Christians, born from above through the Holy Spirit, the name "Allianzler", i.e., Alliance Christians was used often. In our Molotshnaia and Sagradovka colonies we had the same movement, and we tried to get all the information and instruction from them. This, of course, due to unrest and the consequent lack of communication, was quite difficult to do. But somehow from time to time we received messages from them, especially from Sagradovka, where brother Franz Martens was the leader. One sentence from brother Martens remains in my memory, "If you will be weak enough, the work will succeed." In our discussions we had to chew on this sentence quite a bit. But we clearly understood that there could develop a situation where we would be too strong in our own human endeavor, not relying enough on the leadership and the power of God. This was a very good instruction.

The day of Pentecost fell on Sunday, May 17th-30th. The two dates 17-30 indicate that we still were between the old and the new calendars (Gregorian and Julian) which made a difference of 13 days. At occasions like Pentecost we always expected and had visitors from various neighboring villages like Shoeneberg, Einlage, and others. I noticed that there was quite a bit of discussion among the brethren and also among the sisters about organizing a new church. Big holidays like Christmas, Easter, and Pentecost would always be observed with a three day celebration. On the second day of Pentecost it was announced in the service that there would be a special business meeting the third Pentecost day to decide whether or not to organize as a church.

Peter Koehn of Waldheim

The holiday of Pentecost in German is called "Pfingsten" and in Russian "Troitza", which means Trinity. In most of our churches we had more than one ordained preacher, though only one would be the leading pastor.

It was Easter ("Ostern" in German) and pastor Peter Koehn of Waldheim was to bring the morning sermon. Those of us who had seen him knew about his physical stature. Though he had one artificial leg, what an impression he made on the audience with his appearance, his diction, and with his bass voice. It was in one of our big Molotshnaia churches, either Waldheim or Rueckenau. The church was packed with people eager to hear this wonderful man of God bring the Resurrection message. There he stood for a few moments in silence, then he slowly repeated the word "Easter" three times, with a voice and manner which engendered in the whole audience an air of expectancy for the coming message. This was just marvelous.

Here in the audience was a preacher from one of the neighboring villages. When he saw and heard all this and noticed the affect it had on the whole audience, he said to himself, "This is worth remembering and I may use this method in one of the services to come." But until Easter it was a whole year to wait and he was impatient to use this method of opening a service. What could he do? Oh, yes! It dawned upon him that he was supposed to bring the message at Pentecost (Pfingsten). This was his chance! This was his opportunity!

Again the church was filled with eager listeners, though this was a different place. He tried to copy brother Koehn as closely as possible. He waited, he tried to make an impression by his appearance, but how? He was of small stature and he had a tenor voice. Well, he would try his best anyway. So he slowly said just one word with his high pitched tenor voice, "Pentecost" (Pfingsten). He waited. No affect yet, but he must try it once more, yea twice more; and he did. When he for the second time exclaimed "Pentecost", some in the audience were puzzled and there was a slight smile on some faces. When for the third time he with his high pitched voice called "Pentecost", the negative affect on the whole audience became vividly evident . . . an affect this preacher had not expected. When we heard about this we said to ourselves: "Beware of imitation."

The Divine Call

One of our neighbors in Rosental was brother Abram Brauer, a brother-in-law of our dear "Moses"—no, his name was Benjamin B. Janz—whom, along with quite a number of others, God used to bring out of Russia in the years 1923 to 1928 or later; about 22,000 penniless, suffering and almost aimless, discouraged Christians from Russia to Canada, to the U.S.A., and to Paraguay. Benjamin B. Janz was the one who did the job in Russia and bishop David Toews in Rosthern, Saskatchewan. Many others have helped in this great and noble enterprise and we will always be grateful to them.

Brother Brauer tried his best to persuade me to go to the organizational meeting in the morning of the third day of Pentecost. It was not an easy decision for me to make, but I went.

My cousin Abram Klassen opened the meeting with a special period of prayer by a number of our group. He also was elected to be the moderator of this meeting and his brother, Peter Klassen, and yours truly as secretaries; I was surprised. What did this mean? The decision to organize as a church passed and the question came up, how many of those present were ready to become charter members of this church? Each one had to give a personal answer. When I was approached with this question I said, "I would prefer to wait." By now it was time to go home for lunch. I invited one of the brethren to go with me. When at the dinner table we discussed these questions Truda said, "I don't want my husband to go to this meeting in the afternoon." "Why not?" she was asked by the visitor. "I am afraid they will elect him to become a preacher and this I am against," she replied. We discussed this question pro and con, and I went to the business meeting in the afternoon of June 1, 1920.

Abram Klassen was elected as leading pastor of the church and Peter Klassen and myself as preachers. Now I was asked to tell the newly organized church whether or not I was willing to accept the position, to which I replied, "The people's voice is God's voice. I do accept."

Let me take you back six years to Schoenfeld, to 1914, soon after Truda and I were engaged. There in my study, we discussed the various aspects of our future life. Now, after almost sixty years of married life I do not understand why, but I stated to her then, "Truda, I know at present I am not taking the right position towards my Lord, but I have the feeling that He will call me one day and I want you to promise not to hinder me from going the way I feel the Lord is leading me." Yes, Truda promised me this, but now in 1920 she was against it. Why? She said she did not feel she was fit to be a preacher's wife. Well, she has been my faithful wife and companion through these many years. God knows, and He will reward her and many others who faithfully stood by to help in this great task for our loving Heavenly Father.

Any minister nowadays who receives a call from a church to serve as pastor will naturally ask the church about an adequate salary, parsonage, etc. This question was not considered at all in Rosental in 1920. We all knew the church members were poor, they could pay no salary and there was no parsonage. But there were plenty of indications that I could and should expect persecution because of my new position as minister of the glorious Gospel of Jesus Christ. We did not know at that time that in

English speaking countries a man in this position was called "Reverend" or even "Right Reverend". My guiding verses through all these years have been Mark 10:29-30: "Jesus answered and said, Verily I say unto you, there is no man that has left house, or brethren, or sisters, or father, or mother, or wife, or children, or lands, for my sake, and the gospel's, but he shall receive an hundredfold now in this time, houses, and brethren, and sisters, and mothers, and children, and lands, with persecutions; and in the world to come eternal life". Among the promised items is also persecution, and persecution did come . . . plenty of it. I knew the Lord was calling me and I was determined to follow that divine calling. I have never regretted serving my Lord so many years, and I would like to serve Him to the very end of my life.

The War Commissariat of the Communists

At this time I did not have the slightest presentiment or foreboding that in a brief period of time in 1920 I was going to have two new positions, one the divine call to serve God and humanity as a servant of God, and the second one, only a few weeks after the first call, to serve the communists as the head secretary of the war commissariat.

One day a soldier, a "Redguardist" as we called them, came to our house and handed me a small letter. It was from the Head Commissar of the newly established Communist War Commissariat. The signature was that of Jacob L. Loshitzky. I was supposed to appear in his office for a personal conference. What could this mean? Truda naturally was excited, but the fact that it was signed by a man whom we knew gave us confidence that nothing bad was ahead of us. So I went.

The War Commissariat was in the building of the former bank of H.A. Niebuhr. I was invited into a room where without disturbance we could discuss matters. They needed somebody to take over the position as head secretary of the War Commissariat. I would have expected anything else but this. But realizing that this was a situation where I had absolutely no choice, I agreed to become the head secretary of this district. Anyone reading these lines should sense that I did some deep thinking about how I could get out of this situation. And here a happy thought came to my mind. Communists do not stay in one office very long because of the danger that they might make friends with the population, whereas communists must be trained to be rough, not friendly. So I said to comrade Loshitzky, "You know just as well as I do that you will not stay in this office here very long, because they will transfer you to some other place." He agreed with this. "Will you promise me that when you get your orders of transfer that you will dismiss me for any reason you may choose?" Yes, he agreed to do this as long as he had somebody in the office and as long as he was the Head Commissar.

It was good that I was not the only preacher in a small church, so I did not have to preach at every service. At this time I found the preaching pretty hard and after ten or fifteen minutes I had had enough. Truda noticed this and suggested that she would rather stay home when it was my turn to preach, because it was unpleasant for her to see what a struggle I had. But as times passed by this changed, too.

Everyday I had to sit in the office among communists. I had to listen to many of their plans and aspirations. Everyday we would receive a telephonogram (telegram) from our head office in Ekaterinoslav. I, as the Head Secretary, had to receive the telephonogram; I had to read back the message slowly, my name was registered at the Ekaterinoslav office, and I had to register the name of the person who had given me the message. Everyday we had to report back the same way, apprising them of the action we had taken.

There were occasions when we would drive to the Dnieper River to swim and to take a sunbath. A team of fine horses and a carriage were at our disposal. At some of these occasions I had an opportunity to hear these men talk more freely about their aims and plans and ideas. These were things which I would not discuss with anybody, not even my wife. But these experiences helped me to evaluate the whole situation. I consider this period of time as providentially provided by God to prepare me for the things to come and to help some of our people.

It took only a few months for a new commissar to be appointed to our office. Jacob L. Loshitzky was transferred to another office some distance from Chortitza. About a month later he was killed by a group of anarchists who ambushed him and his party while they were driving to another place. His funeral was conducted in our Chortitza Mennonite Church. I attended, but I am unable to report who officiated.

Now I could devote more time to our newly organized church, which was named The Rosental Evangelical Mennonite Church. After our move from Schoenfeld the constant threat of typhoid fever, bandits, the death of so many loved ones, the prevailing uncertainty of the whole situation, the crowded living conditions—these and many other features demanded coolness of mind, a lot of adaptation and determination, a smile, prayer and confidence in God.

Peter Andreyevich Lebedinsky

Again Red soldiers were marching in. The Whites had been here just for a few days. There was heavy fighting and the Whites were driven back across the Dnieper River. A company of soldiers came into our yard with their officer, demanding shelter, food, beds, etc. New trouble. But this seemed to be the routine of our time. What could we do? Somehow . . . somehow we satisfied them.

This officer's name was Peter Andreyevich Lebedinsky. He was a friendly man and seemed to be quite satisfied with our little bedroom where he could sleep. On the wall was the famous Kroeger clock, ticking the seconds, showing the hours and minutes. The soldiers slept in the barn or in the hayloft. It was summer and quite warm.

While there was no fighting just then we had time to engage in a friendly conversation. I will not bore the dear reader with all the subjects we discussed at that time. But Andreyevich made a remark which turned our conversation in a different direction. "I hate the Jews", he said. "Why? What have they done?" I asked. Finally, we came to the person of Jesus Christ. This was my opportunity. I very definitely pointed Peter Andreyevich to Jesus Christ as the Saviour of the world and as his personal Saviour. No, he did not hate Jesus, he was not against Jesus, but . . . he hated the Jews and Jesus was a Jew by birth. This was the obstacle. "You cannot be saved without Jesus. He must enter your heart; you must permit Him to rule your life or you are lost." He was silent for a moment. Then I pointed to the ticking clock on the wall (this same clock now measures the time here in Lodi, California as I write this) "Peter Andreyevich," I said, "Look at this clock! This very hour, this minute, this day is registered in Eternity in the presence of God on your behalf. You either let Jesus come into your heart and life and be saved, or . . . you are lost. This very hour and minute will testify for or against you in Eternity." This was a serious moment but I had to leave him while he pondered this eternal decision.

Time passed by and Peter Andreyevich with his company had to move to another place. Where? I do not know. There were periods of heavy fighting. In the meantime, we, as a family, had moved about one mile or more north in our village of Chortitza to live in the house with my widowed cousin Helena Braun (nee Klassen). She was afraid that the communists would force her to share her house with some very unpleasant residents so she persuaded us to move in with her so that we would occupy half of the dwelling.

At this time (it was either late summer or early fall) there was heavy fighting along the Dniepr River. On the other side (the East side) of the river were the Whites. On the island Chortitza, which we mostly called "de Kaump", was a sizable force of the Cossacks. Peter A. Lebedinsky and his company were sent against these Cossacks. I know the place very well, which we usually called "de Spetz", a place where we so often had our picnics and where we enjoyed swimming. At this place the Dniepr is spread out and during the late summer months or in fall there are places where the water is so shallow that you can walk across the river. This was the place where Peter A. Lebedinsky with his company tried to cross to fight the Cossacks who were using machine guns against the "Reds", hiding behind the rocks and bushes on the opposite side.

What a horrible sight! That afternoon, after classes (I was teaching in the Chortitza Central School and in the Teachers Seminary) I went to see my mother in Rosental. We very distinctly could hear the shooting; there were soldiers on horseback and in wagons moving to and fro. I went to the corner of the street that leads to the Dniepr river, near the Rosental public school. There was a wagon at the corner of the street. As I came closer I saw this wagon filled with dead Red Army soldiers.

I went back, visited my mother and sisters in Rosental and from there went back north to our home in Chortitza.

At sunset the fighting increased and the situation became very dangerous. Peter Andreyevich, having lost most of his soldiers in the river, came back running, dressed only in his underwear. Here at the edge of our village he ran into the John Giesbrecht house. John was about a year younger than myself; we knew each other very well.

"Do you know teacher Schroeder?", Lebedinsky asked John. "Do you know where he lives?"

"Yes, of course, I know this place very well," said John.

"You have to take me over to his place right away. I want to talk to him. Take me over to him right away," he demanded.

"Oh, no, said John, this I cannot do. Just to walk outside the house is dangerous right now."

"You must take me over to Schroeder's place. I must talk with him," Peter Andreyevich insisted. Here John's wife stepped in and told Andreyevich she would not permit her husband to go out on the street at this time. But all this would not satisfy him. Finally, John gave in and brought him to my mother's place. There, with a very anxious tone in his voice he asked to see and to speak to me. When he was told that we no longer lived there he hung his head, whispered a few words, "Not here—moved north" and left. Oh, how I wished I could have spoken to him that night. Where is Peter Andreyevich Lebedinsky now? I tried my best to show him the way. Miracles happen every day. God is able! I believe in miracles.

With the fall of 1920 I became one of the teachers of the Central High School and Teachers Seminary in Chortitza. Two of the teachers had died the previous winter; my cousin John Froese and my dear former schoolmate in the Ekaterinoslav Teachers Institute from 1910 to 1913, Andreas A. Vogt. All kinds of strange emotions filled my heart when I entered the very familiar schoolrooms, where for five years (1902-1907) I had been a student. My dear mother often would sigh about her unruly, hotheaded son Gerhard. She felt sorry for the children that would become my pupils; she also felt sorry for the girl that would say yes to me, to become my wife. But God performs miracles. He has changed many things in me and He will perform miracles of grace today and tomorrow.

That year we had plenty of watermelons in our field so we were able to make a lot of the famous watermelon syrup. Several times the war front moved through our village, consequently there would always be interruptions in our school work. The Red government was gradually prevailing over the other political powers. We were so accustomed to the constant change of authority that finally we became almost indifferent, though most of us hated to see the communists gaining control of the country. However, there was nothing we could do about it.

The Whites occupied our village for about five days in the fall.

After classes in the Central High School one day, again I went to see my mother in Rosental. Somehow the time slipped by much faster than I realized; while walking home I noticed that it was getting dark, but I did not mind this because all the streets and houses were very familiar to me. One thing I had forgotten, though, we now were under the authority of the Whites and they had declared martial law. Near the gate of the P. Janzen property stood a soldier. He stopped me and demanded that I walk with him into the yard where the soldiers had built a bonfire to warm themselves. It did not take long before an officer appeared, yelling at me at the top of his voice. He asked me if I knew that nobody was supposed to walk on the streets after sunset. He demanded my identification papers. I had my school books under my arm and began digging in my pockets to find some identification. Since we had been under the rule of the Reds for quite a time, all I had in my possession was a certificate from the Communist rulers that I was a "school worker" (shkolny rabotnik). The communists intended to show that they represented the working class, so the term "worker" had to be used at every possible and impossible occasion.

When this White officer read this document he became more enraged than before. He angrily threw my certificate into the fire, calling me a spy and not a "school worker". I was pretty sure this time I would get the bullet, when he yelled at me to march out of his sight. I was sure the bullet would strike me down. I did not look back but cautiously proceeded homeward.

In a few minutes I reached my home and here I saw that my dear Truda had her hands full of work; a number of officers and soldiers had occupied our house. Truda had to serve them supper. They seemed to enjoy eating our big, sweet watermelons. But finally they, too, went to bed; some in our beds, some on the floor.

It was sometime after midnight when we heard a commotion and voices calling, "Skorey, skorey", which means, "faster! faster!" It did not take long until they all were gone. Outside we could hear shooting. In the morning we saw soldiers in different uniforms marching the streets. The Reds were back once more.

Prayer Meetings

During this period of time we held two prayer meetings in one week. On Tuesday night in Chortitza in our home, and on Saturday night in Rosental at our assembly place in the former Herman Borm bookstore. It happened that some of our people walking back from the prayer meeting were arrested and put into a dirty, lousy jail, because nobody was supposed to walk on the streets after sunset. It seemed there would be no other solution to the problem than to discontinue the prayer meetings. I will never forget this. The question was asked, "What did they do to you?" "Nothing, they just put us in jail where, during the night we testified to some imprisoned people. In the morning they let us go. Only we brought some lice along from the jail." That did not seem to be too bad. It was decided to continue with the prayer meetings. We had to obey God more than men.

One evening Truda invited our neighbors David and Helena Hamm (Mr. and Mrs.) to come over for a cup of tea. While drinking tea we had the nicest spiritual fellowship, reading and praying. Only a few minutes after the Hamm's were gone, we heard a knocking at the door. Yes, another company of Reds were here. They demanded that I come out and show them where to put their horses. We were not farmers and there was no grain for their horses. One of the soldiers had a live duck which he had taken from some place. It took some time until I came back into the house and Truda was wondering whether or not I was still alive.

The soldiers were rough men and they made all kinds of demands. I marveled at my Truda. She told them, "Listen, I am a teacher's wife and not your servant maid; we are not capitalists. If you will behave and show patience I will give you a meal but if you keep on the way you have done so far, you will get nothing. What do you want?" "We want 'salo'" (salted pork). We did not have salo and Truda told them so. She offered them our German salo which was only headcheese, and they liked it. When this was all over, Truda and I realized that it was a miracle of the Lord to prepare us spiritually through the fellowship with the Hamms for this occasion. How else could she have handled these men in such a situation?

Atrocities

We do not like to talk about them and if I should tell you in detail the experiences we had in this matter, you would have sleepless nights. Now it was mostly the Reds and the Whites fighting and they seemed to indulge in the most gruesome cruelties. I refrain from telling you about them, except for just a few lines from my diary.

Just take a look at the street in Rosental in the morning! Who are those women? They are wearing light home-sewn caps to cover their heads because they have clipped their hair short. No shoes on their feet, just home-made wooden sandals. All the shoes have been taken by the visiting gangsters. All these fine young women and girls are going north to the doctor. Do you know why? What a sad picture! How we felt for them and how our prayers went up for them! The wife of one of our neighbors was molested in one night by nine men. But I must stop here. The picture grows darker. Just pray that this never will happen in Canada or in the United States of America.

One clear summer day a whole wagonload of these men with all kinds of weapons, at full speed drove into our yard, just when I was standing outside near the door. One of them jumped from the wagon even before the horses came to a complete stop, held the rifle close to my head and yelled at me. "What do you want, comrade?", I asked. "Shoes", was the answer. "Shoes! Don't you see that I am standing here before you barefoot? Go into the house and get all the shoes you can find. There have been too many before you demanding shoes." Only a few words of swearing came through his lips. They went into the house but, thanks be to God, there was nothing to take anymore.

One of our problems was the absence of thread. We had a professor of art in the Ekaterinoslav Teachers Institute in 1910, one Peter Timofeyevich, who was asked one day, "Please tell us, what does 'null' mean?" Here came the answer of this fine old gentleman, "Null [zero] my golubt-shik [my dear one] indicates the absence of every presence." That was our situation at the time, the absence of every presence.

Not only the absence of clothing and yardgoods for dresses or suits, but also the absence of thread to fasten a button or to mend a torn garment. "Not macht erfinderisch" we say in German. "Emergency creates inventiveness."

Silk Worms

In my memoirs I have several pages on this subject. There was no thread to be had at any place. In the spring of 1920 we started with the silk worm industry. It was interesting and profitable. The communists who came to search our premises were quite surprised about our adaptation to the situation. It is quite interesting how about 200 silk worm lines can be spun together in one which will give you a thread just thick enough to sew on a button or patch a hole in your garment. Thinking back to this experience I feel like humming the song we learned to sing in Canada:

> There's an old spinning wheel in the parlor,
> Spinning dreams of a long, long ago.

Whenever I had a free period of time you could find me sitting behind the spinning wheel, making silk thread.

Communist Rules

We kept a pig in order to get some meat to eat. There was no grain to feed the pig so we bought linseed cakes, about five pounds each, the residue from it is left when the oil is pressed out of the flax. Now we had two things to regret about this. First of all we soon found out, and we were lucky we did, that we were not permitted to butcher the pig. What do I mean? Well, just this, you may be puzzled because you do not realize what kind of a "wonderful" government we now had. This was really a government "for the people." You might eat too much pork, get sick and . . . You do not know yet what I mean? One of our neighbors butchered a pig without first obtaining a permit from the government for doing so and (!) he landed in jail. You must not forget that from then on everything was declared to be national property; your wife, your children—everything. Only those in the government offices had the right to say what you may keep and what you may not. Many things you formerly considered as your own belonged to the State. You must change your whole ideology . . .

Two of our neighboring teachers landed in jail. For a long time no one would tell them what offense they had committed. Then one day they were told, "We have reasons to believe that your thinking is different from ours." You may have learned many things, but they re-educated you. When you graduate from their schools you will really "enjoy" living under the best government of the world!?

In the summer when we moved from my mother's place in Rosental to my cousin's place in Chortitza I nearly lost everything we still possessed. I was arrested and was brought into the volost where only months ago I had been the secretary. I was threatened by the Head Commissar that they would confiscate everything because I had not first obtained a permit to change my place of residence. I had not learned to change my thinking. I was lucky this time; there were men who knew me very well and they intervened for me . . . we received a permit to move to the Chortitza place.

Mail at the beginning was supposed to be delivered free of charge. Everything belonged to the people anyway, so why pay postage? This seemed to be a very sensible and pleasant innovation. But—first of all the mail did not move very fast, and it did not take long until a new ruling was introduced and we had to pay postage. What a strange world!

Trains also were supposed to be at our disposal free of charge. However, we were not just to loaf around in the country. If we had to make a trip we had to get a permit from the local authorities stating for what purposes this trip was to be made, etc. To obtain such a permit was not easy and took a considerable period of time.

The communists had created "freedom", i.e., free empty places everywhere. This later resulted in hunger and starvation beyond comprehension. This is what the communists wanted, because they knew and they now know that it is much easier to force hungry people into submission than it is to force healthy, strong, well-fed and well-clothed people into submission.

Spiritual Counsel

Up till June, 1920 I had hoped a way could be found whereby we would not have to separate from our Mennonite church. After all these many years we had maintained a nice fellowship with many good friends there. To separate from a church which you have called your own for many years is not an easy matter. One day I went to talk these matters over with my former teacher and pastor, Peter John Penner. I had full confidence in him and I decided that I owed him a visit; I wanted to give him an opportunity to give me his advice. Many of his former students considered him a pretty strict teacher and some people perhaps thought that he was somewhat narrow minded. This was a little over two years before his departure, and I treasure it very highly that I went to see him about this matter.

When I revealed to him the purpose of my visit and the aims and plans of our group he smiled and said, "I understand you personally and the other members very well. Some people may consider me a narrow minded pastor, but I am not narrow minded. I wish you God's richest blessings. The way you have chosen is good and according to my understanding the right one. Your aims and your plans are good. Should you remain in our church you would face constant occasions of opposition; your time and energy would have to be used to remove these obstacles. Now you have formed your own church and your whole time and energy can be used to reach these goals you are pursuing." He laid his right hand on my left shoulder and once more wished me God's blessing. This in itself gave me a wonderful peace and inner satisfaction.

During the remaining two years of his life we consulted him from time to time, and several times he was our main speaker at special occasions, such as harvest festival, etc. I have always considered him a wonderful man of God, a very good teacher and a very true friend of our family.

In my diary of 1922 I find an entry of Sunday, November 5th. It was a special occasion in our church, with nice weather and with many visitors from places such as Schoenwiese, Schoeneberg, and Einlage. Pastor and teacher Peter Johann Penner along with his dear wife, visited my cousin Abram Klassen on Sunday afternoon where we met in a friendly, informal way over coffee (prips), and discussed some of the important church Christian education questions with our beloved "Lehrer" (teacher Peter J. Penner). Under December 11, 1922 is written, "Pastor Peter J. Penner is very ill with pneumonia. I visited him." Friday, December 22: "Pastor Peter Johann Penner died at 8 o'clock in the morning. In the afternoon of this day there was a celebration in the Mennonite church—the birthday of pastor Isaak G. Dyck."

Monday, December 25: "At the Molotshnaia colony, we have been informed, they are celebrating Christmas today, but we are still celebrating according to the old calendar, 13 days later, January 7th. Today is the funeral of pastor-teacher Peter Johann Penner in the Mennonite Church. Many people gathered there for this important occasion. My brother Peter came, too, from Einlage.

The Year's End, 1920

In our school life we experienced many difficulties and interruptions.

It was hard to get the fuel for heating the school buildings and there was almost no money for the teachers' salaries. Poverty and suffering were evident everywhere. Our devoted and courageous leaders such as Henry H. Epp and others did their best to keep the schools functioning and many teachers were trying their very best; but we all realized that unless help could be obtained from somewhere else we would not be able to carry on very long. Starting out in the morning to school on wooden sandals with an almost empty stomach was no easy task to perform. There also came all kinds of interruptions through new orders from the now more-or-less established Communist Government making demands and giving us instructions. The Ukrainian language was supposed to be taught as a language in all classes, which meant seven classes in High School and in the Teachers Seminary. At the faculty meeting we were facing this problem of not having the proper teacher for this new subject and it also was hard to find a place for this new subject in the school curriculum. At the request of the faculty I agreed to temporarily become the teacher of this language.

Our library was in need of more and better books; our teachers in physics and chemistry often found themselves in difficult positions trying to teach without the necessary equipment. We all were glad when the Christmas vacation came and we at least would have a brief period of time to orient and prepare ourselves for this difficult task.

Whatever money would come in for salaries of the teachers was in a very fraternal way divided among them.

There was still some fighting going on, now mostly between the Communists and the Anarchists (Makhnovtsy).

CHAPTER 13

A Trip To The South

Christmas Vacation 1920

There was a prolonged period of time when we did not know whether to count time according to the old or to the new calendar. We finally celebrated Christmas according to the old calendar, January 7. There were not too many preparations for Christmas possible, because we did not have much left to prepare with. And yet, in most of the homes there were some preparations.

The children as usual were singing and preparing their recitations for Christmas and for New Year's. This was deeply rooted in all of our homes, schools and churches, and no one wanted to miss this. Only the previous year, due to the terrible unrest and the subsequent typhoid fever was there an exception.

Even the idea of Santa Claus had not died out yet. The eldest son of my cousin Mrs. G. Braun, Gerhard, whom we always called by that Russian name "Yegor", personified Santa Claus at Christmas Eve by putting on a fur coat, the fur turned outside, with whiskers, so our children would not recognize him. They were quite excited when suddenly Santa Claus entered the room. With his voice lowered to a deeper bass he asked them if they had always been good, behaving and obedient children, if they had been praying, etc. It did not take long for the children to display their knowledge of prayers. Before Santa Claus left he promised the children they would not be forgotten and would receive some presents. It was fun to watch the children's faces glowing with expectancy.

But the days of celebration soon were ended. We had our usual services in the churches but not in the schools on Christmas Eve as our custom was. This was already strictly forbidden. We were satisfied to celebrate this wonderful occasion in our churches and homes.

In the meantime, Truda and I prepared for a trip to the Molotshnaia in order to find out where our parents, the B.J. Peters and other relatives were. No mail was coming through and we knew nothing about them now for seven months. In Chortitza we had Mrs. Cornelius Peters, a widow, whose husband last winter had been brutally killed by the makhnovtzy. She, too, wanted to go to the Molotshnaia. She furnished one horse for this trip and we were able to get my brother John's horse, and this way we started out the last day of Christmas. First we stopped in Einlage at the home of pastor John Martens, whose wife was the sister of Mrs. Peters. The weather turned out quite favorably and we were full of hope to find our dear relatives somewhere in the Molotshnaia.

By the way, the word Molotshnaia derives from the word "moloko" which means milk. The river Molotshnaia was the "Milky River". The root of this word is also found in the word "Molokany", whereby we get the word "Molokans" which is a religious, ethnic group in the Los Angeles area.

Driving southward we stopped for the night at Orechovo. The next day we reached Halbstadt and stopped at Truda's uncle's place, who formerly was mentioned as teacher Henry Loewen. Here we received a very cordial welcome and dinner and also learned that our parents were now living with our uncle Jacob Wall in Lichtfelde. From here Mrs. Peters went her own way while we, just the two of us, drove by way of Tiegerweide—Kleefeld—Lichtfelde. The weather was mild, the roads were somewhat muddy and we no longer were trying to force the horses to go any faster than was absolutely necessary.

Surprise

As the horses were walking at a slow pace south from Tiegerweide, coming closer to Kleefeld, we used the time to read a portion from our little New Testament and we had devotions, thanking God for His guidance thus far and asking for His further guidance, blessing and protection.

We had barely finished our devotions when we noticed a two-wheeled cart pulled by two horses and carrying three men driving in the opposite direction. As they came closer we soon recognized one of the men as being my former student Jacob J. Dick, formerly of Schoenbrunn. His parents both had died and my dear student had chosen a road which could not please God and had caused some of his closer relatives quite a bit of concern. But at this given moment I knew nothing about all of this. Somehow I felt that the Holy Spirit had prepared me just for this moment; so I followed His leading. For a few moments we just talked about our trip, then I asked him to come behind the wagon, where I had a heart-to-heart talk with him. Only years later I found out how the Lord through His Holy Spirit had marvelously directed us in this important matter.

Many of us know how Jacob, like myself and like many others, for a number of years rebelled against God, and how suddenly the Lord gloriously saved him. Jacob and his faithful wife in the year 1934 escaped from Russia via China into India, where for twenty-five years they served as missionaries.

It was Sunday, July 23, 1950 when in the Chilliwack, B.C. Mennonite Brethren Church, Jacob and Anna Dick celebrated their twenty-fifth wedding anniversary. At this occasion Jacob told me that I had been the first one to talk to him, at the approximate age of fourteen years, about his soul's salvation. I do not take credit for this at all but I mention this as a sign of God's miracles through His servants, though imperfect they may be, if only they obey Him.

Lichtfelde 1921

So we finally reached Lichtfelde and drove into the yard of Truda's uncle, Jacob Wall. That was a great surprise to all of the people inside the house. Our parents, along with some of their children had found a place of refuge here, though they were living under quite crowded conditions. But the Russians say: "Better crowded than to be insulted."

Besides visiting with our parents and relatives we also had the privilege of attending the special services of the Lichtfelde church. This was the week of prayer, always observed in our churches at the beginning of the new year. We came to know the leading men of this church Abram Nachtigall, Peter Penner, and others. On Sunday, pastor Peter Koehn of Waldheim brought the message according to Hosea, chapter eleven. I will never forget this sermon. I also was quite favorably impressed with the spirit of unity and humility of these men. For me, as a young preacher, all of these experiences were of great importance.

One of the pastors invited me into his home for a more personal fellowship. This humble and highly gifted man of God proved to be a great blessing to my soul. But he and his dear wife had quite a heavy burden to bear. Two of their grown-up sons, ignoring all of the holy influence of their parental home, had become Communists. Their room was filled with tobacco smoke, they invited their new atheist friends and by all their behaviour caused their parents a lot of grief and pain. Later we received the message that one of these young men became sick with an incurable illness and on his deathbed repented and confessed Christ as his Saviour. But at his funeral the Communists took full charge of the service with music and everything in the Communist atheist manner and spirit.

These days in Lichtfelde with our dear loved ones were so very important to all of us and we tried to utilize every minute for information and consultation and Christian fellowship. All of us had become refugees, all possessions were lost—we had to find a way out of this.

One interesting trait we all inherited from our parents, by which outsiders may know that we are real genuine Mennonites, we do not squander our money or other possessions. This is not a bad trait as long as we do not become stingy.

Our dear uncle Wall was known in our family as one who knew how to save money. Now it seemed to me that he was not quite satisfied that he had always done the right thing in the matter of earthly possessions. One morning we had an open discussion and prayer about this matter.

When the day had come for us to go back to our home in Chortitza it was decided that Mika, Truda's sister, should go with us to continue her studies at our Chortitza Central School. We gladly took her along knowing that she would be of great help to Truda.

Grain from the Molotshnaia

Here in the Molotshnaia villages our farmers had plenty of wheat left and the brethren encouraged me to convey their best greetings to our people in Chortitza with this special message, "If you need help in the form of grain just come with ten or more teams and we will fill your empty sacks with wheat." This message and greeting was received with great joy, remembering the general need in many homes and also about our mental hospital near Einlage "Bethania". So I was delegated twice to make this trip with about ten teams to bring this wheat over to our colony, because the Molotshnaia farmers knew they would not be able to keep this grain and sell it for a good price.

At these occasions it was my privilege to visit many of our Mennonite homes in the Molotshnaia villages. All received us with open arms and we were not disappointed at any place.

On our second trip back homewards with our full loads, we stopped in the village of Petershagen. Our good friends from Schoenfeld, the Gerhard H. Doerksens, now lived here. We anticipated an evening of fine Christian fellowship with the Doerksens and with others. But! No one thought about this before it actually happened. A Red commissar suddenly appeared and gave me the strictest orders to deliver all the grain to Halbstadt, "And be sure not to try any trick in this matter because if I want to I may confiscate all your wagons and horses." That was a shock for all of us, but we had no choice so the next day all the grain was delivered to Halbstadt. With empty wagons we made the long trip back home. Naturally, we all felt very downhearted about this. How would we now pay for the teams for this trip?

At this time our good friend David A. visited us. His brother was in a quite important office in Alexandrovsk. From this district office (Uprodkom) we obtained a very valuable document. It was decided that the same teams should make this trip once more in order to get the grain back, especially for "Bethania".

I had made the last trip during our Easter vacation, but now I was supposed to occupy my place as teacher in the classroom. Bernhard I. Toews was chosen to head the second trip. When they came back with all the wheat restored to us I asked Mr. Toews about the behaviour of the commissar in Halbstadt. He said that this commissar had been raging mad at all of us but had especially mentioned my name and the good connections I had at the "Uprodkom" in Alexandrovsk. This grain had been donated and designated for the needy people in "Bethania" and in our villages, so we really had a full right to have this grain returned to us. We all were very glad to get this wheat because the need was acute.

CHAPTER 14

Judgment And Grace In Lubimovka

Turkenovka and the End of Senjka P. Pravda

It was during this time that some villages would be surrounded by communist soldiers and all known makhnovtzy would be apprehended, and in most cases shot. This was the time when in Zalievnoye they caught our good friend Trifon P. and drove out of the village to shoot him to death in the field. Only by the grace of God he escaped. He then turned to Jesus Christ, was baptized in the Baptist church and from then on became an ardent follower of his Master and Saviour.

Guliaypole was the center of the Makhovtzy. A short distance away, perhaps five miles, was the village of Turkenovka. It was here where the Makhnovtzy in the summer of 1921 were engaged in a hot battle with the communists. S. Pravda with his group was trying to hold back the advancing Reds. Many of these Makhnovtzy were riding on "tachankas" with a lower back, very convenient for the use of machine guns.

Senjka Pravda and Koljka Ermolovsky were in the back seat handling the machine gun while Yerik Grosa was serving as coachman. At a crucial moment one of the front wheels of the tachanka broke to pieces and it was obvious to all three of them that they could no longer fight. Quickly, Koljka and Yerik unhitched the horses and rode off, each of them on one of the horses. Senjka was in a hopeless situation. He could not run with his cut-off legs (many called him "kootzy" because of his shortened legs). He yelled at his unfaithful comrades and helpers: "Na kogo vy menja, Bratzy, pokidajetje?" "Whom do you abandon or forsake me to?" These were his last words. Yerik and Koljka sarcastically answered him back, "It is enough that you have combed us with your nagaika [whip]; you will comb us no more." (In Russian: "Dovoljno ty tshesal nas nagaikoiu, boljshe tshesatj ne budesh.") How often Pravda had abused his subordinates with his nagaika. In Russia they use the word "tshesatj", i.e., "to comb" for whipping with the nagaika. When Senjka saw the advancing Reds, he pulled his gun and sent a bullet through his head, as he several times had told me he would do. When the communist soldiers came and saw his lifeless body, they hacked him to pieces with their sabres. I have this report from men who were there when it happened.

How often S. Pravda boastingly had told me that with his gun he had killed fifty-six or more men. He had shot to death his own brother Mitjka; his only remaining brother Grishka (Gregory) was shot to death by the communists in Alexandrovsk. So this was the end of the three Pravdas. Pravda in Russian means truth, but they had anything but truth.

Lubitzkoje Baptist Church

Lubitzkoje is the official name of this village but common people mostly call it Lubimovka. In this village where many Makhnovtzy lived, a small Baptist Church with seven members was started. We had been dealing with a number of people here. These and a number of others had been approached with the Gospel and we felt that they were under conviction. But in the end it took somebody who lived amongst them to start the work, and God sent this man in the person of Vasily Ivanovich Shachovtzov.

Until 1918 he was a prisoner of war in Germany. Russian evangelists came and preached the plain true Gospel of Jesus Christ. Vasily never before had heard the Gospel so clear and plain. When he came home to his family there was both joy and disappointment. His wife and his mother living in the same house called neighbors and friends to see him and to welcome him back home.

My former student Jacob J. Dick, who along with his wife has been a missionary in India and has done spiritual work among the same Makhnovtzy in Lubimovka, told us about this event of Vasily Shachovtzov's coming home.

"Vasily came home in the year 1918 along with many others, mostly walking. Among the returnees was also Andrey Kiril Drany, who later became the presbyter of the Russian Baptist Church in Sherebetz. When brother Shachovtzov arrived back home, his young wife and child (the child was born after he had left for the front), his mother and brother, were very glad to see him. But when Vasily expressed his joy at being home and also announced that he had brought the Lord Jesus in his heart along, they were baffled and felt they had to call the priest of the local Greek Orthodox Church, who came and declared him a sectarian and ordered him out of his own house; his family should not even eat with him. So our brother Shachovtzov had to live in the barn, isolated from his loved ones, his food being brought to him by his wife. Brother Shachovtzov accepted the situation as it was, working on the farm and living in the barn, and he kept on consistently loving his family and neighbors. It did not take very long until his wife, under the conviction of the Holy Spirit accepted the Lord Jesus Christ and moved to live with him in the barn. No harsh words were spoken by anyone, and so it happened that by and by his mother and brother, too, became Christians. Now they were all of one faith. All moved to live in the same house, and they told the priest to stay away from them, as they all had access to the Lord without him. The priest through the revolution had lost much of his authority which, under the czarist government he had enjoyed.

Vasily was not sitting idle. He visited people and convinced many of them of their great need of salvation through Jesus Christ. All those in Lubitzkoje with whom I spoke told me what a zealous Christian Vasily was. He was no eloquent orator but he would read the Bible and explain it to the people as best he could and pray with them. He also conducted prayer meetings, usually on Saturday night, and Sunday services as well.

Khariton and Lukashka

It was on a Saturday night when Khariton and Lukashka, the latter dressed in that fancy coat of many colors I told you about before, both being under the influence of homebrew (samogonka), were walking on the street. When they came closer to the place where they saw a light in the house, they realized that their former comrades were gathered here for their prayer meeting. They decided that this was their chance to play a trick on them. They walked up to the house, opened the door and Khariton just stood in the doorway. Lukashka from behind gave Khariton a strong push so that he fell prostrate on the floor of this room where the people were kneeling in prayer. Having done this, Lukashka disappeared. Khariton got up; Mishka (Michael P.) helped him to sit down and tried to persuade him not to disrupt the prayer meeting. But Khariton insisted that he wanted to smoke and took out of his pocket his tobacco bag with paper and rolled a cigarette. Mishka would not permit him to light the cigarette so there was a struggle. While this was going on, the rest of the people in the room were kneeling on the floor and loudly praying for Khariton's salvation. When the meeting ended Mishka escorted Khariton home and helped him undress for bed.

We will never be able to explain the miracles God performs. The next morning Khariton came to see Mishka. He began to excuse himself for the disturbance he had created the previous night. In many instances Khariton had participated in rough doings of the Makhnovtzy, but here the Holy Spirit had started to work in his heart. When he apologized Mishka comforted him but told him of his need of the Saviour. God performed another miracle. From then on Khariton began to attend the meetings of the Christians, but strangely enough his wife, who so often had suffered when Khariton was drunk, now began to oppose his turning to Christ. But the Holy Spirit was at work and both he and his wife became dear Christian people. The Church in Lubitzkoje grew from a small number of seven until in 1925 it had a membership of over sixty.

Letters from Former Anarchists, Now Christians

Not exactly in chronological order, I would like to give you these letters in English, which we received in the years 1924 and 1925. Quite a few letters have been lost while moving from one place to another.

Village Lubitzkoje, March 21, 1925.

Dear Brother in Christ Jesus!

Today is a holiday for us. You will ask, what holiday? We received the letter from you addressed to brother Peter P. and we really can call this day a holiday, because all of our brethren came together to us in the house and several times we read your letter and rejoiced; we also remembered you and all your words that you spoke to us which we still remember.

And also imagine what the people of our world are talking about: some Baptists, neglected and disregarded by all people and considered as dirt, suddenly receive letters from America! [they were mailed from Canada] Many are asking us what you are writing to us? Some are just ridiculing us. Others take a serious attitude toward us and to the brotherly fellowship.

But there are also those who would like to misuse our name and our fellowship. For instance, not long ago there was a woman who came and asked for your address. She is calling herself a sister, but I want to tell you that she is far from the Lord. My question was, what she wanted your address for, and she said: "I want to have correspondence with this brother." Later she told us that she had written to you asking for financial help. Brother! If you have received a letter from her then you should know that she is far from the Lord.

Dear Brother! I will never forget those days when we with you sat there in Chortitza and under the howling of the wind and the whistling of the bullets and whips (nagayky), we in a friendly conversation could discuss important questions. At my question: What is the essence of your Mennonite doctrine of faith? you answered me so simply: "Golgotha (Calvary). On the cross Jesus was crucified. Believe that He died for your sins." Even though I after this for quite a period of time resisted the Holy Spirit Who was working at my heart, the seed was thrown into my heart and the Lord made this seed to grow. I often remember this conversation.

You remember Gregory F.? (The one who was butcher at our headquarters in Schoenfeld) He now, too, has peace with God in Christ Jesus. In a marvelous way Jesus has found him. First his wife came under conviction and invited the brethren on a Sunday to come into their house to conduct a service. Gregory was at home. When he saw the brethren coming he did not know what to do and went up into the attic so he would not hear or see anything. After this it took several months, when he suddenly came into our meeting and gave his heart to the Lord.

When we sing that song: "Oh, the Bitter Pain and Sorrow" which in our Russian hymn book Gusly is under the number 209, we really remember our spiritual blindness, how many times the Lord spoke to us through His servants [in Russian the word "slaves" is used] that we should repent. B.J. Peters spoke to us, also Gerhard H. Doerksen. (Where is he?) We always answered back, "All of Self and None of Thee".

Brother! You are writing that you do not have any thieves in your vicinity and no lice and no fleas. There are fewer thieves here now, too, since we have repented! But the lice and fleas are still biting, also the bedbugs.

Please write us if it is possible to do farm work there. How is the soil? Is it possible to come to Canada? We often think about emigrating to America. V.V. Vin. also is preparing to emigrate to America.

Dear Brother! I already have written to you that we have received the money you sent to us and now I want to tell you once more that we are very thankful and from the whole congregation a sincere "Thank You", Yegor Petrovich, also brother Luke Kravchenko for your financial help which you sent to us. With this money we have bought twenty copies of the New Testament at 50 kopeks each, one

Bible for three rubles and 50 kopeks, also we bought some yardage material for a suit for brother Jacob G. Friesen.

We send you our greetings from all our brethren in Christ Jesus, both Russians and Germans. Also a heartfelt thank you from me personally and from Peter P.; you have given us such a joy by writing us a letter. Our women also want to send their greetings—Alexandra and Zinovia. Greetings to mama and papa Peters, also to Truda, Anna, Mika and Susan. Also our son Peter sends greetings to your son Peter—Petia [the diminutive is used] also to Greta. Also greetings from brother Jacob G. Friesen. Today he is in Friedental.

Please write again. We will impatiently wait. Can we get a Bible concordance there? If possible send us one. Greetings to Greta (Truda's sister) and brother J.W. Reimer. I learned to know him through brother Enns. With brotherly greetings,

Michael P.

These dear converted Makhnovtzy could never forget what shameful lives they had led. Before departing from Russia to Canada I asked brother Jacob G. Friesen, a member of our Rosental church to visit these new converts and help them spiritually, which he did.

Lubitzkoje, 1925, July 12.

Dear Brother in Christ Gerhard Petrovich!

Your letter brought us great joy and encouragement in the work for Christ. "The field is already yellow and the harvest is ready!" We hear the divine call that we should work more for the Lord. This verse is so appropriate. When we look at the harvest field we see the yellow field, but in spite of the fact that tomorrow is already the holiday of Saint Peter, we have not started yet to harvest because for two weeks now we have always rain. Also when we look at God's field and see the surrounding ungodliness it seems to us that we should call out with a loud voice: Let us labour more unitedly! How guilty we are before our Lord for this! Our leading men in Moscow are printing a magazine, a monthly, which brings us much encouragement, but also some grief because there is too much of disputing and quarreling; for instance, who is better, the Baptists or the Evangelicals? In our respective churches where there are these two denominations represented, there is plenty of disputing.

In our district for awhile there were meetings and quite a bit of talking about emigrating to America. Some men were chosen to investigate this matter. Only one trip was made to Ekaterinoslav. The plans were to emigrate to Paraguay, South America. V.V.V. also is planning to emigrate.

On the second day of Pentecost we had a big celebration! There was baptism of 18 persons. They were received into the church fellowship. We had many visitors from Kopany, Novo-Ivanovka, Zaljivnoje, Vosdvishenka and from many other places.

Two weeks ago brother Jacob Friesen went to the other side of the Dniepr River to Chortitza. We do not know where he is now.

Cordial greetings of love in Christ from the brethren Vasily I. Shachovtzov, Gregory K. and Trifon P. The brethren Khariton and Peter promise to write you, too. Also a thank you for your greetings to Theodore Borzenko. He is still far from the Lord. Also brotherly greetings from Gregory F. You are asking if he remembers how he was threatening and scaring father B.J. Peters? Yes, yes, and yes, we all remember this as a nightmare and we now often reap what we have sown. Often people remind us about this and perhaps also in eternity the Lord will ask us: "Do you remember S. Pravda?" This for us is a reminder similar to the one the Lord Jesus gave the apostle Peter when He said: "Simon Peter, dost thou love me?" With brotherly love M.L.P.

October 3, 1925

Dear Brother in Christ!

First of all I greet you all in the name of Jesus Christ and convey to you hearty greetings. I am very thankful to you that you do not forget us. Also greetings to you and your family from my wife Valia. She, too, now has turned to the Lord. We wish you much success in the work of God. I thank my Lord for all His love in this matter, that He has united us in His blood and though bodily we are far one from another, in the spirit we are close together. I also thank God that He was not ashamend of me and has not left me a sinner in this world. Oh, the bitter pain and sorrow! How ashamed to think back about the days of our sinful blindness. I also thank the Lord that your children from the youth on are serving the Lord. I want to report to you the great joy in the Lord, that He is still seeking the sinners. The wife of Gregory F. and Gregory F. himself have turned to the Lord. And with this, good-bye, pray for us and we will pray for you. Your brother in Christ K.H.Z.-enko. Khariton.

What a dangerous man he was! What a miracle just to receive a letter from him like this!

April 18, 1924

Dear Brother in Christ G.P.

We have already received two letters and I must confess that I am very guilty before you for my silence. But you know our condition. First of all there is the obstacle of the distance to the post office and second is our negligence.

You naturally are interested to know what is going on and especially about our Christian life and the work for Christ. The church of God is growing, but along with this also the darkness is gathering. But that sunbeam or ray of the sun from Christ which came into our hearts, being redeemed by His Holy blood, nothing can darken that. Very often in our family, also in the fellowship with the brethren in our conversation and in our prayers we remember you. In the last letter we received from you, written February 7th, there was included a brochure which brought us much joy. You do not imagine what a joy it is to a hungry man to have even a small piece of bread. You know how it is in Russia in the spiritual matter. Dear Brother! You are now working—this we can see from your letter—and in the Bible Society. Do not forget us there in a free country, we who in the services often have to tremble and to shudder at the appearance of the red cap [police]. Do not forget us in your prayers and if there is a possibility also send us some spiritual bread. You are asking about Khariton Z. We thank the Lord that he today is with the children of God and is a member of the church since September, 1923; he is helping in the fellowship with the help of God in the field of Christ. For a period of time at your recommendation your colleague brother Friesen was laboring amongst us. During the winter he was in Kameshevakha, Novo-Ivanovka and Novo-Solovka.

Many of our brethren are thinking about emigrating to America, especially brother A.F.N.—do you know him? He even asked me to write to you if there is a possibility to help him in this matter, with your advice and whatever it takes.

To write to you about the life of a Russian believer is not necessary because you know well enough what it is and you have had your own experience.

It would be very interesting for us to learn about the Americans, their life and their country, where so many legends are being told about. There we say life is incomparably better than ours. But I suppose the enemy of the human soul is there also. But there is a better world, a wonderful world (Psalm 391, Gusly). This is the place we all should endeavor to reach from America and from Russia. We convey greetings, our dear brother, to you and to all the brethren in Christ whether Russians or Americans, for there is no difference between all of us, but we are all one in Christ, Col. 3:11. A hearty brotherly greeting; also all our brethren and sisters send greetings to you. A hearty greeting to your wife Truda from Zinovia; I must report that I had a little son Paul (this is what Zinovia is writing). He lived only a short time and died. Also greetings from Alexandra (Sasha). She also had a son Elija.

How are you living there? We are waiting for an answer.

Signed M.P.

The following is a letter from Peter P. I am sorry I can find only half of the letter. Peter died in 1933 of hunger and persecution.

Lubitzkoje, Oct. 3, 1925.

Peace be unto you, dear brother in Christ. Your letter of August 20 I received September 15th. Yesterday we had visiting brethren from Sherebetz and we read your letter together and were surprised about your Canadian brethren.

For the 14th of October we are planning to have a week of Bible Conference in Sherebetz and the brethren Isaak Petker and Ens from the Molotshnaia are supposed to be there. I am planning to be there, too, and I will read your letter to the Brethren.

In respect to the letter of I.S. Prokhanov we do not know much about the whole matter. We take the same attitude as you do, also our leading brethren take this attitude towards this matter.

The work of God amongst us is growing. As you know our church started in 1921 with only seven members and now we have about 60 members. In the scope of all over Russia the spiritual work is going satisfactorily. In the spring (at Pentecost) we had a conference in the city of Amur, close to Ekaterinoslav with the permission of the government.

You are asking whether we have had any baptisms. Yes, we have had several baptisms. Yesterday also three believers were baptized.

We thank God, our Lord that His hand is not shortened to save souls and His ear is not closed towards our prayers (Isaiah 59:1). You are asking about my brother Vanjka (Ivan-John), about his attitude towards the truth. His attitude is the same as most of the worldly people in our time and whose minds Satan has blinded. (II Cor. 4:4.)

Brother A.F. Naumenko has moved somewhere and has found himself a job as treasurer in an establishment. In Sherebetz I will find out the addresses of our leading brethren like brother Aliokhin (Kharkov) and the brethren members of the all Russian Union of Baptists and I will send you the addresses, so you can have a correspondence with them.

Our brethren have connections with an American brother by the name of Porter, a former representative of the American Relief Administration, of whom they say that he often is visiting Russia. If you need any help to gather more sheaves on the field of God, just write us to the Russian Union of Baptists and they will be able to help you. From your letters we notice that the Russian brethren in Canada have grown cold in their love. They gather only once in five weeks. This is very low. And in regard to tobacco, vodka, fighting, etc., this is not Christian at all. Christ has told us that when a member does not obey the church then he should be regarded as a heathen or a publican. (Matt. 18:11.) Here in our church matters like this are taken care of. Our brethren are watching with a sharp eye. Peter P.

This letter is written by brother Jacob Friesen.

Lubitzkoje, March 23, 1925.

Dear Brother in Christ,

Your letter brought us great joy. It was received by the brethren at a time when I was not here. For the brethren here this was a great holiday. They asked me to draw you a picture showing what joy this was. Brother Peter P. was busy hauling manure on the field as fertilizer; they had a visitor from the Orthodox Church, a relative. But when they brought your letter, brother Peter left his work, also his visitor; a few of the brethren came together and read the letter, weeping. [Please forgive me when I say that reading these lines after all these years, my eyes are filled with tears, too.] *This letter was also read in the congregation and they expressed their thankfulness to God and to you there in America. This letter, like the pigeon of*

Noah brought them the olive branch, is a testimony or a sign that behind the ocean there are still hearts who are warmed by the love of God in Christ and are also full of joy for Christ and for us.

As I have already mentioned, I was absent when your letter arrived; I was in Friedental, distributing spiritual literature and also conducting discussions on Biblical subjects; we also held evangelistic services. The results of the meetings are not known to me yet because Satan was hindering me in my work there, but I pray to the Lord for all the people in Friedental, and I believe there are people that will find the Saviour ... Generally speaking, I must say that in the Lutheran colonies the work of God is almost dead. They have only a few services, only in Mistukovo-Friedental the pastor does conduct services. All the other colonies he is visiting only three times a year; a very sad situation. In the colony No. 6 they are waiting for me to come. Before Christmas I was in Lubitzkoje, conducting evangelistic services, also Bible study. The Lord blessed this effort and twelve souls repented. [They want to repent.]

After Christmas, for about a month I was in Soloshtshansk. Besides all this I also visited Zaljivnoje and Voskresensk villages (khutor) close to Zaljivnoje where brother Trifon P. is living. I also visited Buriakovo with brother Philip Korkhovoy; we also had services at these places. For a week and a half I conducted services in Little Tokmatshka. The Lord has richly blessed the work of the Sherebetz Brethren Union, which consists of 22 congregations. Very often we here have Bible Conferences for the preachers. We had such in Sherebetz, in Novo-Ivanovka, Kuprianovka (near the Mennonite village Jakovlevo), in the city Orekhovo and in Petropavlovka—a week at each place. We believe that the Lord will send us the Holy Spirit on our country Russia; that's why He has given us time to prepare our spiritual strength. The speakers and leaders at these conferences were the preachers—brother Poettker from Wernersdorf, brother Enns helped in Sherebetz, (Enns from Alexandertal). Besides all this the congregations exchanged their preachers so they would get acquainted one with another.

Besides the twelve members added in Lubitzkoje there are many thirsty souls which have been touched by the Lord.

Perhaps you remember when you were at sister Sashka's house at the dinner of the christening of her daughter Vera. At this occasion you spoke the Word of God. There also was her aunt Darotshka, who always loved you for this. Now sister Sashka is asking you to pray for her so God would give her much wisdom in dealing with these thirsty souls. Here are some of her questions: What attitude do your relatives take towards the Saviour, the Lord? Has Willy been converted? How about Susan and how about Greta's children? Where is Doerksen and his daughter Sarah?

This morning I had a conference with sister Sashka and we discussed the marvelous plan of God for humanity and especially with us. Why did you, G.P. Schroeder, become a teacher at Schoenfeld? How was it that you became acquainted with brother Peter P. Sashka's husband (who at that time was a Makhnovetz)? Why did you give Jacob G. Friesen the advice to go to Lubimovka? Where will this river of blessings end? Brother Peter P. says that he often is imagining that he can see you coming on the road from the Molotshnaia and he is waiting for you. Also, please send us your photo.

I, for myself, must say that the Lord has given me a joyful and beneficial work in training the young people in singing, etc. Sister Sashka often remembers the time when you at Schoenfeld at Christmas would have services and you had beautiful singing. She is grieving over the fact that she at that time did not have the joy of salvation in the fellowship with the Lord that she now has.

Our assembly room is becoming too crowded because the Lord is adding new members to our church. We have to find a suitable place to build. This week, the Lord willing, I want to start evening classes with the Young People "about the Great Day of the Lord." If at all possible send us some books for our edification and in Bible study. Here in Russia we are not very rich in spiritual literature.

Signed, Lubitzkoje, 23 March, 1925

Brother and sister P. and Jacob G. Friesen.

I often have to think back how these men still in spiritual darkness would embrace and kiss me, when we would sit at a table. What a tremendous power of God it took to bring them out of darkness into the light of Christ. One thing we must yet mention, that all these believers were sent into slave labour or other places where they after a period of time would have to die. There is no Baptist Church in Lubitzkoje now. Not one of the men mentioned in these writings is alive. We have received messages from these places so we do not want to say too much. Trifon P. was sent to slave labour in the 1930's. Michael L.P. was also "repressed" and never came back. In the message we received about him, this word "repressed" was used. The latest information we have now in the beginning of 1974 is that more persecution against faith in God is evident in places in the South.

CHAPTER 15

The Beginning Of Famine

No Rain

1921 was a very dry year. It seemed one calamity just would pile up on the other. The farmers were unable to do a good job in plowing the field because of the lack of horsepower and no grain for seeding, and on top of all of this came a terrible drought. We did not get back the amount of potatoes we had put in the ground in the spring. The fields were barren. It was evident from every corner that we were facing a hard time of hunger and starvation.

One day in the spring, I drove to Alexandrovsk and here Mr. Cornelius Janzen very secretly told me that he had hidden quite a few of the "Raduga" books. Raduga means rainbow and this was the name of a Christian bookstore managed by our good friend brother A. Kroeker. When the communists began to confiscate all Christian literature, you could see the fine Christian books, periodicals and magazines used as wrapping paper somewhere in the market. Brother C. Janzen asked me if I could take them along and distribute them among Christians and non-Christians. I was willing to risk it. Just taking a look at all those books and tracts and literature made my heart beat with joy and yet I was quite apprehensive about the danger this would involve. We put all this literature in a box on my wagon and I proceeded back home.

One dangerous spot was the bridge at Einlage across the Dniepr river. As I came closer to the bridge I took a piece of my white bread which somebody had given me in Alexandrovsk. We at this time did not have any white bread. Approaching the bridge I took out the bread and began to eat. The soldier with his rifle was standing there near the bridge. When he stopped me I greeted him, "Good morning, comrade, how are you? Would you like to eat a piece of white bread?" His eyes were beaming; of course he wanted a piece of bread." Just proceed across the river", he said. I waved him "good-bye" and proceeded on my way home. Many souls have been blessed by reading these books. I know one definite conversion through the use of one of these tracts.

Truda's parents, the B.J. Peters, had moved from Lichtfelde to Rueckenau and it was our desire to see them and the other relatives once more. We did not have good horses and we did not have the money to stop in fancy hotels or eat at good restaurants. But we made this trip in August. Over night we stayed somewhere; people were kind to permit Truda and the children to sleep in the house while I preferred to sleep outside on the wagon, near the horses. We had a nice time of fellowship with members of our family, grandma Toews and others, here and in Gnadenfeld.

In Ruekenau we also visited pastor Jacob Reimer and Dr. Tavonius. Somebody here asked me how we were getting along in Chortitza. I told him everything was just fine. "Did you have a good crop? Did you thresh quite a bit of grain?" My answer was very frank. "We had no crop. We have threshed almost no grain whatsoever and we are facing death from hunger." "How, then, can you be so happy? That is a strange attitude." My answer was, "We know that the Lord still is able to save us, even from death by hunger, if it be His will. We trust God also in this matter."

On October 29, 1921 we had a Bible Conference and how happy we were to have the brethren Adolph Reimer, Henry Enns and David P. Isaac from the Molotshnaia to lead us in this conference on prophecy.

Brother Reimer was a very capable and a deeply devoted man of God who had been preaching in many places in Southern Russia, and to the soldiers at the front lines. He was deeply devoted to this great task of bringing the light from God to people who had been living in spiritual darkness. Soon after this Bible Conference he went to other places such as Kiev. There, he got sick. Although he reached home, he was not even able to give a report about his last conference to his wife. He died soon after this last conference.

But now, October 29, 1921 we had this wonderful Bible Conference in the Mennonite Church in Chortitza. Brother A. Reimer also visited us in our home. I still have the full outline of this Bible exposition on prophecy. We received great blessing at this fellowship and especially treasured the fact that this conference could be conducted in our big, old Mennonite church, because we had the longing to have fellowship with all children of God.

Teachers' Conference in Halbstadt

On December 10 I, together with the teachers Abram Vogt and Hans Janzen of Schoenwiese, went by train to Halbstadt to a teachers' conference, where forty-six teachers participated. One incident of this conference is still fresh in my memory. In the front seat of this schoolroom was the political commissar, with a pistol, observing and watching everything that was being done and said. The study was about nature science. The weather conditions of the various localities were discussed and in this connection we had to talk about the sky. You remember that song ". . . and the skies are not cloudy all day". We talk about sunny California or about sunny Alberta. We are fortunate to have in the English language the distinction between sky and heaven. But not so in the Russian language, where we have the word "nebo" for sky or heaven. The moment one of the speakers (not I) used the word "nebo"; the political commissar was on his feet with his hand on his pistol. Then with a very excited tone of voice he exclaimed, "No more words like nebo. There is no heaven, no God, no soul". All these words very carefully must be avoided. This was one of the first lessons we received under the Soviet government.

From Halbstadt I was able to get a ride to Rueckenau to visit our relatives there unexpectedly. One thing that was much in discussion already at this time was the emigration from Russia to Canada. While in Halbstadt I was able to visit my former colleagues Peter Sawatzky and Jacob John Dyck.

It so happened that at this time David P. Isaak, former employee at father B.J. Peters' store in Schoenfeld, was visiting here in Rueckenau and was just about ready to drive back to Sagradovka where he lived. This way I had a chance to get a ride with him to Chortitza. It was very, very cold and there was still some unrest in many places in Southern Russia but we arrived safely home and I bought an axle with springs and wheels from D. Isaak to build a little wagon for our use.

At this time many people began to die from hunger and older people and children on the streets and elsewhere would cry for bread. One pud of flour (about 37 pounds) would sell for 1,000,000 rubles. One pound of butter was worth 65,000 rubles. Many people were glad when they had a little bit of bread for Christmas.

Even at this precarious time we had started a Sunday School in a private home in Chortitza. Sixty children were attending and were still quite lively and happy. We practiced for a Christmas program, preparing also to have a Christmas tree with a few little presents for the children. We noticed how willing our people were to help these children and teach them the songs and explain God's Holy Word to them. We collected some flour from people who still could and were willing to help, and baked cookies for the children.

The Christmas program was presented in the former store of another cousin of mine, Mrs. A. Wiebe. Each child received a cookie or two. Also in the big Mennonite Church a Christmas program was presented and we had a big Christmas tree. In our assembly room in Rosental, a Christmas program was presented.

On Christmas day we met at my mother's home in Rosental. On this occasion letters from some of our relatives in Canada were read and discussion centered on emigration to Canada.

We also celebrated the watch night, the night before New Year's, which in German we called "Sylvester". There was singing, preaching, music and a love meal followed, which consisted of a piece of rough rye bread with what we called coffee or "prips". Instead of coffee, roasted rye or barley was used. At this time we were still full of hope, enthusiasm and courage. The songs and recitations proclaiming the Word of God were very precious to all of us, and with a prayer we left the place hoping against hope for the best in the year 1922.

Part of the first week I spent in our neighboring village Neuendorf, conducting meetings in private homes with a love meal at the home of Hans P. Epp. We had wonderful Christian fellowship with pastor Abram Hamm participating. The meals still were very good but I already was facing a problem. My stomach and intestines no longer were able to retain and digest the food. For this reason I often had restless nights. We had a service on Sunday morning and on Sunday afternoon I caught a ride home to Chortitza.

On Monday, January 10 we started with classes in our school. Not all the students had come yet but we started anyway. I had my classes at the high school and also at the teachers seminary. The campuses were adjoining.

Arrest of Brother John

On the 27th of January, a Friday, this being my day off, I decided to help Truda in getting a little bit of thread. I took the spinning wheel and began the job of producing some silk thread. Then came my brother Peter to tell me that they had arrested my brother John. Immediately, I got up and along with brother Peter went to the volost to find out why he had been arrested. When we got there we learned that he already had been transferred to the village about twenty miles south—Belenkoje. The Revolutionary Tribunal was in charge of this affair. It was a very serious situation. The school was closed on account of the cold weather. The next day, Saturday, we received the message that more of our men had been arrested and sent to Belenkoje. There was nothing we could do, so we gathered at a prayer meeting. It was a very cold night.

The following day, Sunday, I went to the Volost to talk to a man in authority in these affairs, whom I knew. He promised that he would drive to Belenkoje and try his best to help those that were arrested. At 3:00 p.m. we had another prayer meeting where the Lord gave me the boldness to pray with joy knowing that God would help.

The next day I went to Rosental to my mother who was sick in bed, praying for her son John. We read from the Holy Scriptures, knowing that the Lord never makes a mistake, but that everything is in His hands and He will help.

Before we go on I must give you an explanation about the footwear we used at that time. Many of us were wearing scuffs or what we in low German called "Schlorren", and in high German "Pantoffeln". These scuffs or Pantoffeln were the only footgear most of us had during the revolution. The soles were mostly made of wood and over the front part of the foot a leather covering. In normal times we mostly wore leather shoes of good quality.

Schlorren-Len', Schnurrbarts-Len'

There was in our village of Rosental a woman whom most of us called by the above mentioned names. Len' is an abbreviation of Helen or Lena, but they called her just Len' and because she always was wearing Schlorren or scuffs, people gave her the name Schlorren-Len'. Also, she had developed quite a bit of a mustache which in German is called Schunurrbart so some people would call her Schnurrbarts-Len. (English meaning: mustache-Len.) She was a domestic working in various places and made her living that way.

When famine came she would not be able to obtain work. Who would pay money for hired help? Everybody was struggling for his life, so hired help was not used at all. The only way for her to make a living was to go and beg.

About this time my brother John, realizing that he could not bring his family through the winter, sold part of his machine shed and a part of the farm buildings for a very nominal amount of wheat. This seemed to be a wise move, if he did not want to see his family die of starvation and we were happy for him that now he would have enough bread through the winter for himself and for his family. On the other hand, this became quite a problem for him because people, knowing that he had obtained wheat, would come and demand bread from him.

One day Schlorren-Len' came and asked my brother John to give her some bread. "You have bread. You have wheat and I am asking you to give me some bread." Here was the problem. My brother, not knowing what to do, told her that he had only a very limited amount of wheat which would barely be sufficient to bring his family through the winter, asked her to go to the Soviet authorities who in some places, had organized some help for the poor and hungry people. Having received such an answer Schlorren-Len' said to my brother: "So you refuse to give me bread. You will remember me," and she left.

Complaint Box

At this time the Soviet Government had at some places installed special boxes which they called "shalobny yashtshik" or complaint box. The people were asked to put into this box a paper with a complaint about anything or about anybody. They did not have to sign their names. You guessed it; Schlorren-Len' did just that. She put in a slip of paper with a statement of complaint that John Schroeder had refused to give her a piece of bread, while she knew he had bread. At the same time he had tried to instigate hatred against the Soviet Government by telling her to go and demand bread from it. This was the accusation and it was a serious one indeed. For this he now was sitting in Belenkoje.

In Belenkoje the men were placed in a hut with straw on the floor for them to rest. As far as I remember there were at that time at least fourteen or more men in jail from our villages. During the day they had to appear before the judge who was a nineteen year old Jewish boy from Chortitza. His brother was a student in my class at Central School. Now this boy, S., was the main judge of the Extraordinary Revolutionary Tribunal. This tribunal was mostly called "Troyka". Famous are the Russian troykas, which means a team of three horses, but here it meant a committee of three men, who day after day were the sole judges over many people, dealing with life and death.

During the day the prisoners would be interrogated and, in most cases, there was only one judge. My brother John was interrogated by S., and John told me how the situation was. There were others, not Mennonite men, two of them by the name of Petrenko. There was a Mennonite pastor Peter Julius Heinrichs from Neuendorf.

With night approaching the prisoners could hear the soldiers in the adjoining room preparing for the shooting. There seemed to be two parties for this job and one party would quarrel with the other party, each demanding the right to do the shooting that night. Their motive was mostly the clothing and other belongings of the prisoners which would automatically belong to the men who did the shooting.

In the evening, when it was all dark around us—inside and outside—we could hear the two Petrenko brothers with tears saying goodbyes one to the other, also asking the other to take care of his family should he remain alive. They each made these promises. There were those asking pastor Heinrichs to pray with and for them, because they all could expect this to be the last night.

Postmaster Bandarovich

Among the prisoners was also the postmaster of Chortitza, Bandarovich. After he had been interrogated by the judge, the other prisoners asked him what the accusations against him were and he answered them with one word, "tshepukha", i.e., nonsense. He stretched out on the straw on the floor and soon fell asleep. When evening came and the soldiers began to prepare for the shooting, everyone seemed to be alert and nervous. Only postmaster Bandarovich was sleeping and did not realize what was going on. Another hour passed by, then the door opened and men with a kerosene lantern entered the room. They had the list of the victims to be shot that night and the first name they called was—Bandarovich. But Bandarovich, still sleeping, did not hear that his name had been called. They called twice and a third time. Finally, they began to curse and to swear, asking somebody to show them who this Bandarovich was. When somebody pointed at the sleeping postmaster, one of the soldiers kicked him with his foot, after which he opened his eyes and began to look around. The soldier asked him, "Are you Bandarovich?" He of course had to answer that he was. "Get up, take your belongings and move out of the room!" he was ordered. Now Bandarovich realized the full meaning of the situation and he began to beg. He was a poor man. He had done nothing wrong, he had a family . . .

But there was no other way. When he still hesitated they grabbed him, took his belongings and went out into the other room. The prisoners could hear him cry and beg for his life. He was ordered to undress. You must realize that this was winter and it was a very cold night. When he had undressed they led him to a machine shed in the same yard. There was a rock in the corner. Here the victim had to kneel down with his face towards the rock. There was only one shot and it was all over for Bandarovich. It did not take long for the soldiers to come back and take one victim after the other out of the room and in the same manner shoot them. How many, we do not know.

Brother John—Free

That was Sunday, January 29th. The next morning we received the message through somebody that there was hope that my brother John would come home as a free man. How happy we were when towards evening of the same day my brother John came home, completely exhausted, but a free man again. The joy was great, and though the distance between our two houses was over a mile, I went over to greet my dear brother John who was once more among the living, and we praised God for it. The next day, we gathered as a family at my mother's house to give thanks to God for John's safe return.

The day after that we went to Neuendorf to visit some dear people there, but especially pastor Peter J. Heinrichs, who also had come home. We had a nice fellowship together but the struggle between life and death was very evident on brother Heinrichs' face.

Hunger and Hope for Emigration

In letters and conversations one thing began to be the main topic of discussion, and that was, emigration to Canada, the second topic was hunger. Bible conferences and Bible study groups were organized not only among our specific church people but also with the General Mennonite Conference members, with pastor P. Neufeld. As the food situation became more and more acute, we were forced to find ways and means to get bread. If only we could get a few pounds of flour we could mix it with either boiled beets or linseed cakes, called in Russian "makukha". You may sometime want to find out how it tastes. Very little was coming in as payment for teaching.

About this time my brother John became very ill and was unconscious for a period of time. This was the reaction of his body to all he had experienced in Belenkoje. In his unconscious condition he was humming the song, "Jesus my Life's Joy."

At this time we had a ministers conference at my cousin Abram Klassen's place. As a church we had the two out-stations in Schoeneberg and in Hochfeld, so their pastors A. Froese and Bernhard Dyck attended this conference, too. Among other things, the recent events at Belenkoje were discussed and prayed about. Hunger was evident everywhere. Pastor Bern-hard Dyck of Hochfeld gave me a few rolls baked from whole wheat flour, which were sent by sister Dyck for Truda, because Truda at this time was expecting her fourth child. What a precious present this was, even a few rolls.

Telegram About Professor Miller

A telegram arrived telling us that professor Miller of America was com-ing to Southern Russia with a supply of food. Many had been waiting for such a message for quite awhile and it was carried from home to home with great joy.

The following Sunday, February 5th, when we had the General Assem-bly in our church, with representatives and visitors from various places, one of the brethren from Schoeneberg brought us one pud (37 lbs) of pota-toes. The following day, while teaching at the Teachers Seminary our sen-ior teacher Dietrich H. Epp brought the message that the representative of Holland, Mr. Willings, came through the city of Alexandrovsk to be on hand when at the city of Berdjansk a ship with 24,000 pud of products would arrive for the hungry Mennonites. Also, it was mentioned that Prof. Miller of America would arrive with 32,000 pud; of this 12,000 pud was for Chortitza. Do you blame me for registering all this in my diary? The joy was great! People would have hope again to live. The same eve-ning we had a session at our Teachers Seminary because a request was made by the authorities for us to maintain a farm of 37 desiatins (about 105 acres) to help in the upkeep of the school.

CHAPTER 16

Hunger—A General View

Of all the perplexities, afflictions, trials and tribulations we had experienced, hunger seemed to be the worst. Let me suggest that you read Lamentations 4:1-10. I do not remember when we had read so much from Lamentations as at this time. It seemed to me the same experiences we had in Russia at this time had been the lot of those living in Jeremiah's time. Here in this chapter I would like to emphasize some verses.

Verse four "The tongue of the suckling child cleaveth to the roof of his mouth for thirst: the young children ask bread, and no man breaketh it unto them." Then from verse five, just one sentence, "They that were brought up in scarlet embrace dunghills." Now let me quote verses nine and ten. "They that be slain with the sword are better than they that be slain by hunger: for these pine away, stricken through for want of the fruits of the field." Verse ten, "The hands of the pitiful women have sodden their own children; they were their meat in the destruction of the daughter of my people." How often we have quoted these verses. Slain with a sword or a bullet took a moment or two or three, a minute at the worst and it was all over. But starvation and hunger were much worse. There was nobody to help us. The government would not help and we had the feeling at that time, and later we learned that it was true, that the government was in favor of hunger and starvation. Why? The simple reason: It is much easier to force into submission people who are hungry.

Hungry people will not rebel. They will not instigate revolution. A person that is hungry will just suffer hunger and die. The mental effect was terrible, just to think that you with all your education, at an age when you are considered in the prime of your life, are unable to provide food for yourself, for your wife and children. In the evening you go to bed hungry. You take a look at your family already in bed. You know they have gone to bed hungry. It takes a long time for you to fall asleep because of the gnawing thoughts of hunger, of helplessness, of being destitute. You are perishing . . . you are going down . . . you have to die . . . slowly. You are getting weaker and weaker . . . These thoughts drive you almost to insanity. In the morning you awake with the same thoughts. You are hungry and you know your family is hungry. What will you do? What can you do? You answer your own question: There is nothing, nothing, nothing you can do. You walk from one room to the other; you walk through your kitchen and you remember what an abundance of food there used to be in this house. The possibility of want, of suffering from hunger never entered your mind . . . But now it is here. You are h u n g r y!

You go to visit other people and on your way you say to your wife, "Let's not talk about food or about eating while we visit these friends because the more you talk about it the hungrier you get. We knock at the door and when the door opens we are greeted by friends with pale faces and expressions of suffering. After the greeting the first question they ask us is, "Have you eaten at all today?" There you are, you start talking about eating right there and then. You are unable to stop it. You walk on the street and you see hungry people; older men, women and children just standing around. Others are sitting with pale faces, and the one question, the one word that comes through the lips of these hungry people on the streets is, "Bread, bread, will we get bread?" I meet these people on the street walking to school and they approach me with the same question, "You are a teacher, perhaps you have some information. Can you give us any hope about the American help that is supposed to come? Will we get bread soon?"

Those who had cattle, calves, cows and heifers, butchered all they could. Our neighbors had a calf and they butchered it, but they were trying to get everything out of this butchered calf that they possibly could, not just the meat. When Truda and I went over to visit the Hamms we saw how they had taken off the hide of the calf, had poured boiling water over the hide and with razor sharp knives had shaved off the hair. From this hide they made something that had food value.

Horses were butchered, young or old horses, as long as the people could get something that would sustain life.

I will never forget an incident that happened about this time. I was walking in Rosental southward, up a hill we called "der Hemmberg".

There was a man driving uphill in a one horse cart. That poor horse must not have had any feed for quite awhile and right near the hill that horse suddenly dropped dead. I stopped and looked at an amazing scene. People from everywhere, with knives, hatchets and other tools came running, pushing, shoving and yelling at each other, and before this man could save anything they had cut up that horse by chopping off the head, legs, etc. The whole horse was cut to pieces and carried away piece by piece. Everyone wanted a piece of that dead horse just to prolong life.

A Cat Story

Would anyone ever think about butchering a cat? Normally, no, but at this time the cats were used for meat. It was very hard to find cats in our village.

Let me tell you a story about a cat. In the spring of 1922 in our hayloft I discovered a mother cat with three young kittens. I almost trembled with excitement to have made such a discovery. This seemed to be a treasure. I acted very carefully and managed to take the three kittens away from the mother cat and brought them into our house. Of course there was rejoicing not only in our house but also with our neighbors. Everyone was glad to see these three young kittens. But we had not estimated the cleverness of a mother cat, how she would walk around the house and from a distance call her young kittens. One day when the door was open this mother cat managed to take away two of the young kittens which we were unable to find again. One of these young kittens, a male, remained in the house and we were very careful to watch him so he would not escape. To make a long story short, this became a very valuable cat, an asset, not only in our house but also in the neighboring houses. He was used to catch mice and it really was amazing how he could catch them. When he could eat no more he would put the dead mice in a pile and look around with satisfaction. The reader should not get the impression that we ate the mice. We needed their eradication.

One day pastor A. Froese from Schoeneberg came over and asked if he could borrow this cat for a period of one month to catch mice in his house. So our Tom cat went to Schoeneberg for one month. Then my cousin, David Klassen, came and asked if he could have our cat. When in 1923 we emigrated to Canada, we gave this cat to the David Klassens and they were glad to receive such a valuable present.

Not only cows, horses, calves, and cats, but also dogs were eaten in many places. If hungry people could catch a dog somewhere, they would eat it in order to prolong life.

At this time doors and windows in our houses were not only shut but also locked so nobody could come in. One day when I came from school I inadvertently left the door open and two small boys following me entered the kitchen. They begged for something to eat. My cousin, Mrs. Braun, with whom we were living in Chortitza, had a little tiny dog and this dog was gnawing at some bones which Mrs. Braun and her two sons Yegor and Henry had left after eating their noon meal. There also was Mrs. Braun's cat. When these boys saw the cat they begged and begged with tears, "Please, auntie, please auntie, give us the cat, we are hungry." They saw a bone or two under the chair which the dog had gnawed on for quite a while. These two boys jumped for and took these bones and it was a pity to see how they were gnawing with their teeth on them to get out of them some food value. That is hunger. Hunger is very painful. Hunger may drive you to insanity.

Krugel Family

There was a family in our neighborhood by the name of Krugel. They were very poor people and had suffered from hunger severely. In our village Rosental-Chortitza whenever a horse, cow, calf or pig would die, people would come and take pieces and boil or fry it, then eat. Quite a few people died from the poisoned meat they ate, especially from pork.

Mr. Krugel heard that in some villages like Rosengart, only about four miles from Chortitza, farmers would not use the meat of a calf when it had died, but in the winter would just throw it out of the barn on the snow. So he walked to Rosengart with the one desire that he would find somewhere a dead calf. But he had suffered so much from hunger already that his whole body was weak and when he finally reached the village of Rosengart he just dropped dead. The message was sent to Mrs. Krugel and her family. After a short time a farmer from Rosengart brought the dead body of Mr. Krugel to Chortitza. This was in the beginning of March of 1922, and some days the weather was nice with warm sunshine. On this particular day the thirteen-year-old daughter of the Krugels was sitting on the threshold of the house when they brought in the body of her father. This poor girl had already suffered so much from hunger that when she saw the men bringing in the body of her father, she just leaned over and she, too, was gone.

Mrs. Krugel came over to see me, asking if I would be so kind as to conduct some sort of a funeral for her husband and daughter the next day. But early in the morning she came and told me that the funeral would have to be postponed because she was unable to find anybody who was willing to dig a grave. Everybody was afraid to do a strenuous job like digging a grave without eating a good meal first. Some men told her to give them at least two pounds of bread each, then they would be willing to dig the grave. She had no bread, consequently she could not do it. The bodies remained on the floor in the house, without coffins, of course. Nobody would even mention a coffin.

The following day Mrs. Krugel came and told me that we could have the funeral now, the grave was ready. How did she get this accomplished? She just went to the volost (county) office and reported to the authorities her predicament. These authorities sent out several soldiers, and the first able-bodied man they met had to go and dig the grave. The bodies without a coffin were taken and put on a small wagon. Somebody had to jump into the grave and take the bodies and bury them. Nobody was interested in going to a funeral, so only a handful of people were there. That was the funeral of hungry people, Mr. Krugel and his daughter.

Gophers and Birds for Food

People were doing many other things to survive and to prolong life. They invented traps to catch birds, especially crows, and used the meat of these birds for food. They also dug in the forests for some special roots. I do not know what kind they were but they did get some roots to live on. Also, in the spring there was quite a bit of hunting after gophers and there were some boys who were quite clever in catching and dressing gophers.

In the year 1937 when I was the state missionary in North Dakota, I made a trip to Pittsburgh, Pennsylvania to the Russian Baptist Conference. I stopped in Chicago where our nephew Waldemar Rempel was working at a printing office. We went to a restaurant and ordered a meal. Just when the meal was put on the table a certain thought came to my mind and I asked Waldemar, looking straight into his eyes, "Do you remember how the gophers tasted in Russia in 1922?" Waldemar remembered this quite well and we gave thanks for the nice meal we had on the table in Chicago. In 1922 Waldemar, perhaps at the age of 11 years, was one of the boys who was quite skilled in catching and dressing the gophers for a meal.

We, as a family, have not eaten gophers, but we have eaten a number of other things that did not taste good at all and I asked Truda to sew me a little bag (a "glove") to put over my tongue so I would not taste the food. But I never tried this experiment.

There was a constant struggle between the stomach and the tongue.

The tongue would say: "Do not take it", and the stomach would say: "Give it to me"!

Cannibalism

In Lamentations 4:10 we read, "The hands of the pitiful women have sodden [boiled] their own children: they were their meat in the destruction of the daughter of my people." That happened many, many years ago. Cannibalism existed then and it existed in 1922 in Russia. Perhaps you do not like to read all this because it does not make pleasant reading—it surely does not give me any pleasure to write about it. But maybe it is well to remember how destitute, how poor and how hungry we were, and how we thanked God for His omnipotent hand that was upon us, helping us in many situations that were not pleasant at all. Yes, cannibalism existed and well-fed people and children were in great danger in many places because of cannibalism.

Butter at this time was selling at 110,000 rubles a pound. We sold a few pounds of butter and bought sunflower seed cakes at 25,000 rubles a pound.

On February 7, 1922 I had to teach in the afternoon and two of our colleagues, Dietrich H. Epp and Jacob Martin Dyck went to Alexandrovsk to meet professor Miller from America and to arrange whatever help they could obtain from him. The next day I took a few pounds of wheat and did my best to convert this wheat into flour on our coffee mill.

Soup Kitchen

February 9th: Professor Miller had not arrived yet but he may come soon. This was the message of the day. Preparations were being made to establish a soup kitchen and a bakery when the American Relief Administration brought the necessary products for this. We received a letter from our relatives in Canada that they were sending us food drafts at ten dollars each. What a joy to know that somebody was trying to help us.

On Saturday February 11th we had a teachers conference in Schoenwiese and this gave me an opportunity to visit the parents of my former colleague, Andreas Vogt. Hunger was increasing more and more. We noticed it in our church services, especially in the matter of singing. Hungry people do not like to sing. Singing takes physical strength and this was lacking. So the singing was becoming very weak.

A brother from our Einlage group came to see me after a Sunday service. He told me that he was under very strong temptation to go and steal bread. His family was suffering severely from hunger and he

knew a place where he could perhaps obtain the needed food if he would
be willing to steal. Perhaps it was well that I could tell him about our
own experience, how we suffered from hunger and that we had decided to
die from hunger rather than do anything that was wrong in the sight of
God. It was my privilege to pray with this man and to help him overcome
the temptation and suffer a little bit longer until the Lord would send the
help in a legal way.

Mika, my wife's sister who was staying with us while studying at the
Teachers Seminary, went to school but soon came back on account of the
severe cold weather; there was no school that day. Many people were without fuel to heat their houses. The situation was getting worse day by day.
The hungry people were just standing on the streets, knocking at doors
and asking for help. We had absolutely nothing anymore.

The weather turned milder again, so early in the morning I went into
the village to look around to find something to eat for my family. It
seemed I was looking in vain to find something. My colleague and my
former teacher Henry H. Epp traded me twenty pounds of ordinary beets
for two pounds of butter. These beets were used to put into the flour to
bake bread. The next day we, as a family, went to my mother in Rosental
and had a meal with her and with my sisters, because we had absolutely
nothing to eat at that time.

Here we heard a report that it would take at least another ten days
before the American Relief Administration would move in. Many were
dying of hunger. "I am glad another day has passed and we are still
alive." This is the entry in my diary for that day.

Looking for Food

One Sunday evening Truda and I went into the village searching for
something to eat. We had obtained some money but there was no food
available. We were told about two places where we possibly would be able
to buy bread. We left our children at home and on our wooden scuffs we
went about on the slippery, icy sidewalks in hope of finding some bread.
When we came to the first place, about half a mile from our home, we
found it locked. We turned to the street again and when we came to the
second place we saw it was still open. So we had at least some hope. Perhaps we could get a pound of bread or two for the family, but when we
got there we were told that they had just sold the last pound of bread.
With heavy hearts we went back homeward. By this time it had become
dark on the streets and it was dark in our hearts and in our minds.

As we came closer to our home we were asking one another, "What will we, what can we, what must we say to our hungry children?" When they noticed our approach they came to meet us, and at this time our hearts became heavier than before. But our children seemed to be happy. They were saying something we did not at first understand. "Papa, Mama, we have bread!" "Where did you get bread?" We asked. My sister Lena had come and brought us half a loaf. My mother had told her, "Lena, I am pretty sure Gerhard and Truda with their children have nothing to eat today. Take half a loaf of bread to them." So the children and we, with thankful hearts and with tears, each ate a slice of bread before retiring for the night.

The bread Truda baked at this time was flour mixed either with linseed cakes or beets, or the remnants from our coffee kettle which were left after drinking the coffee—the residue being from burned barley or rye. But we did not eat as much bread as we wanted because Truda had already divided it into slices or pieces for each one of us so there would be enough to last until the next baking. One morning at the breakfast table I had to shed tears when one of our children, looking at me said, "Daddy, I know you are still hungry. Please, daddy take a bite from my piece." Could I—would I do that? Oh, no I could not take bread from my child. If we had to die we would die together.

Many of our neighbors and friends were suffering just as much as we were, or even more, so on many occasions Truda would take some of the food off our table, mostly in liquid form, and pour it into a pitcher and say to me, "Please take this over to Mrs. Harder." This woman was already swollen from hunger. She could hardly talk. She was always short of breath. I would take the pitcher with soup over to Mrs. Harder, and only then would we eat our own meal, knowing that once we started to eat we would not be able to restrain ourselves from eating everything on the table.

As it happened one time when I brought this soup over to Mrs. Harder she had a visitor, another neighborhood woman. Mrs. Harder took the contents of my pitcher and poured it into her own pitcher. She put it on a shelf waiting for the neighbor woman to leave, after which she would eat it. When I went to the door she came with me, sending greetings to my wife, and perhaps we exchanged a few sentences before I actually left the place. When I finally left the neighbor woman had gone too, but through the other door. When Mrs. Harder went to her cupboard to take the pitcher and eat the soup Truda had sent her, the pitcher was empty.

Baking bread was always a happy occasion whenever it could be done, but you had to very carefully watch the oven because somebody might come and steal the bread from it. We could tell some interesting stories about this. Some prospective thieves would not hesitate to break through a brick wall just to get bread.

My dear wife Truda was in what we in Russian call "poloshenjieje" meaning that she was expecting her fourth baby and pretty soon, too. We were always quite apprehensive especially when the night came. Everything seemed to be getting darker day by day, but we remembered a Russian verse, "The darker the night, the brighter the stars, the deeper the sorrow, the closer God." We would have to walk about one mile to the hospital. Waiting for things to develop I sat down and copied a song, giving it a somewhat different appearance, rearranging things. Later I was glad to find the same song here in English under the title, "In the Glory of Life's Morning."

Spiritual Work

We were waiting for professor Miller from America to come, but in the meantime there was a lot of spiritual work to be done. People wanted to be visited in their homes for prayer and I was eager and willing to do this, if only my physical strength would permit it. Finally, the message came that professor Miller had arrived in Alexandrovsk on February 22nd. We sold our cream separator for twenty pounds of wheat and fourteen pounds of millet meal. Some people still had plenty to eat and they were locking themselves up in their homes while eating their meals. Christians were sharing to the last bite with hungry people under the motto: "We live together and we die together."

There were some men who always had been chain smokers, and they at this time had to decide what they would spend their money for, either for bread or for tobacco, and strangely enough, some men would prefer to spend the money for tobacco. As one man said, "I do not care even if we have to die, but I have to have my tobacco."

One day a man from a neighboring village who still had plenty of wheat and food, admonished me to trust more in God than I did. This was a very bitter pill for me to swallow, and I told him, "You have no right to tell me this. Bring me a sack full of wheat from the abundance you still have and I promise to trust God a little bit more." Yes, we did trust God, but we found out that we could not trust some of the people who still were in possession of earthly goods. One farmer brought Truda a loaf of white bread because she needed it now more than I did. Some Christian people were very considerate in this matter.

It was reported to me about a certain man, J., who had been mean to his wife, even having beaten her. How awful! She was a sickly woman and the next day I walked over to see this man and I had a very serious conversation with him. As far as I could tell he repented and promised not to do it anymore. We had prayer together.

Professor Miller Arrived

On February 24th I went to Rosental to make wooden sandals for some members of our family. This turned out to be a real happy day for all of us because the message reached us that professor Miller had actually arrived and now we would get bread to eat. Katie, at that time four years old, would always sing, "Only trust Him, only trust him", and along with this song she would pray, "Saviour, bring us one 'kul' of flour." One "kul" in our weight would be 180 pounds, and we had to laugh that she had the courage to pray for that much help. Later this materialized when the food drafts from Canada and from the U.S.A. arrived.

There also came a good message through our neighbor Peter Berg in regard to emigration. We all had been waiting for a more definite message in this matter and it seemed there was now more hope that we eventually would be able to emigrate to Canada. Along with this message also came the unpleasant reminder to pay taxes for our horses, etc. Because I was a minister and teacher I was supposed to pay three times as much as the ordinary farmer would pay. I was not supposed to have a horse.

About this time we had a faculty meeting of the Central School and I was informed that from now on I would no longer be a teacher. Other teachers received a similar notification. Under the new rules no person who held any office in the church could also be a teacher. At this time I went over to professor Miller and received from him some information regarding emigration and about some other matters.

Our churches also had to register and present to the government their constitution which was the first indication that the government would interfere with the freedom of religion.

Our Son Gerhard Born

March 1st, 1922. Truda was restless during the night and at 4 o'clock in the morning we on our wooden sandals had to walk to the hospital. It was not cold outside but our heads were filled with all kinds of thoughts and emotions as we walked. Preparations had been made for us, and Truda was accepted as a patient. At 10:00 a.m. our son Gerhard was born. We, of course, were very happy to have another healthy child, but at the same time the danger and the fear of dying from hunger was still hanging over all of us. As there was a free bed in the same room I asked the doctor and was granted permission to stay with Truda overnight in order to be of some help to her. At home I fixed the baby buggy to have it ready when our little son Gerhard would come home from the hospital along with Truda.

On Sunday in the congregation there was a general feeling of sadness, hunger and hopelessness. Bread was needed very badly. Though this was the first Sunday of the month we did not have the Lord's Supper as we usually did.

On Monday I was supposed to bring Truda home from the hospital, but we had absolutely nothing to eat in the house and I did not know what to do. I was able to trade nine pounds of homemade soap for two pounds of flour. Later in the day I was able to buy ten pounds of rye flour at the E.P.O. store (a Co-op). So there was some hope. About noontime I brought Truda home, using my little horse Siskin Tshishik and our little two-wheel buggy. So the family was together again.

But there was no time to rest. In the afternoon I walked to Einlage, about five miles, and from there took the train to Alexandrovsk, just for one purpose, to sell four pounds of butter which the next morning brought me 220,000 rubles a pound. I also obtained, from an office, the money for the teachers' monthly salary. I wondered why they trusted me with all that money but no questions were asked and I brought it to the teachers. Our little son Gerhard was developing very nicely, but Truda got sick with fever and I myself developed a bad cold. Many people at this time were dying from hunger.

We received notification that there were several food drafts which had arrived for us, but they were in the city of Ekaterinoslav about fifty miles distant from Chortitza. How would we get those food drafts?

I am thinking back to the time when Truda was in the hospital. She was there five days under very adverse conditions. There was not enough food. There was no real service for the sick. Every morning she would receive her share of bread, just a piece of rye bread, and at noon some soup or whatever, but of very little real food value. Every morning I would take her some milk from home, and when I saw her pale as she was and weak, I felt sorry that we could not provide better for her. At the same time she would look at me and ask, "Have you eaten this morning?" What should I say?

I do not remember what provisions were made for the laundry but we remember that one morning all the diapers were stolen and when Truda with the baby Gerhard arrived back home, they came minus the diapers.

About this time Truda got quite sick. She had boils and was coughing. One day both of us went to see the doctor, who happened to be Dr. Theodore Hottmann who later was tortured to death in a most cruel way by the communists. I, too, had boils from my waist down. After he had examined us he told us that he could not prescribe any medicine for us, but that we needed better food.

Carloads of American Food

Like wildfire, the message went through our village. The American food had arrived at the railroad station. This was March 13, 1922. In my diary I find these words written, "Hooray! Three carloads of American food at the railroad station." Many of us went to see these railroad cars.

When they opened them and we could see the products sent to us from across the sea we rejoiced in our hearts, and when I came home and told my family what my eyes had seen we resolved that we would never forget this day, but we would remember it as a memorial of our being saved from death by hunger; we saw tangible evidence of this fact. For supper we drank our "prips" and ate a piece of what we at that time called bread. We all seemed to be in a happy mood and the question was asked, "Where will we be next year?"

We received a letter from Truda's parents in the Molotshnaia that they too were without bread.

The following day we had a wonderful prayer meeting with many praises and thanks expressed because of the help sent from abroad.

March 16th was the first day we received some food from the American soup kitchen. It was somewhat cold and we had to stand in line for quite a time to get our share of about one-third of a pound of white bread and a dish of soup. It was hard to stand there in line for a long period of time, but we were happy and thankful to God for this help.

Trip After Food Drafts

On Monday, March 20th my brother John and I started out on a fifty mile trip to Ekaterinoslav to get food drafts for us and for other people of our village. John had one horse and other people provided two horses, so we had a team of three horses for this strenuous and dangerous trip. The first day we made about twenty miles to Hochfeld. Here we stopped and stayed overnight in the home of pastor Bernhard D. Dyck, a brother of the well-known Arnold Dyck.

Brother Dyck had his own feed mill where whole wheat, rye and barley flour were made. He also made flour from the seed of the Russian thistle.

Have you ever seen Russian thistles? Have you threshed out or beat out the branches of this weed and then seen the little black seed that comes out of it? There is some food value in this seed. It was also put through the feed mill by brother Dyck and then mixed with the other flour used for baking rolls or bread, which appeared somewhat dark in color but tasted very good.

In the evening we had a service in the church and I was asked to bring the message. The following morning we got up quite early and at half past five we drove on from Hochfeld to Ekaterinoslav. We reached this city at about 1:00 p.m. There at the A.R.A. (American Relief Administration) we received the food drafts. In the evening it began to rain. We stayed overnight at Peter Isaac Dyck's place. I also visited Mrs. Julius (Helena) Bergmann and her family who were my former pupils. They all were suffering from hunger, too.

The next morning we started on our way back. The roads were very muddy and we had quite a load of food drafts. When we reached the bridge at the Sura River we met pastor Peter Fast from Einlage, who was stuck there on the road with his truck full of food drafts. According to my diary he had twenty-six food drafts at a little better than one-hundred pounds each. From here we drove on but we could not reach Hochfeld. It was raining. We could not sit on the wagon because it was too heavy for the horses, so we mostly walked beside it. With my wooden sandals it was very uncomfortable. My feet were wet and my left foot hurt very badly. My toes were sore and it became pitch dark. We could not move on.

We pulled the horses a little to the side of the road and stopped. The wind was blowing. The horses were hungry but we had no feed for them except a little bit of straw. We tried to give this straw to the horses but we had to hold the straw in our hands or else the wind would blow it away. So the horses, all harnessed and hitched to the wagon stood there all night. We crawled into the wagon and covered ourselves and the food drafts against the rain. We were always looking out for the stars, watching for the morning star to appear, because we had no watches with us. It was getting colder. We noticed how the blankets that covered us were getting stiff from the frost.

At about four o'clock in the morning I took the reigns and started driving towards Hochfeld again. I will never forget this night. Quietly I was humming the song, "Nearer, my God, to Thee, nearer to Thee . . ." We both were very cold and it began to rain again and at the same time it was freezing. As time went by, just before the sun broke over the horizon, we recognized the place and saw that we were close to the road that turned to

Hochfeld. We said, "Praise God, we soon will be there."

But it was here that brother John's bay horse gave out and could not pull anymore; the other two were not too strong either. So we had to stop there once again. It was about three and one-half miles from Hochfeld, so we had to make a quick decision. I, as the younger one of the two, unhitched one of the horses and rode bareback the remaining distance to Hochfeld.

I will never forget how we were received there. When they saw me sitting there on horseback, stiff and hardly able to move, they lifted me from the horse and took me into the house. Sister Mrs. Dyck washed my feet in very warm water. They gave me hot tea to drink and something to eat. After this they put me to bed, covering me with all they had to make me feel comfortable and warm. In the meantime another man, D. Pauls, with a team of horses and a friend drove out to bring my brother John and the load of food drafts to Hochfeld. This was real Christianity in action. I shudder even today to think of the danger we were in. So many of our men had died on the road. When somebody discovered that there were men with food, they often murdered them and all their possessions would go to someone else. We had been in this danger all night, but now we had a pleasant visit with our dear Christian friends.

The next morning (Friday) there was a slight frost and the roads were somewhat better. We started out at 7:00 a.m. from Hochfeld to Chortitza. We stopped at one place to feed the horses and reached our destination at 4:00 p.m. Our children were jubilant over the supply of flour, bacon, tea, and evaporated milk. We could never find out why those Americans sent us so much tea—about three pounds in one package. We had to take back the horses to their owners and the food drafts to their respective recipients, one of them being pastor and teacher Peter John Penner. Others were teachers Dietrich H. Epp, Jacob John Epp, and widow Julius von Kampen. You might guess what we had for our noon meal the next day, white dumplings made from American flour. From the American soup kitchen that day we received cocoa, so we had a very delicious meal and our children said, "Now at last we can eat to our hearts' content." We were very grateful when we sang, "God is Love" (Gott ist die Liebe), thinking about our Canadian and American friends who had made this possible.

The following week I got sick from all the strain of the previous week, but we did not mind being sick because we now had hope for life. The same evening I went along with some brethren from Schoeneberg and walked back ten miles to serve at a meeting.

Thanksgiving Service

On Sunday afternoon of April 2nd there was a big Thanksgiving service at the Mennonite Church for the help we had received from America, and also Canada.

A wave of thievery was spreading over our villages. It seemed that hunger and other hardships we experienced were the causes of all kinds of lawlessness. Owners of cows had to watch the barn, otherwise in many places the cows disappeared in the night.

About this time we moved from my cousin Helen Braun's place to her sister's, Mrs. A. Wiebe. There we had four cows in one barn, which meant that I had to watch every fourth night.

May 1st was a great holiday. It was Revolutionary Day, a great celebration for the communists and their victory. There were parades, speeches and music.

On May 7th we had a conference at the volost and I was appointed the technical worker for products taxes. I had to figure out the tax on products for each resident.

The corn and beans we had planted were coming up, but as soon as a plant would come to the surface the gophers would do their destructive work. So many of us, even on Sunday, instead of going to church had to be in the fields to chase gophers.

One of our men in town had to straighten out a boy of seventeen. The reason: theft. How he straightened him out I cannot tell you. But this was a time when more radical means were being employed.

A note in my diary says, "Many Mennonites are occupied with thievery, women and girls included. Strict measures and merciless punishment have been advised by the government, either to beat them up or even kill them if necessary to stop the stealing."

In one of our villages in the South (I will not mention its name, though I have everything fresh in my memory) there is a well respected family. One day an opportunity presented itself when the machine shed door was open and the neighbor's pig came running in. This was a chance for these people, or so they thought, to get some meat. They butchered the pig, very secretly, of course, and hid everything so nobody would find out about it. When the owner of the pig noticed that his pig was gone he began to search for it and all the indications were that his own neighbor, a Mennonite, had stolen the pig, only the owner could not produce any proof.

At this time the authorities at various places had arranged for a correction committee to operate in the villages with the main idea of fighting thievery. I have been in touch with some of these men. They were instructed to interrogate the suspects and, in case the suspect would not confess his crime, were to beat him. In the case of the stolen pig, the suspects were brought before the assembly at the village head office. They were asked to confess but both husband and wife denied their guilt time and again. They were warned that they would have to face the correction committee, which we called only the "pruegel" committee, or the spanking committee, but they still denied any connections in the loss of the pig. I have all the details of what happened next, but the picture is too unestethic. They had to undress down to their underwear and then the beating started . . . Only then did they confess and the meat of the butchered pig was produced.

In another Mennonite village, about seven miles distant, lived a young man, Peter G., whom I knew very well. In his younger years he became an orphan and, according to our Mennonite rules, two guardians were appointed for him, my father being one of them. When he married he loved to come over to our place and visit. But when hunger was so prevalent, Peter somehow had taken something that did not belong to him. I am deeply sorry about this story. When Peter fell into the hands of the correction committee they beat him so severely that he died. These are very dark and sad events in our Mennonite history, where Mennonites would beat other Mennonites to death.

On Monday, May 15th, Benjamin B. Janz arrived in Chortitza and we had a meeting in our school about emigration. We were very happy to have him with us.

The following day we received notification that more food drafts had been sent to us, but at this time I was getting weaker day by day and could hardly walk a mile. The struggle against hunger continued. In our family only my wife and children would get a limited amount of food through the American soup kitchen. There was not enough food for men, so only women and children were getting this food assistance.

Representatives from Sagradovka who were sent to Alexandrovsk came back with the message that for the time being they could get no help from the American Relief Administration. Very discouraged, these men went back to Sagradovka.

I was supposed to work in the field to plow and to seed millet, but I was so weak I could hardly walk.

One day I was called by a representative of our village, Jacob M. Dyck, to discuss with him matters of emigration and how to arrange some of the details of emigration to Canada.

Ascension Day is always on a Thursday. I got up about 2:30 a.m. and although I had eaten almost nothing, I along with our deacon Cornelius Friesen walked to Schoeneberg, about ten miles south. We had another younger deacon by the name of Jacob Funk. I will never forget how C. Friesen and I each had a cake or two of waffles baked from corn meal and how we ate while walking the ten miles to Schoeneberg. As soon as we were outside the limits of our village, we took off our wooden sandals and walked barefoot the rest of the way.

When we arrived at Schoeneberg some of the men met us and said, "Hurry, because the people are gathering and it is time to start the service." We asked the ladies to give us a basin with water to wash our feet before we went to church. After we had done this we went to the church and preached there. We also had a baptismal service for seven people that were uniting with the church, and along with this was the Lord's Supper.

At the Lord's Supper, as the bread was passed (and there were pieces of nice white bread, some larger and some smaller pieces) I was tempted to take the biggest piece to satisfy my physical hunger. When I noticed this I silently asked the Lord to forgive me, because I was hungry.

After the services we all were served a meal of soup with potatoes and rye bread; how good this tasted! Then we were ready to walk back home. They gave us each half a loaf of bread to take along home. During the recess the conversation among the members present was mostly about the emigration to Canada.

I wonder today why the people in Schoeneberg let us walk the stretch of ten miles for the second time that day, not thinking about how tired we were. Some of them had good horses and could have taken us home in a wagon. But we walked the same distance once more that day, and I do not remember that we ever complained about this matter. We were accustomed to it.

About this time we received a letter from my cousin John Schroeder, near Steinbach, Manitoba, strongly advising us not to come to Canada because the conditions in Canada were not good. The main objection seemed to be to the fact that they now were forced to learn the English language, and many of the older Mennonites preferred to emigrate to South America or to Mexico rather than to learn the English language.

I well remember what I wrote in reply to my cousin in Canada, who in many ways had helped us and to whom we were very thankful. But I wrote to him, "We do not intend to stay in Russia. If it is impossible for us to leave Russia and emigrate to Canada we prefer to die. Please do not send us anymore food drafts. We prefer to die rather than stay in Russia . . . if we cannot move to Canada." What effect my letter may have had on our relatives in Canada I do not know, but I know the effect cousin John's letter had on all of us and especially on my old mother and on my sisters. Their names were on our passports with the privilege of emigrating to Canada as credit passengers, without paying one dollar for the trip. However, my mother and sisters decided not to emigrate to Canada, and they stayed in Russia for another three years. This was a very difficult problem for us to face because we saw the dangers of continuing to live in Russia.

CHAPTER 17

Summer 1922

At this time we still conducted our services in Rosental, Chortitza, Schoeneberg, Hochfeld, and other places. You would be surprised if I told you all the details of our walking tours to many places such as Hochfeld, twenty miles away. That always took special strength, to walk the twelve miles to Alexandrovsk just to bring the message of salvation to some hungry people. We at this time experienced the sustaining power of God both physically and mentally. But there were days when we would get so weak that we thought we just could not do any work anymore.

We needed money to pay the 110,000 rubles for one person to register for emigration to Canada.

This was still the time of suffering from hunger; the new crop could not be reached yet and many were still dying. On June 1st I drove to Alexandrovsk with my little horse "Siskin" (Tshishik in Russian) and there sold our best set of dinnerware and other things we had treasured, which we decided we could not keep any longer. The food we received from the American soup kitchen was not enough. I sold this dinnerware and a few other items for 15,000,000 rubles. There also was a food draft for us, and I was able to buy some flour and beans. In my diary I wrote, "What a wonderful God." But when I came home I was all tired out, hungry, and with a pain in my left leg.

The next day I had to spend in bed, sick with a fever from the cholera injection. As the disease of cholera spread we all had to have the injection. People were dying from cholera. The elder pastor Perk of the Seventh Day Church in Alexandrovsk died of it. Also, the hospital attendant Tichon, died of cholera. More people were getting sick with the disease and we all were quite apprehensive about this danger.

Pentecost, June 4th, 5th, and 6th were three days of celebration in our churches and in our homes but with hungry, empty stomachs evidenced once more. There was a special meeting on Sunday afternoon at the Mennonite Church with guest speakers. Our main attention was directed to the lack of food, starvation, cannibalism, and stealing. In our particular church we used the time to admonish the members to help one another, to live an honest life, and to trust in God. The third day of Pentecost we had a baptismal service at the Dniepr River and the subsequent Lord's Supper in the church where the new members received the hand of fellowship.

No matter how dark the horizon seemed to be, some of our young people planned to be married. When later we came to Canada we heard this expression, "He or she fell in love." We could not quite understand why they would *fall* in love; why could not people just love and not fall. But we found out that this was an idiom of the English language. There were two young couples, Peter J. Funk and his bride-to-be, Tina Knelsen, whose names we have mentioned before, and also the son of my cousin, Peter P. Wiebe and his fiancee, Louise Loewen.

Some of the young men were drafted into the army and they had to march. One day when there was a period when the boys were permitted to stand at ease, one of them asked the officer what year it was. The officer's reply was, "Everybody knows that this is the year 1922. Are you that foolish not to know this?" "Oh, yes," said the young man, "I know that this is 1922 but since when is it counted 1922?" Here the officer began to swear and with a very angry voice he said, "It is from the birth of Jesus Christ." The Communists cannot deny this fact, and it is quite interesting to know that every Russian, when it comes to the name of the first day of the week—Sunday—will say, Voskresenie, i.e., Resurrection. We like this name for Sunday: Resurrection. And even atheists all over the world, speaking Russian, use this name.

Suicide

There were reported several cases of suicide, but these were not real suicides. The head of a cow was placed on a post at the edge of our village along with the following "suicide" note, "It does not pay to live any longer. Before the communists came to power I received plenty of hay and grain, but now the only feed I get is dry straw and my boss is never satisfied with the amount of milk I give, since he says he must deliver so much milk as a tax to the Soviet government."

At another place a dead chicken was hanging on the fence. The "suicide" note in this case stated that it could not satisfy the boss, who maintained that he had to pay so much tax for each chicken. "He hardly gives me anything to eat but makes demands for more eggs, so I had no longer any choice but to commit suicide."

We all knew what this meant and woe unto the person or persons who had done this. If somebody had learned the name of the actual writer of these notes it would have gone very badly for him. Life became more and more difficult under the communist government.

Our Trip to the Molotshnaia-Rueckenau

For a long time we had had a desire to visit Truda's parents and relatives in the Molotshnaia. But this meant a trip of about two-hundred-fifty miles under all kinds of difficult conditions. Besides our four children, there was a lady, Mrs. Sudermann, whose home was in the Molotshnaia; she asked us to take her along. Also my cousin David Klassen, who was a school teacher, had a special attraction in Rueckenau, which was Mika Peters, Truda's sister. Before we left on the trip we had to get a certificate from the American soup kitchen in order to get some food during our stay in Rueckenau. And how could we make this trip with our little horse "Siskin" doing all the pulling? I borrowed a small wagon from my cousin Abram Klassen. We had to take some feed for the horse along in the form of hay, stuffed in sacks, which would serve us as seats for the time being. We had very little grain such as oats or barley to take along as feed for the horse, but where there is a will there is a way.

On Wednesday, July 26th we prepared everything and the following day about 2:00 a.m. we started on this long and difficult trip—four adults and four children. We could hardly go any faster than two to three miles an hour. For the night we stopped at the village Yanchikrak. We slept outside somehow and the next morning we started out again very early. We stopped for two hours at Lugovoy where I had an old friend, djied (meaning "old man") Tshuprina. We had to feed the horse and we had to eat a little, too. From here we proceeded southward through some German villages—Gruental to Andreburg to Prishib to Halbstadt. At Halbstadt we stopped at uncle Henry Loewen's place. Uncle Henry Loewen had been Truda's teacher, also giving her lessons in music (the organ). We had a very cordial invitation to stay overnight, which we did.

It was a sad picture to behold the fields in the Prishib area. Although they had very fertile soil in this district the fields looked neglected without any good crops, only a few patches of corn and a few sunflowers remained.

The following morning we left from the Loewen's place at 7:00 a.m. and started on our last stretch to Rueckenau, where we arrived around noontime. David and I very seldom sat on the wagon but mostly walked alongside. Only at very exceptional places did we sit during this long trip. The harvest had already started and at places we would get a little more food for ourselves, and also some feed for the horse.

David had left us in Halbstadt to visit somebody in that vicinity and he came to Rueckenau about an hour later. He had a special aim and purpose for making this trip and he did not wait long to make this known to Mika's parents, i.e., asking them for permission to marry their daughter.

These matters were not done in a hurry in our families at that time. It was already evening when he received the positive answer to his most cherished desire. This was Saturday, July 29th. The following day we naturally attended church services and in the evening we had the celebration of the engagement of David Klassen and Mika Peters. I was asked to deliver a short message which I did, using Psalm 85:11 as the text for the sermon. It was a very pleasant family evening with Mika's sister, Susie, leading in prayer.

During our visit in Rueckenau I was offered a teaching position at the Alexanderkrone Central School, but I did not have any interest to bind myself to anything in Russia anymore. Our aim and our interest were to emigrate to Canada.

Also, I had an occasion to visit elder pastor Sudermann from Bedjansk, and many others such as pastor Jacob W. Reimer who later married Truda's sister, Greta Rempel. Among many of these people we found quite a few who doubted that our emigration to Canada would materialize.

We also visited Truda's gradma Toews in Gnadenfeld and her aunts Tina and Susanna along with uncle Peter. We did not know at this time that this was our last opportunity to see uncle Peter and Truda's brother Hans, who both died that same year. And how important to read in my diary how uncle Peter, during our visit there, gave his personal testimony about Jesus Christ as his personal Saviour.

We, at this time, could drink American tea with American sugar, and we also went to Halbstadt to get the food drafts that had arrived for our parents, from Canada.

In the afternoon we had a very welcome visitor in the person of our former neighbor from Schoenfeld, John Warkentin, who also was suffering from hunger and was trying to find something to eat. Some of the former residents of the Schoenfeld area were traveling back and forth from Molotshnaia to Schoenfeld to find something to eat.

On Sunday, August 6th, there was a special memorial service in the church for the deceased pastor and evangelist Adolf Reimer. In the afternoon of the same day we started on our way back home, but this time we took a different route. We had heard about the conversions among the maknovtzy in our Schoenfeld area so we decided to make a little longer trip in order to visit these dear friends in Christ. Uncle Peter went along and also Truda's brother, Gerhard, who would go with us only as far as Schoenfeld. While stopping at Blumental we were told that one-hundred-eight people had died from hunger in this village.

We drove to the city Orechovo and from there to the village Buriakovo. Here we stayed overnight with a certain dear Christian friend by the name of F. Korchovoy, who told us quite a bit about the spiritual movement among the Russian peasants in this district. We were full of expectation of what we would find in the village of Lubimovka.

Our First Visit with the Converted Makhnovtsy

The next morning at four o'clock we started on our way to Lubimovka where we arrived at 8:50 a.m. What emotions filled our hearts when we came into the village which was full of anarchists, with a small group of believers—Baptists. They had started a church and quite a number of these men had formerly belonged to the army of Makhno.

We stopped at a distance from Michael P.'s house. They were in the process of threshing their small crop with a rolling stone. A person must see this in order to understand it. Two horses were pulling a sizable stone, which was attached to an axle, rolling over the grain.

I took our small son Gerhard who was now five months old, in my arms and asked the rest of our people to remain in the wagon. With my little son in my arms I walked up into the yard of Michael P. He was not alone—others were helping and when they saw a man coming, carrying a baby in his arms they wondered what this could mean. When they recognized me, they were jubilant. They threw their tools down and stopped threshing, put their horses in the barn, and then they began to embrace and to kiss us, as only Russians know how.

One man by the name of Gregory K., whom I had led to believe in the Lord Jesus Christ one day while he was sitting on the shore fishing, along with his son was on the way to the field to bring home a load of sheaves. When he saw us he stopped his wagon, jumped over the fence and told his son, "Drive on and do what you want." We sat down right there near the house on the "prizba," a clay bench, and began to visit.

There was great joy in meeting each other again. All the passengers from my wagon were taken into the house.

They would not let me go through Lubimovka without a service. Their pastor was Vasily I. Shachovtzov, and that evening we had a nice service in spite of the fact that it was threshing time. Many came to hear the former teacher from Schoenfeld deliver the message from Revelation 20:15, "Written in Heaven." What a joy it was to see these former bandits who were now servants of Jesus Christ! You could see and feel how they were full of love for one another and for all men. What they lacked was a deeper understanding of the Holy Scriptures and the singing was not too well organized, either. They were now children of God and no longer in the army of Makhno. They really treated us as best they could. We had plenty to eat and even our children told us how glad they were to experience the extreme friendliness of these people.

The next day, August 9th, Truda's brother, Gerhard, Uncle Peter, and I went to see the teacher, V.A. Pivovarov. We talked about the school property they had taken from Schoenfeld and the many items they had taken not only from our school but also from our parents, the B.J. Peters. It was really a heart-breaking experience to see all these buildings, taken apart and brick by brick—along with many other things—moved over to Lubimovka where they built a nice public hall with the materials taken from Schoenfeld. They expressed a willingness to pay something for all the things they had taken, including the things taken from the Peters' property. This made us happy because now our parents would get enough to live through the next winter. But this never happened. They never paid anything for all the things they had taken.

After eating a good meal at the Michael P.'s we were ready to depart, but before we left Mike asked me if I had a sack; they were going to give us some of the newly thrashed rye. When I gave Michael our sack he lifted it up and laughing heartily said, "Look, brethren, this is the kind of sack Yegor Petrovich has. This is a real pope sack." (mishok popivsky). When the priest, whom they often called pope, would visit the various places he carried with him a big sack in which to put the things people gave him.

The next place we intended to visit was Zalivnoje, then the road would lead us through Schoenfeld. This was the first time we had seen our dear home village since departing from it. Many of the buildings had been demolished, the orchards destroyed, the school and many other buildings destroyed. The vines on the property of our parents, instead of growing along the walls which were no longer there, were falling into the basement, and all the nice apple trees and the other trees were gone. With very mixed emotions we left the place, and from the hill I once more looked back at Schoenfeld and said, "Good bye, good bye my dear Schoenfeld." There would never be a trip back to Schoenfeld to live.

In Zalivnoje or Brasol, we wanted to see Trifon P. He was also a former bandit and a very dangerous one, but now was a real follower of Christ. While entering the village, driving very slowly with our little horse Siskin, we saw the former chief of police, who was called Uriadnik, Ivan I. Zubkov. We stopped. We were in such dresses and suits that he did not recognize us. Then we began to talk and he told us that there were saints in the village now, meaning the newly converted bandits. "Yes", I said, "we have heard about them and we are very glad." "And I am against them," he said. I said, "Ivan Ismailovich, I fully understand you but this can only be comprehended by people who have had the same experience. You will never understand this until you come to the Lord Jesus Christ." He may have had faith in the Russian Orthodox Church but not faith in the Lord Jesus Christ. What happened to him later, I do not know.

Trifon's Conversion

At Trifon's place we must visualize a big tree in the middle of the yard. It was a warm evening, Trifon's wife greeted us very friendly and called us brother and sister in Christ. "I am sorry Trifon is not home but I will run and call him. He will be very glad to see you." While she went to call Trifon we were waiting under the shade of the big tree. Our horse Siskin was happy to have a nice place to rest for a while.

It did not take very long before Trifon arrived. He shook hands with us, looked us straight in the eye, and with a somewhat lisping voice called me "brat" (brother-Russian). Then he asked me, "Can you believe that God can change one of the roughest sinners and make him a child of God?" "Of course," I told him, "I believe this and it is also verified in the Bible." Then he embraced me and kissed me. The horse was put into the barn where he received his supper.

We sat outside near the house, while Trifon's wife was busy preparing supper for us, with all the good things she could put on the table. In one corner of the yard they had a dugout cellar, where she stored the milk, cream, eggs, etc. It seems to me I still can see her literally running to this cellar and coming back with the nice things to eat. They also had a samovar (tea urn) which would soon produce for us the nice Russian tea. The table was set outside the house under the shade of a tree. But before starting to eat, we all arose from our seats, and Trifon began to pray. This made a very deep impression on me. Only about two years ago he was one of the roughest bandits out of whose mouth swearing and all kinds of dirty words could be heard. Now he was a dedicated child of God. We had dealt with him so many times before and then had heard about his miraculous conversion, but now we wanted to hear the story of his conversion from him personally. This is what he told us.

It was in the summer of 1921 when the communists were tracing and destroying all the opposing elements in the country. Zalivnoje, Lubimovka and other places were known as centers of the anarchists. So one day the village Zalivnoje was surrounded by soldiers of the Red Army, and all men known to have been in the army of Makhno were taken and shot to death without any further trials. It did not take long until Trifon was caught and placed in a wagon with several communist soldiers who drove out into the field to shoot him. How often Trifon himself had participated in acts of brutality, but now he was the victim.

I asked him, "What did you think and what did you do?" He told me how he thought about his whole life; also he had been thinking about sister Kuklenko. Mrs. Kuklenko, a Russian Baptist had often told him, "Trifon, Trifon, watch out what you are doing. You are sinning against God and God will not let you go on. He will punish you."

At this Trifon always would answer, "What kind of a God?—there is no God." Now he was to be executed and, while he was thinking about sister Kuklenko he began to pray. "What did you pray and to whom did you pray, since you did not believe in God?", I asked him.

"Yes, I actually was praying, but not audibly. I did not want these communist soldiers to hear and to know what I was doing", Trifon answered.

"What were the words of your prayer?" I asked.

To this he answered, "I prayed this prayer: God [in Russian 'Bog'], if Thou art, Thou knowest I never have believed in Thee, but if Thou really art, reveal Thyself to me today, right now, and if it be Thy will, save my life and I promise from now on I will serve only Thee." So with this sentence he jumped from the wagon into a corn field. He was always fast on his feet. He zigzagged because the soldiers were shooting at him, and somehow by the miracle and providence of God he escaped. He told me how the rest of the day he spent in the grain field; it was hot and he was thirsty. He rubbed some of the ears of grain and slowly chewed on it, but he was thirsty. There, hiding in the field of grain, he continued to pray and waited for darkness.

Then he began to slowly crawl back to the village. He did not dare to walk, but crawling on hands and feet he came closer, not to his home because he was afraid the soldiers might be waiting for him, but to sister

Kuklenko's house. He knocked at the window and a voice from inside replied: "Kto tam? Who is there?" "This is me—Trifon." "What do you want?", he was asked. He asked her to open the door. When sister Kuklenko opened the door he fell on his knees right there in the house and exclaimed, "Sister, there is a God."

They prayed together and Trifon lived a number of years after this. After hearing this wonderful testimony, which I also call a miracle of grace, we were getting ready to drive another two or three miles to the next Lutheran village, Kankrin Number Five.

Number Five Kankrin was the village where father B.J. Peters hid at the home of the Wansiedlers. Uncle Peter and Truda's brother, Gerhard, were still with us. It must be mentioned that wherever we went all these Russian Christians almost begged us to come again and to give them more instructions in the Bible. In village Number Five Kankrin we tried to find a place to stay overnight, even to sleep someplace on the hay, but the wealthier farmers would refuse us. They were very unfriendly in some places. So we had no alternative but to turn to the poorest, and Wansiedler was one of them.

The next morning at three o'clock we very slowly started out from this unfriendly village with our little horse. Uncle Peter and Gerhard went in a different direction, so from here on we were alone. We went through Kankrin Number Four to Kopanie and to the village Kirpotino to the home of our good friend Dmitry Esaulenko. He always had been very friendly toward us and now, too, he tried to make our stay there as pleasant as he could. They had a good crop that year and before our departure he put a sack of about ninety pounds of millet in our wagon as a present from he and his wife.

The Russians were known for their hospitality. At the next place, Stepnaja, a prairie village, it was reported that they had several cases of cholera so we did not stay too long, just long enough to eat a little and feed the horse.

At six o'clock in the evening we arrived in Alexandrovsk, and later went to the home of our friends, the Janzens at Schoenwiese to stay overnight. We were very glad that after traveling on that hot day we could find a place to rest. The family slept in the house but I slept outside near the wagon.

The next day, August 11th, Friday, at 4:00 a.m. we started on our last stretch of twelve miles homeward over the Dniepr river and through Einlage. The Lord made all things well and we praise His name for ever and ever. What rich experiences we gained on this trip and how this had strengthened our faith in God. This trip, too, was a miracle of grace. Everywhere it was only God's grace that led us in every mile we made.

Signs of Life

Our neighbors and friends were glad when we arrived back home. The crop was pretty good that year. The melons, the watermelons, the potatoes and vegetables were very good, and in the afternoon we brought a full load of watermelons home.

The following Sunday we had quite a few visitors and we enjoyed their fellowship. They all wanted to know about the details of our long and hazardous trip. In the afternoon we had a meeting in our high school to discuss matters pertaining to the new school year. Also we had a private meeting about emigration to Canada. I wrote a letter to our representative A. Friesen in America about certain points of our forthcoming emigration.

There was much work to be done and it seemed to pile up on Truda and me. I was supposed to visit some sick people, also some relatives, and my mother's sixty-seventh birthday was August 19th. There were meetings to be conducted in neighboring villages and this meant walking long distances. We had to dig out and bring home our rich crop of about 740 pounds of potatoes. What a wealth! Our millet had to be threshed, which was not much, but it all helped. From Schoeneberg I got eighteen pud (37 lbs. each) of barley. The previous spring I had provided some barley for seeding and one of the farmers there had planted it. This was of great help. We also had quite a bit of corn to harvest. Truda helped in this and I had to admire her, because she had never done this before. As a businessman's daughter, she had not done work like this. When husking the corn, our children were always happy when they found one of a different color.

One day David Klassen came to visit us. He now was ready to go back to Rueckenau to his fiancee Mika (Mary) Peters, and on August 26th they were married. Only a few days later, on August 29th, now happily married, they came to visit us. A second celebration of their marriage (Nachhochzeit, or afterwedding) was arranged at the home of David's parents.

On a Saturday at the beginning of September, deacon C. Friesen, his wife, and I drove to Hochfeld, with my horse Siskin, to participate at a wedding, and on Sunday a baptismal service. When we came home that same Sunday there was the wedding of Peter J. Funk and Tina Knelsen, whom we mentioned before.

There were more signs of life; in Kronstal it was arranged to have a big Mission Harvest Festival in a machine shed, which was nicely decorated. People from far and near had come for this happy occasion. Several choirs sang, also declamations were rendered and a special offering. At this occasion I asked those who still had some Russian spiritual litera- ture, including Bibles, to give them to me because I still intended to do some spiritual work among the former Makhnovtsy. As a result, I got several books and Bibles.

A Mission Harvest Festival was also observed in Schoeneberg the last Sunday of September, but the weather was cold and the enthusiasm was not evident on this occasion.

We received orders to clear from the fields all cornstalks and whatever was left in the fields, because the following week the American tractors would start to plow. This is quite an item in my diary because this was the great help which our Canadian and American brethren brought to us. These men also educated our farmers in the handling of the tractors. This was all very well-meant and arranged—too bad the communist govern- ment would take these very necessary things away from us.

There were also signs of life in the negative aspect. People were watching each other too closely in their eating, whether they ate more white bread, etc. So jealousy appeared at various places. They just showed their human side of life.

Two of our young men were drafted to serve the Soviet Government. One Sunday these two young men decided that they would not march on Sunday. So, on another Sunday, the whole line of new recruits was stopped by the Commander and these two, with three other young men who had joined them in this matter, were called to the front to face the Commander. You can imagine with what trembling hearts these five young men came out. The Commander evidently did not know what to call them, so he called them, "You Mennonite Baptists, you can go to church and worship God." The other recruits had to march, but these were permitted to go to church. This was quite a boost for our young men and for us when we heard about it.

The second Sunday of October we celebrated Mission Harvest Festival in Rosental. Many had come from neighboring villages and we enjoyed a sweet fellowship together. A special meal for all was prepared by the women, the famous Russian borshtsh, only without meat, as I have noted in my diary. Also a fruit soup called "mus" was prepared.

A letter arrived from our parents in Rueckenau, informing us about the sudden departure of dearly beloved uncle Peter P. Toews. He was such a genuine friend to all and everybody loved uncle Peter.

CHAPTER 18

The Desire To Emigrate

Emigration

There was more talk about emigration. A telegram was received in which the main question was: "Would the prospective emigrants be willing to make that trip from Russia to Canada via Libau, Latvia?" This would cost about one million rubles per person, and this question in the telegram seemed to bring us new hope for emigration.

There was a pastors conference in the Mennonite Church, with several outside speakers present. The main speaker was pastor A. Wilms from Fuerstenwerder, Molotshnaia. In the evening pastor Wilms spoke in our church. The main topic of discussion was, "The Spiritual, Moral and Religious Life of Our Young People and Children." It was decided that special services should be conducted in the various churches for young people and children. This was an effort, not by a small church group but by the combined Mennonite churches. This was definitely a step in the right direction, but we knew that soon all religious work with and for young people and children was prohibited by the government.

There were pastors from Zagradovka whom Truda invited for a dinner. They offered me a teaching position in their high school. I almost decided to accept that position, but after consultation with the local members of our church I decided to stay in Chortitza.

We were able to earn five million rubles. The American tractors needed somebody with a horse and a wagon to transport the fuel and other items, so Abe Harder, a young man from Chortitza, took our horse and wagon for one day and that brought me five million rubles. One pound of butter on the market was worth 1,800,000 rubles.

A telegram arrived. What could it mean? The representative of the Canadian Pacific Railroad Company had arrived in Moscow! The ships were ready as soon as the emigrants could get to Libau. That was October 26, 1922.

Up until the revolution, and even quite a long time after the revolution, we had our religious education in our schools. But now that was prohibited by the government, so the question, time and again, came up about having a sunday school in all our churches. Another disturbing factor for all of us was the fact that in our schools the influence of communist teaching was noticeable, especially in the singing of songs against God. This was also noticeable in our teachers seminary.

There was a court session against a number of our men who could not pay the products tax, because they just did not have the money. They were put into prison and would not be freed until they had paid it. For some of them it meant selling the last cow or horse.

November 7, 1922, a great celebration with speeches and singing was held to mark five years of Communist rule in Russia.

Our young deacon Jacob Funk and I walked to Schoenwiese. Here we conducted several meetings with the Lutheran brethren in private homes. The leader of this group was the blind brother Kaiser. A number of years ago a drunk man was passing by, and while brother Kaiser was looking out of the window the drunk smashed it with a vodka bottle. The glass splintered into brother Kaiser's eyes and he became totally blind.

About this time there were rumors that our emigration to Canada might start in a few weeks. We sold our piano to my good Jewish friend, David A. for 400,000,000 rubles. Quite a bit of money but it was not worth too much.

A Trip to Prijut

The two brethren, Abe and Jacob Neufeld from Prijut, were visiting in Rosental and they asked us if one would go along with them to conduct evangelistic services. The distance to Prijut was about seventy miles. I did not want to go along because I did not have the proper clothing for such a trip. But finally Matthew 6:33 persuaded me to first of all seek the Kingdom of God, so I agreed to go along. I did not have the proper clothing and only wooden sandals made by myself. For the night we stopped in Nikolaipol at the home of J. Dycks, a relative of the Neufelds. In the evening we had a service in Nikolaipol. Their assembly room looked very neglected and unattractive. At the Dycks' I borrowed an old patched-up pair of shoes which I would not want to put on my feet today, but at that time were better than my wooden sandals.

In Ekaterinoslav we visited the Jewish Christian missionary Peter Smoliar. Having studied in Germany he was supported by a British Mission Society. He gave me a new Bible, also a small woolen suit for our son Peter. This suit was from England.

Wednesday, November 22nd in the evening, we arrived at Peter Neufeld's home. They possessed a very nice, comfortable house, a barn full of cows, as my diary notes, "Ten cows and heifers, four horses, good clothing, and plenty to eat." This was so different from what we had in Chortitza.

When I went to see the pastor of the church, the house was full of tobacco smoke and at the beginning it seemed we would not get along, but I continued to invite him to participate at the meetings and finally he even invited me to preach in his church on Sunday morning. God works miracles. The services in the Neufeld home lasted until Sunday. We visited many places including the neighboring village of Wiesental.

On Monday the 27th of November they brought me to Kronsgarten, not too far from Ekaterinoslav where seven-and-a-half years ago I had served in the Red Cross Hospital. Here we conducted services in the local school; I visited many friends old and new, and on Wednesday, November 29th two young men by the name of Henry and Peter Bartel took me to Ekaterinoslav. In Kronsgarten at that time there were signs of relative prosperity, compared to Chortitza.

Again I visited the Jewish missionary, Peter Smoliar, and had dinner with them. Brother David Braun from Hochfeld was there to take me over to Hochfeld. On our way we had to stay overnight near the Sur River. We found a place to eat and to sleep, but some bad premonition was disturbing me that night. I had a nightmare. I did not know what it was, but later I found out that the same night my wife Truda and children had been in great danger, having been robbed by a young woman who had shown Truda a certificate that she was a member of the Baptist Church of Tomakovka, asking to stay overnight. I could tell you many details of this event.

On November 30th, Thursday, I was back in Hochfeld and once more visited with our congenial friends the Bernhard Dycks and with others, too. This dear brother later in the 1930's had to go to a slave labour camp where he perished, as well as my cousin Abram Klassen and millions of others. Communists want to set the world free and what they actually are doing is enslaving millions.

The following day Bernhard Dyck took me home to my family in Chortitza. It was about noontime when we arrived. I was so glad to be home again and to greet my family and it seemed to me I had a special greeting for our son Peter when I gave him the woolen suit from Ekaterinoslav, from missionary P. Smoliar. When I greeted him, this little son of mine began to cry, and my family was in tears. The children were sick. They had no winter clothing. It was a hard situation. When I went to the volost to report this to the authorities, they only smiled. They did not have much to say. Somebody told me that these men had already made remarks that this would teach Schroeder a lesson to stay home and not to travel around carrying the poison of religion to the people. So they were glad, I suppose, that this had happened to my family.

In the afternoon we had a conference at my cousin's, A. Klassen's place and these brethren tried to comfort me. But I already had found my comfort in God's Holy Word in Hebrews 10:34 where we find that the Hebrew Christians had taken the spoiling of their goods joyfully, knowing that they (and we with them) have in heaven a better and enduring substance. As a family we appreciated the concern of our brethren and sisters very much.

Pastors and Bible Conferences

More interest in religious matters and a real spiritual appetite seemed to be evident in most places. We had a Pastors Conference which started December 2nd and lasted over the weekend. The following weekend we had a Bible Conference with people coming from the neighboring villages, and pastor J. G. Tiessen from the Molotshnaia. Many realized that we had missed having these conferences and many were eager to get more spiritual food. Our dear teacher and pastor Peter J. Penner was sick with pneumonia at the time and we missed him very much.

On December 13th I caught a ride to the city of Alexandrovsk. With me on the wagon was also my good Jewish friend David A. The owner of the wagon had quite a load, and we had to sit in the back in uncomfortable positions; but we were satisfied to get this ride and it gave me an opportunity for about two hours to visit with David A. I tried to explain to him the coming events and especially the involvement of Israel in these coming events, because we strongly believe that there is still a great future for the Jewish nation. The main point of emphasis was the fact that all this glory would not come without Jesus Christ as the real Messiah and I asked him to accept Jesus as his Saviour. He took all of this with a friendly attitude but made no commitment.

The price of a pound of butter in the city now was 3,600,000.00 rubles.

The following week they had a Bible Conference in Einlage where I also participated. This gave me an opportunity to visit with my brother Peter and his family and to speak of spiritual matters.

After the Bible Conference I went to Schoenwise to the Headquarters of the American Mennonite Relief Administration and I was told that two Mennonite men had stolen some goods from the A.M.R.A. I felt sorry to hear this; the men were caught.

On my way back I again took some books from C. Janzen along, which were from the Raduga book center and destined to be destroyed. I gave these books to spiritually hungry people.

Friday, December 22nd there was a big celebration in the Chortitza Mennonite Church this being the birthday of their elder bishop, Isaak G. Dyck, who was our neighbor across the street and a dearly beloved man. This may seem to be a matter of little significance, but those who have gone through persecution in religious matters know what this means, just to gather in the church in honor of a dear servant of God. Later, the same church was taken away from its members and converted into something like a theater. There is no freedom of religion under a communist government.

A message arrived from Moscow that our emigration was postponed somewhat and was not expected to materialize before next spring.

Christmas, 1922

As the day of Christmas approached Truda was baking cookies, and I had to go to the drug store to buy ammonia and peppermint oil. These little entries in my diary cause me to think of how different it was now, being able to go and buy items which a year ago we would not even think about. Things had improved in certain matters. We even got a Christmas tree through some friends who brought it to us, and Truda fixed up old dolls and other things as gifts for our children for Christmas.

We had to pay a tuition fee for our seven year old daughter Margaret—154 pounds of millet—not money, because money was of very little value.

One of our young women came collecting things, mostly flour, to give presents to children in our Sunday School. Clothing was very badly needed, also meat and lard. The oil we had used to cook food, like mustard oil, had shown its bad effects on our bodies, especially on our kidneys.

Truda was busy almost day and night. She had to sew "new" dresses for our daughters from her old garments and my sister, Tina's. And how nice these dresses looked. Somewhere I was able to buy a dozen small candles for our Christmas tree for two-and-a-half million rubles.

On Christmas day our son Peter got up at 4:00 a.m. Margaret and Katie got up later, and it was a great joy to see them when they were permitted to enter the room where all their presents were neatly prepared. We all said this was beyond our asking and understanding. Our children also had to go to Mrs. Braun's, my cousin, and recite their Christmas wishes and receive some presents. David and Mika Klassen came from the other end of our village just to see how our children would react to all the joyous events.

A group of our church choir members came very early to sing under our window. This was a very effective custom we had in Russia, especially when singers would sing under the window of a sick person.

For meals we now had those nice German "Zwieback" baked from American or Canadian white flour. We also had that sweet fruit soup. One thing that was still missing was the bratwurst and cooked ham. For this we still had to wait. We had a wonderful time together in our home and at my mother's place in Rosental, where the children played happily together.

Christmas in Chortitza, 1922

In the evening there was a big Christmas celebration in the Chortitza Mennonite Church. This, too, was of great significance to us, because only two years ago the robbing, killing and destroying bandits had filled our villages and now again we could gather in the church, have a Christmas tree and sing. That old Mennonite Church was filled with people young and old to celebrate the coming of Christ to this earth at Bethlehem. After all these celebrations we went back home, tired and eager to rest after all the excitement.

Christmas was celebrated three days with services in the churches and elsewhere, if at all possible. We had our morning service in our assembly room and for the evening there was a special program with nice recitations, singing and a sermon. For the third day of Christmas as a family we went to my brother Peter's place in Einlage, where we conducted two services, and stayed overnight there. I went to visit some people in spiritual need and with many problems. Only in the evening of the fourth day did we arrive back home with our horse "Siskin" who had to help in this celebration.

New Year's, 1923

According to the new calendar it was already January 14th, but we celebrated New Year's according to the old calendar. There were the usual meetings in the churches. Outsiders would come for our Watchnight celebration which was mostly conducted with a love meal. On New Year's Day we also visited a number of sick people, and in the afternoon my brother, Peter, came with a number of people. He took my horse Siskin and drove to Burwalde, about five miles to our Mennonite Dr. Hildebrandt, who really was not a medical physician but was very efficient in setting bones and giving massages. There was hardly a Mennonite settlement in Russia without a doctor of this calibre.

A pound of butter now was worth five-and-a-half million rubles.

There was much work to be done and my health seemed to fail me. I had to spend several days in bed. At this time people from near and far came to help and to comfort us. Pastor Bernhard Dyck of Hochfeld brought me thirty-eight million rubles and twelve pounds of millet, which I was supposed to give to the "Bethany" sanatorium in Einlage.

About this time we received a letter from Truda's uncle, Gerhard Peters of Dinuba, California inviting us to come to California, and offering to rent his fruit farm to us. Just imagine what an offer for a person destitute, hungry, and without the proper clothing this was. This letter really cheered us up. There still was some hope!

About the end of February 1923, I went to Hochfeld to visit some people and to conduct special services. Here I was able to buy a pair of shoes for one-hundred million rubles. Just for the sake of comparison I want to mention that a pound of butter now was worth seven million rubles, which means that these shoes cost me a trifle less than fifteen pounds of butter. It gives one a strange feeling after about two years without shoes, to wear them again. The walking is so different and the feeling on the feet and the whole body is so different.

We had an invitation from the Mennonite Brethren Church in Nikolaipol to conduct services there. An interesting sidelight to these meetings was the fact that we had to bring our own wood to heat the place, also we brought our own kerosene to illuminate the room. We were glad to do this if only we could proclaim the glorious gospel.

Back in Hochfeld we met Mrs. Rempel from Kronsgarten whose husband two years ago was shot to death; the previous year her son had died, and now she had received the message that her daughter Mary, whom we had known quite well as a fine Christian girl, had vanished on her way to

Germany. She was a courageous girl and perhaps had decided that she was going to find a way out of Russia where she had suffered so much and for so long. The latest message that was received about her was that she had come close to the border and there somebody must have apprehended and killed her. No other message was received and we tried our best to comfort Mrs. Rempel, and we prayed with her.

While in Hochfeld we visited a number of people. Church members often have to be taught how to conduct themselves according to the general code of ethics and especially according to the code of Christian ethics. Some men were using quite rough language, others had to be admonished on how to behave in the presence of women; also in the relationship of husband and wife. This is a matter that is not pleasant to do but is much needed.

Two young men accepted Christ as their Saviour in one of the meetings in Hochfeld. We rejoiced with them in their salvation.

Before the next Sunday I was able to get a ride back home and it was fun to see the reaction in the family when I came home with shoes on my feet. Our children were eager to get a chance to untie and to pull the shoes off my feet and to brush them. There was almost a little quarreling among our children as to who would get this privilege. Of course, we did not have the nice shoe polish we have in Canada and in the U.S.A., but our children kept my shoes shining and it was a great event to have shoes again.

Plans for Emigration

During a trip to Alexandrovsk one day I had an opportunity to visit with pastor Peter Unruh from the U.S.A. Somehow I received the impression that the Americans (this is what is written in my diary) were trying to help us in material matters but they considered us inferior and were inclined to control us in all matters of life. It sounded like superiors dealing with inferiors. We did not like to have that kind of feeling. March 1st at 4:30 p.m. we had a meeting in a school house regarding citizens of Hollandish origin. I was elected moderator of this meeting.

I also went to the doctor for a medical examination for emigration to Canada. The physician checked me out as being in fairly good health.

Once more we received a letter from uncle Henry Schroeder in Saskatchewan, with the advice not to come to Canada. We did not care too much anymore what they wrote, because we no longer had much to lose. As a matter of fact, we already had started to sell pieces of furniture and other things, anticipating our emigration to Canada.

There was a meeting in our elementary school with a communist instructor by the name of Fischer, who came from Germany to give us instructions and directives in the new teaching methods. If we were not exactly to teach against God, then at least we were to teach without referring to God.

The following Sunday, March 11th there was a wedding of two members of our church; Peter P. Wiebe and Louise Loewen. Perhaps I should mention that Louise Loewen's mother was the proprietress of the place with the big famous oak tree, which is known historically and protected by the present government of the U.S.S.R.

Monday, March 12th I was called to pay for the emigration at Jacob Martin Dyck's. The amount was not too much, 24,500,000 rubles; also for the membership in the Union of Citizens of Hollandish Origin two million rubles. Now, it was a task for me to find all this money.

Two days later we had a meeting about emigration and this was quite a conglomeration of all kinds of people, all Mennonites of course, but the language some of them were using, it was a shame, to say the least. They were not ashamed to use such dirty language in the presence of women; it was such nonsense to listen to them, and they all intended to emigrate to Canada.

Again we received a letter from one of our Canadian relatives who invited us to come to Canada. Yes, they even promised that they would support us, "if we, according to our faith would join their church." Such an invitation did not attract us to Canada; we would emigrate to Canada anyway, but we would not join that particular church because their promise of helping us was offered under certain conditions, and that is not Christian.

About this time in Alexandrovsk at the A.M.R.A. office I received some clothing for myself, which was very badly needed. Also I had a friendly conversation with pastor Peter Unruh in religious matters.

The following three months were mostly occupied with a lot of walking back and forth to various places, to other villages, to Alexandrovsk, etc., just to buy and sell things, visiting people in spiritual matters, but mainly preparing for our emigration.

On Good Friday, April 6th we had our regular service at 2:00 p.m. Two Russian Baptists from the village of Sherebetz were our visitors. They had traveled quite a distance to buy some horses to prepare for the seeding season.

On Easter Sunday, April 8th as a family we drove to Einlage to my brother, Peter's, place. We had a service in Einlage. The choir sang but not very well, because they had no piano or organ, somebody had given them the pitch way too high, but they sang. Peter's wife, Lena, had prepared a good dinner and in the afternoon we all (both families including all the children) walked across the Dniepr river on the big bridge which is 147 feet above the water, to the east side of the river to the famous Taras Bulba cave. We all crawled into this cave. It was very interesting and a very pleasant day in Einlage. This was our last Easter in Russia.

For the second day of Easter brother Abram Klassen and I, with one of our church members, went to Hochfeld. We were received, but not very graciously, because we had not brought our choir along. What demands people can make! We had a service not only on Monday but on Tuesday also. The weather was excellent.

Thanksgiving Service in Nikolaipol

On Monday, April 9th we drove to Nikolaipol to participate in the afternoon celebration thanking God for bringing us through so much suffering and persecution, but especially through the time of hunger. There were three speakers on the program in the following order: first, the leading pastor of the church, elder Henry Epp brought a very good message; then myself, and as the third speaker, pastor Dietrich Rempel. Attendance was very good and the thanksgiving for bringing us through so many difficult situations seemed to come from the hearts of everybody.

The following day a meeting in the Chortitza Elementary school took place, where those who needed help were to register, because some help was expected to come from Holland. This was no hard task for us to perform because it seemed we all were willing to receive some help no matter where it came from.

At several places there were thefts of horses or cows, and many owners of horses and cows became very apprehensive.

The price of butter had now risen to eight million rubles per pound.

Two of our brethren visited the Neufelds at Prijut, and brought us a gift in money, one hundred million rubles. How handy such a fine amount of money would be at the right time! We had to make all kinds of payments and needed the money. Oh yes, the next day I went to the volost to pay taxes. Now, please note this: for the privilege of having a cow, we had to pay eleven million rubles and the following week I was supposed to pay another one hundred million rubles; for the horse eighty million rubles, and for myself twenty million rubles. So this was where our money went. My cousin Abram Klassen sent me eighty-five million rubles. All this money was now very badly needed.

CHAPTER 19

Our Final Days in Russia

The communist government appointed several men as hostages in case something went wrong with the government. These men were mostly considered the best, or the most honored and respected men. In this case they were, Peter Koop, Jakob M. Dyck, P. Klassen, Peter Penner, and Isaak Krahn. In case something went wrong, these men would be either put into prison or executed. Somewhere a thief had been caught and these five men were now responsible for watching him so he would not escape. It seemed a mockery, just to ridicule or to humiliate these men.

Trip to Lubimovka

One day in April, I walked to Alexandrovsk with the intention of catching a ride to Lubimovka. But there was no chance for me, so I had to walk the twelve miles back again. A week later when again I was in Alexandrovsk, I was able to get a ride with two men, William Schmidt and John Renner, who, for twenty million rubles, were willing to take me along to their Kankrin village number five. It began to rain but we made the trip without incident and arrived in Number Five quite early. I went to visit the Wansiedlers who appreciated my visit very much. I felt sorry for Mr. Wansiedler because he was a slave of tobacco. The Wansiedlers also showed me where Mrs. Gruenke lived. She was the widow of my former colleague, teacher Gruenke, and had since remarried; the name of her present husband was Reinhold Fuehrus. I was very glad that I could visit them, and Mrs. Fuehrus was of great help to me at this time, because she was able to give me a lot of very valuable information about life in this vicinity. They invited me to stay overnight, which I did. The following day I visited some sick people in this village and prayed with them.

Mrs. Fuehrus was willing to go with me to Zalivnoje which was a distance of only two to three miles, to visit my dear brother Trifon and his wife. Here I was received in a very friendly manner and I stayed overnight with them. In what miraculous way the Lord had saved him! People hardly could believe that he was the same man. The same evening we had a Bible study and prayer in his home.

Later, when we were living in Canada, in the 1930's, we received a letter that Trifon for his faith in God had been sent into slave labour, and there all these dear men perished. Not one of all those who were members of our Russian Baptist Church in this area is still alive. They all had to pay with their lives for their faith in Jesus Christ. The Soviet Government had no use for anyone who believed in the Lord Jesus Christ.

The next morning after breakfast I started out on my way to Lubimovka. With a bag of Bibles and other Christian literature on my back, I walked southward in the direction towards Schoenfeld. An elderly man was my companion for about two miles. Although I knew him and he had known me, he did not recognize me in the outfit I was wearing.

When I came closer to Schoenfeld I was eager to see what had transpired there. Almost everything was now demolished. Two men were at the walls of the main building of my beloved Central School. They had crowbars and other tools which they used to break off the bricks and put them into their wagon. Also, our church and many other buildings had been destroyed. Here Truda and I had been married and here we had experienced many blessings. Now everything was in ruins. There was the Neufeld-Rempel place. Some of the buildings were still standing and new residents were living there. I met one of these men and he was very inquisitive as to what I might know about the original and real owners of the houses. He said they were afraid that the proprietors might come back, and for this reason they would not build or make any other changes in the buildings. But they did, however. They tore down and built as though everything really belonged to them.

I also passed by the two farms of Nikolai Tiessen and Peter Tiessen who had been murdered. I could not help but feel sorry for all the things that had happened here.

From a distance I could see on the roofs in Lubimovka the material that had been taken from our houses and used to build the homes of strangers. I could stand this strain no longer. It was a warm day. The road was dusty. I threw myself on my knees and began to pray, "Oh Lord, fill my heart with Thy love for all these men and women, else I will not be able to accomplish a thing." I realized the nearness of God and the strength of my faith. As I walked into the village I could see from every angle some of the former bandits. But my destination was the house of Michael P. who also was a former bandit, but who always had revealed a milder character, and now he was a Christian. It was a miracle of grace, too, that both of them, he and his wife Zinovia, nee Evtushenko, now had only one zeal and goal, to serve the Lord. They loved us and we always loved them and only this way we could influence their lives.

Maria Evtushenko, Zinovia's mother, at the time when Truda and I were getting married in 1914, often had warned Truda, because she knew that occasionally I would have a glass of wine and even stronger drinks, because she had had bad experiences with Savely, her husband, in this matter of drinking. I appreciated this and never thought of her as some-body who tried to do something against me. By the grace of God my appetite for alcohol had vanished.

Michael and his brother-in-law, Peter P., were not home but I went into the house and it did not take too long before both of these men returned from the field where they had been working.

Baptismal Services in Lubimovka

What did I really find here in Lubimovka? I believe it was the provi-dence of God that I had come then and not earlier as I had planned. Here they had arranged for a baptismal service the next day, which was Sun-day, May 6th. The leading pastor of the village of Sherebetz, A.K. Drany, whom the people always called Presbyter, had come with a group of sing-ers and their choir director for this occasion. They all were very good sing-ers and I could not help but think about the roughest bandits that had come from this village of Sherebetz. They had now one common interest, the advancement of the Kingdom of God and the growth of the Church of Jesus Christ.

In the evening, Saturday night, we had a big meeting where presbyter A.K. Drany brought the evening message and where I also was asked to deliver a message. Here were many whom we could show the way of salva-tion, and many came and thanked God for the blessings. Several gave their testimonies in order to be baptized the following day. They were examined but only one of them was received into the church. Others had to wait because it was already midnight when we finally came to rest.

There was a light night frost, but no damage was done to the fruit. Thirteen souls were there to receive their Holy Baptism. There was a long period of examining the candidates, and I have the names in my diary. Outside in the yard were many wagons with the horses tied to them while nibbling the hay. Some had even come from the neighboring Lutheran village to participate in the services.

First, there was a general meeting in which everybody was permitted to participate, but when they began to examine the candidates for baptism and membership, only church members were permitted to attend. Among the candidates was also my friend Khariton whom I have mentioned often. At this time Khariton was not yet accepted. They wanted to see him bring more fruit of repentance.

In the afternoon we had very nice weather and a very big crowd of people were walking on the street of Lubimovka. Many people were standing on the sidewalks and in the yards along the street fence. Many of those who, by nature and in their hearts were still adherents of Makhno, were watching us.

At the head of the procession were the two presbyters, A.K. Drany of Sherebetz, and Vasily Ivanovich Shachovtsov of Lubimovka, both bare-headed. Behind these two men was the choir with its director. Behind the choir came the candidates for baptism and behind them many people followed.

If you could have heard this joyful invitation by the mixed choir, you would believe that they really meant what they were singing. One man standing on the sidewalk said, "Look there, even the teacher is with them", referring to me. One of the men was calling Peter P. who was walking alongside of me, "Hey, Petro, [Peter], come, we will give you some homebrew." Peter answered back, "No, I will not come. You had better come with us and you will get quite a different kind of homebrew." I could hardly believe that this was really I who was walking among all these people. But this was a very blessed occasion for me and for many others. Listen to the singing:

"Whosoever heareth," shout, shout the sound!
  Spread the blessed tidings all the world around;
  Tell the joyful news wherever man is found,
"Whosoever will may come."
Chorus: "Whosoever will, whosoever will!"
  Send the proclamation over vale and hill;
  'Tis a loving Father calls the wanderer home:
"Whosoever will may come."

These singers really were sending the proclamation over hill and vale. It was amazing to note how this message had its effect on many needy sinners. After singing all three stanzas of this Psalm, (every hymn is called a Psalm in Russian) there was a brief lull, and this seemed to increase the interest and attention to the next Psalm:

To the work, to the work, we are servants of God,
Let us follow the path that our Master has trod;
With the balm of His counsel our strength to renew,
Let us do with our might what our hands find to do.
Chorus: Toiling on, toiling on, toiling on, toiling on:
Let us hope and trust, let us watch and pray
And labour till the Master comes.

They did not believe in being lazy or negligent. This was a call to labour for the Master. But so many were still unsaved, and they were listening now. After singing all four stanzas of this hymn, they sang:

Sinners Jesus will receive, sound this word of grace to all.
Who the heavenly pathway leave, all who linger, all who fall.

At the water, before the baptism was performed by presbyter Andrew K. Drany, I was asked to deliver the message. Here the choir sang again. I preached from Romans 5:1. We had a very attentive audience, it was a great day. People were turning from deep darkness unto the glorious light of Jesus Christ.

After baptism several men prayed. The benediction was spoken and we all started on our way homeward from the little river Tersa. The people began to disperse, and in the minds of the observers and listeners who were not yet born again through the Holy Spirit, there were quite a few questions. I was not surprised at all when suddenly a man by the name of Mishka Shinkarenko, stood before me and said he wanted to ask me a question. He addressed me with the word "teacher" because most of the people remembered me as a teacher at Schoenfeld. He asked, "Teacher, I do not understand this. You know just as well as I do what these men have done; how they went into the homes of many people and how they threatened them, beat them, tortured them, robbed them, put their pistols into the mouths of people, scaring them so they would more easily give them what they demanded; and now they walk around here praying and singing Psalms. I do not understand this!"

After he had asked me this long question I looked at him, smiled and told him, "Mishka, you have asked me a question and I want to ask you a question, too."

"Oh, yes, he said. "What is it?"

I asked him, "Tell me, Mishka, which is better, what these men were doing in the past, or the things they are doing now?"

Then he took a deep breath and repeated that Russian word "kone-tshno, konetshno, several times (this word means "of course, of course"), "the things they are doing now are much better than what they have done in the past."

So I told Mishka, "If this is better, and we know it is better, then let us not reproach them for what they did before, but let us help them so they will never turn back to the same bad and evil road again."

"Oh, yes," he said, "I understand, that is right, you are right in this."

When this question had been cleared away, he pointed at his nice dark suit and asked me if I recognized it. Of course I did. Several years ago when I was still teaching in Schoenfeld and I realized that we could not keep all the things we possessed, I gave him the nice dark suit which he had kept very well. And he looked so nice in this my former suit, while I stood before him in an old patched up suit. I did not feel a bit sorry about that suit if only it won souls for Christ.

On our way back to the village of Lubitzkoje, presbyter A.K. Drany asked me if I would be willing to serve at the Holy Communion table be-cause he had to go to another village to serve there. So in the evening we gathered around the table of the Lord. I officiated and read from I Corin-thians 10:15-20, the emphasis being on the Christian life, to separate from the things of this world. The apostle Paul put it in these words, "You can-not participate at both the devil's table and Lord's table." These men had been feasting at the devil's table, now they gathered here at the Lord's table and this was a reminder not ever to turn back to the former. We had a very blessed evening at the Holy Communion table.

I was quite aware of the fact that at that time I was minister of the Men-nonite Evangelical Christian Church, while they were Baptists, but no-body ever mentioned these things at that time. We just felt that we belonged together. We were one in Christ.

That evening at the Michael P. house, we sat almost until midnight, discussing important questions with Michael and Khariton. The latter was not baptized yet, but he was willing to wait and he later became a member of the church through holy baptism.

Our Last Prayer Together

The next morning, May 7th, very early Khariton was already at the door when I was not quite ready yet. He came to bring me the payment for a Russian book, *Na Putie* by Timoshenko, and he asked me if I would take time to have prayer with him for the last time, because only weeks later we already were on our way to Canada. As we knelt there on that ordinary earth floor, we embraced and prayed together. I admonished him to confess all his sins to the Lord, which he did. As he embraced me once more, kissing me, I had to think back how often he, in his intoxicated condition, would embrace and kiss me, telling me that he loved me. Now he was a Christian and I had no reason to doubt that he loved me.

Zinovia P. had breakfast ready, we had our last prayer together standing around the table. Pastor A.K. Drany, also V.I. Shachovtzov and the singers were ready to take me back to Sherebetz.

While driving the approximate distance of twenty miles to Sherebetz we saw some bushes not too far from the road. One of the female members of the choir asked me if I was interested in seeing the place where Koljka Yermolovsky had shot himself to death. Only two years ago the Communists began to clear out the Makhnovtzy; they had surrounded Koljka Yermolovsky hiding in this very bush. When he realized that he could not escape he shot himself. Thus ended the life of the murderer of my friend Peter G. Neufeld. How Koljka boasted that he in such and such a manner had killed my friend Petjka (as he called him). Here in this bush he had ended his life of violence. How serious life is!

When we arrived in Sherebetz I was served a nice dinner and then had to go to the railroad station to catch the train to Alexandrovsk-Schoenwiese. Looking for the last time upon this village of Sherebetz my mind returned to the days of terror—how many of our Schoenfeld people had been murdered by men from this village! And now we had such wonderful Christian fellowship with some of the people here.

In the afternoon on the train I rode along with a blind man by the name of Paul. It did not take too long for us to travel to Alexandrovsk, but at one place before we arrived the train stopped abruptly. We got off to investigate and soon learned the reason why the train had stopped. A young woman, married only for two weeks, had thrown herself under the wheels of the train. She was still breathing but there was no chance for her to live. What a sad event indeed, for a young life to end so abruptly and in such a tragic way. Where will you spend eternity?

Schoenwiese

This Mennonite village is a suburb of the city of Alexandrovsk, the same city which the Soviet regime had renamed Zaporoshje, and of which Schoenwiese had become a part. In our childhood and youth we had always loved to go to Alexandrovsk. We usually rode on the steamship *Chortitza* or *Leonida*. At that time a ticket cost only a few kopeks, and one kopek in normal times was worth about half a penny. That was always so much fun, when we stopped at de Kaump or the island Chortitza. But that time had gone and many things had changed, and mostly not for the better.

When I arrived in Schoenwiese I found out that there would be a farewell service in the Mennonite church for the American pastor Peter H. Unruh, who had served there for an extensive period of time under the A.M.R.A. (American Mennonite Relief Administration) and was now ready to return to the U.S.A. After the service in the church they served coffee with very nicely baked things such as Zwieback. At that time this was quite an item to mention in my diary—May 7, 1923.

The following day turned out to be a very pleasant, warm day. I took care of some business in the city and also went to the A.M.R.A. and had quite a long conference with pastor David Hofer of Chicago, and with pastor Peter H. Unruh. The latter gave me some pieces of clothing for my cousin Abram Klassen, and for myself. For ten million rubles I caught a ride back home. This being Tuesday, we had a Bible study at our place, using Hebrews chapter four as our text.

Beautiful Chortitza-Rosental

God's creation was so beautiful in Chortitza-Rosental at this time. The flowers were in full blossom, the air was filled with a nice aroma, the fruit trees were covered with new fruit, and the vegetables were making good progress in growth.

I went to my partner Dietrich Pauls to get my horse, Siskin, so Truda and I could drive out to the field on the hill to plant a few more beans. Reading this item in my diary, also some other entries, I cannot understand why we bothered about anything in this realm at all. But I suppose we were so used to doing these things that they automatically were a part of our lives.

One of my brother John Schroeder's newborn twins by the name of Hedwig died, so I dug a grave for this baby, helped by my brother-in-law, Jakob Kasdorf. The latter was the husband of my oldest sister, Anna, who died in Russia in 1936.

About a year later thousands, even millions (in 1938 the Soviet press reported that they had taken thirteen million people) of people were taken to slave labour camps where they were told that they had not been sent there for reformation but for destruction. The four children of my brother-in-law are now in Paraguay and one daughter is still in Russia. Nobody ever learned what happened to him. This was my last real chance to have fellowship with him, while digging a grave for the baby on May 10th.

The following Sunday in our church service we had a visitor by the name of John Rempel from the Molotshnaia who brought us some information about the situation in that part of our country.

Our Last Trip in Russia

By this time we, along with David and Mika Klassen, were planning to make one more trip to the Molotshnaia to see our parents for the last time. Rueckenau was perhaps ninety miles away. Some of our neighboring church members teased me, that finally I, too, would make a trip, indicating that I was traveling too much. That was plain sarcasm and we understood each other well.

David brought a horse and I borrowed one from my brother John. We built a little roof over part of the wagon, and on May 17th, very early in the morning, we started out on this long trip. That was Thursday and Ascension Day. When we stopped in Schoenwiese at the Cornelius Janzen place we had to listen to quite a hot sermon from brother C. Janzen, because we were traveling on Ascension Day. We justified ourselves before him with the fact that we were going to the Molotshnaia where the people had celebrated Ascension one week earlier.

We drove southward and in the evening arrived at the German Lutheran village called Gruental, where we found shelter for the night in the machine shed of a man named Folz. The next day about 11:30 a.m. we arrived in Rueckenau.

Family Reunion

We all were very glad that we could have this family reunion once more in view of the fact that soon we would be on our way across the ocean. Other members of our family were also planning to emigrate. We were saying good-bye to our dear Southern Russia which we loved with all our hearts. Now we were preparing to go into the very uncertain conditions of Canada. The specific day of our departure was not yet appointed but we knew it would not take very long now, and later this turned out to be July 2nd, 1923.

The same afternoon Truda's brother, Gerhard Peters, with a team of two cows hitched to an ordinary farm wagon, drove to Gnadenfeld to bring Truda's grandmother, Mrs. Peter (Katherine) Toews and her two daughters, Susanna and Katherine, to Rueckenau. We rested in the afternoon and in the evening we were eager to hear the details about the departure of our loved ones, uncle Peter Toews and Truda's brother, Hans (John) who the previous year had gone to be with the Lord. We also sang and somebody played the guitar.

On the following day, shortly before noon, grandma Toews and the aunts arrived and soon after the Nikolai Rempels from Mariental arrived with their family. They too, had a team of two cows, the only difference being the fact that they had a spring wagon. Now the house was full and it seemed the visiting would know no end. For the night some of us found a good place to sleep on the hay in the machine shop. So ended this day, Saturday, before the day of Pentecost.

On the first day of Pentecost we naturally went to the Mennonite Brethren Church in Rueckenau. I was asked to deliver the opening message, which I did, using Hebrews 3 as the text. Pastor Jacob W. Reimer, who only a few months later became my brother-in-law by marriage to Truda's eldest sister Margaret, widow Rempel, gave the message according to the Book of Acts, chapter 2.

During these days it was our privilege to also have fellowship with Dr. Erich Tavonius, M.D. who was a sincere Christian and supporter of God's work here on earth. It was a wonderful experience to sit with these brethren, J.W. Reimer who often was called "Revelation Reimer" because he loved to expound the message given in the Revelation, and Dr. E. Tavonius. They used to sit in brother Reimer's front room studying the epistle of Ephesians. Being young at that time I felt that I was sitting between two spiritual giants who by each verse from Ephesians were lifting me to higher spiritual levels.

On the second day of Pentecost, we again went to church where the Holy Communion was also observed. In the afternoon, a number of us gathered in the beautiful orchard of brother J. Reimer. Later on pastor David Hofer of Chicago, Illinois, and his wife arrived by automobile. The topic of discussion was mainly emigration to Canada, and the fact that our experiences here in Russia were of such a nature that ordinary people in Canada or America might not be able to understand us. Be prepared for this!

Our brother-in-law, Nikolai A. Rempel (later of Chilliwack, B.C.) left with his family for home.

On Wednesday, May 23rd during the night I was in the barn feeding the horses. At 2 a.m. we once more gathered in the dining room and had our early breakfast with our barley coffee, called prips. This was our last prayer meeting in Russia with our loved ones in Rueckenau. Truda's sister Anna volunteered to go along in order to help Truda in various ways preparing for the trip across the ocean.

Our last trip from the Molotshnaia to Chortitza was uneventful. Good weather, good roads and a fairly good place to stay overnight in Schoenwiese where we stopped at the home of Frank Toews. We arrived home about 11:00 a.m. and everybody seemed to be happy. We were happy for the safe arrival and our children and neighbors were glad to see us back, safe and sound. Praise God!

There was plenty of work to do around the house to prepare for the trip, and Truda, with the help of her sister Anna had her hands full with the sewing. I had some arrangements to make about our possessions in the field where we had put in a crop of wheat, barley and especially watermelons. We also had to sell things we still possessed. Everything went into the millions and billions of rubles, but as I stated earlier money was not worth much. One pound of butter now was already close to ten million rubles and one Canadian dollar was worth 160 million rubles.

This year we had the privilege of celebrating Pentecost twice. The previous Sunday we celebrated Pentecost in Rueckenau according to the new calendar, and in Chortitza we celebrated it one week later. The messages we heard were a blessing to us and the prayer meetings were wonderful, filled with the Holy Spirit. In the afternoon there was a special testimonial service with many of the visiting Christians participating as well as our own members.

Baptismal Service at the Dniepr River

On Monday, the second day of Pentecost we went to the Dniepr River to administer the ordinance of holy baptism. Ten new members were received into the church that day. There were many visitors from most of our neighboring villages, including Schoenwiese, Schoeneberg, Neuendorf and other places. At the morning service one outside speaker gave a very long and monotoned sermon. It was hard to follow him in his thoughts. This day closed with a Holy Communion service in the evening. . .

May 29, 1923

The third day of Pentecost there was a great song festival, with people coming early from Hochfeld twenty miles away—two wagon loads—and from Kronstal and other places. We had a very inspiring morning service. Four choirs, including our own, rendered a total of forty-four songs with speeches in between and an especially good sermon by brother Neufeld from Steinfeld. Time and again I wondered whether or not this was our last such wonderful occasion in Russia, and I had to supress my tears.

Final Preparations

At this time I was served with a notification that it was time to pay 355 million rubles for the passport to emigrate to Canada. We were getting excited; would it really happen that we would live in a free country? How often we were burdened in our minds because one really never could express what was deep, deep in one's heart—what one felt and desired. So most of the time we had learned to be quiet or even to smile and simulate satisfaction, while in our heart we were deeply dissatisfied. This began to disturb and to bother some of us. How would this look when we came into a free country? Had we become hypocrites? No, of course not. But there was a steady struggle going on and from this we soon hoped to be free. We still had to hide our feelings, but in our hearts we were jubilant over a country that was willing to accept us and where there were brethren who had arranged everything for us. I could shout for joy

In normal times we had in Rosental Chortitza seven sizable flour mills, which we in German called Dampfmuehle, i.e., steam mill. Whenever we needed a sack of flour we would just give the order and the flour would be delivered to us at the house. Now, preparing for a long, long trip where for about ten or more days we would have to provide our own food from Chortitza up to the Latvian border, most of us prepared bags full of rusks. But first we would have to have flour to bake the rolls (Zwieback)then make rusks of them. Where could we get the flour? Not in Chortitza. Only in some of our neighboring villages such as Schoeneberg or Osterwick was I able to get the needed flour. Our Chortitza flour mills were not operating.

Pay more money! How much? What for? Oh, just taxes for the few acres of land I had operated. Nineteen million rubles.

One warm and quiet evening a group of us sat outside the house of my cousin, Mrs. A. Wiebe. We visited, sang and discussed the various aspects of life and of our forthcoming emigration. We all loved each other and it was only natural that we wished we would not have to part. Some of this group tried to persuade me that it was an unnecessary thing to leave Russia. The same things we have in Russia will also come to Canada; and in addition to this we only have to remember that the coming of Christ is so near, and He will snatch us from the Russian soil just as easily as on Canadian soil. My answer to these dear loving members of our church was Matthew 10:23, where Jesus told His disciples, "When they persecute you in this city, flee ye into another . . ." What we will find in Canada we knew; what may come we did not know; but we believed the Lord lead us to Canada. This was my answer to these dear people. And not for one single moment have we ever regreted that we emigrated.

Annia

We had taken into our home a fourteen-year-old girl by the name of Annia Golian. Through the efforts of my cousin Abram Klassen about four to five years ago, she, along with her mother and other members of her family, had come from Moscow, where living conditions at that time were very poor. We had planned to adopt her and take her along to Canada. Her parents by this time both were dead. But Annia, being a minor, had to listen to her older brother and sister and they would not permit her to go along with us. We felt sorry for her, for she would have liked to go with us. She had to live with her married brother. While we were in Canada she wrote us several very loving letters. Then no more letters arrived and only later we learned that she had died of typhoid fever. Dear Annia Golian! Annia had shed many bitter tears because she had to stay in Russia.

A telegram from B. B. Janz arrived stating that the first seven hundred emigrants should be ready to leave soon.

Mother and Sisters

One day before we left I went to visit my mother and sisters in Rosental. We had them on our passports, both my brother John and I. They had nothing else to do but to pack their suitcases and go along to Canada as credit passengers. But they had decided to stay in Russia. On his deathbed my father had admonished me not to forsake my mother and sisters. I promised to carry out his wishes if at all possible. But now I told them that under no conditions would I be willing to stay in Russia. If they wanted and needed my help, they had to follow my advice. If we stayed in Russia we all would perish. Now in retrospect, more than fifty years later, I must say that it was the right thing to do. Only a few months after our arrival in Canada they asked us to help them emigrate. We were willing and we did help them to do this, but it took three more years before they, along with my brother Peter and his family could come to that blessed land of Canada. O Canada, glorious and free!

On June 12th we had a special meeting about emigration in Einlage, where teacher Henry Andres from Nikolaipol, having arrived from

Moscow, informed us that the first train with emigrants would leave from the Chortitza railroad station on June 22nd.

Truda was very busy with sewing, mending, cooking, etc., and with the help of her sister, Anna, she made good progress. Anna sewed and sang with her lovely voice "Faith is the Victory." How true this was and is. Just have faith!

There were big auction sales of those who were emigrating and everything was sold very cheaply because the people knew that we were moving to Canada and took advantage of this situation. This is only human and we did not mind this at all, if only we could get out, the sooner the better.

Truda's brother, Gerhard, with Mr. Herman Enns from the Molotshnaia, had come to learn about the emigration. We went to see my former colleague, artist John P. Klassen who was a representative of the board and had brought some information from Moscow.

Finally on Friday, June 22nd, 1923 the first train with seven hundred or more emigrants left from the Chortitza station and my brother, John, with his family were on this train. Now we knew that the emigration had started and we would be on the next train. We sold whatever was not already sold and exchanged some of the money for Canadian and some for American dollars.

About this time our good friend pastor Jacob G. Tiessen from Kleefeld, Molotshnaia with his wife and family of eleven children and a daughter-in-law, fourteen in all, arrived as pre-arranged. They stayed with us the remaining days. They had asked for the privilege of leaving with us on the same train, and permission was granted. It was important for the Tiessens to leave now, else they would have had to wait for another year. It was a very pleasant experience; we had to be together during the closing days in Russia and to make the whole trip to Canada together. When the train was in readiness for us at the railroad station, we all went to clean the dirty freight cars. We washed the whole inside of the cars with boiling water. We also took boards and made ourselves beds and seats for the long trip.

It was hard for us to say good-bye to so many loved ones, especially to my mother and other relatives and friends and church members, when this day of July 2, 1923 arrived. Hundreds of people had gathered around the train of twenty-eight cars to say good-bye. We sang a song, though we were not supposed to, but nobody seemed to care. We also prayed.

We Love Russia

We loved and still love Russia and especially the Russian people. Leaving was a very difficult decision for us to make. We had received our education there, we had many connections with dear people, some of them in very high standing. We had gone through many very difficult experiences in Russia, but we intended to stay there. Only when we saw that the government of the Soviets very definitely turned against God and took away from us the dearest principles of freedom, turned us into slaves, did we say, "Let us get out! This is enough!"

Epilogue

How often, when we were still young and even later, we were reminded that, at a certain occasion in Gethsemane, Jesus told Peter: "Put up again thy sword into his place: for *all they that take the sword shall perish with the sword.*" Matthew 26:52. Yet Nestor I. Makhno, who took the sword and through whom so many died, escaped the sword, lived quite a number of years in France where in 1934 he died a natural death. That, too, is a sign of God's grace towards all of us. And we are satisfied that in this matter the Lord has extended His grace to a sinner.

Many of us have hoped and argued that eventually communism would mellow down and the rulers and dictators of communism would become more tolerant. But only the opposite is true. They have changed their system from time to time, because this at the given moment was expedient for them, but speaking in general terms, they are still aiming at world dictatorship. Intellectuals, who do not adhere to the principles of communism, in many cases have been taken to places where medical injections were given them, which would in turn make them almost insane, so they would be taken to insane asylums.

Parents, who are training their children in the faith of God, in many cases have lost their children, when they were taken by the communist authorities to communist children's homes.

Most of the churches that now exist are registered and under strict surveillance by a special agent or director of religious matters. All officers of the church have to be acceptable to this supervisor of the government. There is no separation of church and state in the Soviet Union. Indications are that at present time more restrictions are being imposed on Christians.

There is a strong group of Christians who have been called the Initiative Christians or in Russian "Initsiativniki", i.e. Christians who are following their own initiative derived from the Word of God. Many of them are either in prisons or in slave labor camps. The important thing about these dear brethren is, that they do not seem to feel sorry about themselves because of much suffering imposed upon them by the present government, but they take it as it comes and will not give in one half inch on the unreasonable demands of the soviet government.

We have been corresponding with people in Soviet Russia. It is better not to reveal too much about this, but we notice that here, too, freedom is very limited.

I feel sorry for many citizens in the U.S.A. and in Canada, who still do not appreciate the great freedom we have here. And at present time it seems to me that these two great nations are deliberately digging their own graves. Some of our people in the U.S.S.R. were forced to dig their own graves before being shot down. But here we have freedom and living conditions which no other nation in the world is able to match, and yet the signs are prevalent that in government places, in schools and in churches people are not satisfied, but would like to copy from communist countries. "Give us darkness rather than light, give us slavery rather than freedom", etc. We are very grateful for the privilege to live in a free country like Canada and the U.S.A.

Appendix

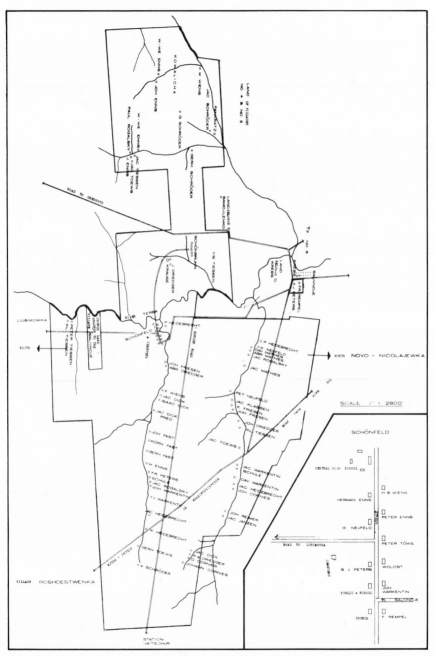

This is a copy of a map of Schoenfeld made in Russia in the year 1912, which was brought along to Canada by Henry B. Wiens, Leamington, Ontario.

Brethren, Come Rejoicing

Translated from Russian by G. P. Schroeder

1. Brethren, come rejoicing, glo-rious is the day.

Sisters, God exalting, sing for grace He gave

Once we were yet strangers, we are friends in God;

We are one in Jesus, one through Jesus' blood.

Sing, o sing loud Hallelujah!
Sing, o sing loud Hallelujah, Sing, o sing loud Hallelujah

We are saved and justified
We are saved and justified, We are saved and justified

And our names now stand forever
And our names now stand forever, And our names now stand forever

In the heav'n-ly book of life
In the heav'nly book of life, In the heav'nly book of life.

2
We have come together not at Sinai,
Not with fear and trembling, not afraid to die.
From the cross comes comfort,
  through the grace of God.
We are saved from anger,
  through the Saviour's blood.

3
Now by faith and love we live in unity;
In the blood washed marching to eternity.
Glorious hope is filling hearts
  with joy from God,
We will live forever washed
  in Jesus' blood.

Whiter Than Snow

1. Blessed be the Fountain of blood, To a world of sinners revealed;
2. Thorny was the crown that He wore, And the cross His body o'er came;
3. Father, I have wandered from Thee, Often has my heart gone astray:

1. Blessed be the dear Son of God; Only by His stripes we are healed.
2. Grievous were the sorrows He bore, But He suffered thus not in vain.
3. Crimson do my sins seem to me, Water can-not wash them a-way.

1. Though I've wandered far from His fold, Bringing to my heart pain and woe,
2. May I to the Fountain be led, Made to cleanse my sins here below;
3. Jesus to that Fountain of thine, Lea-ning on Thy promise I go;

1. Wash me in the blood of the Lamb, And I shall be whiter than snow.
2. Wash me in the blood that He shed, And I shall be whiter than snow.
3. Cleanse me by Thy washing divine, And I shall be whiter than snow.

Blessed Calvary

Translated from Russian by G. P. Schroeder

1. Come, brother, let's go to Calvary! The Godsent Messiah is nailed to the
2. Come, brother, let's go to Calvary! He suffers great pain there for you and for
3. To Calvary, brother, let us go! "Forgive them my Father, they know not what they
4. Come, brother, let's go to Calvary. His eyes turned to heav'n but no light can He

_mf_

1. tree. A glorious Gospel He came to proclaim, The sick did He heal, but
2. me. He thirsteth and vinegar they give Him now, Whose waters of life so a-
3. do!" He's praying, take heed that His pray'r may ascend, For you and for me to a
4. see. "My God, why oh why hast forsaken Thou me?" My friend, so from sin you and

1. now He is slain
2. bundantly flow.   Kneel down, wor - ship Him!
3. glorious   end!
4. I may   be free.

Our Prayer For Russia

Hear us, Lord our God, we intercede today,
Millions suffer, help them, earnestly we pray.
Godless rulers torture them, O God, how long
Wilt Thou let them suffer this great wrong?

Chorus:
O Lord, save Russia through Thy pow'rful Word!
Oh Lord, save Russia, send Thy Spirit's sword!
O God, save Russia; sinners will repent.
On us all a great revival send!

In Thy Word is comfort, light, eternal life,
Joy and peace instead of all this earthly strife.
Satan's kingdom with Thy Word must conquer we,
Russia with its millions be set free.

[Chorus]

O God's servants, will you heed this challenge now?!
With His sword in hand, please make this sacred vow!
By the Holy Spirit led to victory
We will help to make the sinners free.

[Chorus]

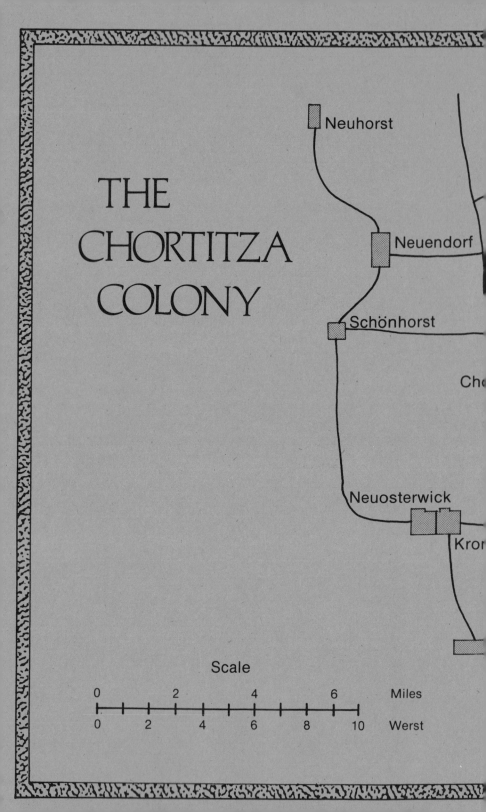

THE
CHORTITZA
COLONY

Neuhorst

Neuendorf

Schönhorst

Ch

Neuosterwick

Kro

Scale

| 0 | | 2 | | 4 | | 6 | | Miles |
| 0 | 2 | 4 | 6 | 8 | 10 | Werst |